Citizenship and the Origins of Women's History in the United States

Teresa Anne Murphy

PENN

UNIVERSITY OF PENNSYLVANIA PRESS

PHILADELPHIA

Published by
University of Pennsylvania Press
Philadelphia, Pennsylvania 19104-4112
www.upenn.edu/pennpress

Printed in the United States of America
on acid-free paper

10 9 8 7 6 5 4 3 2 1

A Cataloging-in-Publication record is available
from the Library of Congress

ISBN 978-0-8122-4489-2

Contents

Introduction

Thomas Wentworth Higginson wrote to Caroline Dall in the spring of 1854 to let her know he was bowled over by her biographical sketches in *The Una*, which he collectively labeled "Essays toward the History of Woman." The questions that were being raised by the woman's rights movement, questions inspiring Dall's writing, were the most revolutionary ones of their generation, Higginson claimed. Encouraging Dall to continue her historical writing, Higginson argued that the challenges posed by woman's rights would force the wide-scale revision of all history and all scholarship. "On Slavery or Temperance, for instance, nothing new can be said. But in regard to Woman about all that is true is new. For instance, all statistics must be compiled over—& all history re-written."[1] Given the rather modest nature of some of Dall's historical sketches, Higginson's praise might seem a bit hyperbolic. But Higginson was right. The demands for full citizenship that permeated the movement for woman's rights in the 1850s required a wide ranging reevaluation of social relations. And social relations, in order to be legitimate, needed a history.

While suffrage is the demand usually associated with this movement, a broad notion of citizenship actually suffused the concerns of woman's rights activists in the antebellum period. As Nancy Isenberg has pointed out in her important study of this question, activists took on not only issues of voting, education, and jobs, but also problems of property, the media, and public performance in challenging ideas about what a female citizen could and should be. Full citizenship implied universal rights, but the acquisition of those rights necessitated changes in the terms by which women were included in society. Full citizenship meant the ability to participate equally with men in the political, economic, and intellectual life of the nation.[2] Higginson was right in thinking that supporters of woman's rights would need to revise current statistics and rewrite history in order to make the argument for such societal changes. And this rewriting would involve

not only more general histories but also the histories of women that had been circulating since the time of the American Revolution.

Women's history had developed as a genre in the waning years of the eighteenth century when a sense of nationhood and related ideas of belonging began to expand in regions throughout Europe and the Americas. The genre emerged, however, not with a cry of defiance or shout for woman's rights, but as a lengthy exploration of women's intellectual and political shortcomings. European men who wrote women's histories in the eighteenth century drew on the assumptions of stage theory that had tied the general advance of civilization to manners and, more specifically, the deportment of women to make a strong plea for the importance of female domesticity in national development. In works that circulated widely in the colonies and the early republic, European authors such as Antoine-Léonard Thomas, William Russell, William Alexander, and John Adams argued that the citizenship of women should be constructed in a very different way from that of men.[3]

Women's activities during the American Revolution spurred some revisions of those narratives, but it was not until the 1830s that a sustained and spirited challenge began to unfold. Lydia Maria Child, in particular, was inspired by female reformers who were questioning the assumptions that had driven the narratives of women in the past. As debates about women's legal, civil, and political rights began to unfold during these years, proponents and critics more explicitly used examples drawn from history to legitimize their positions either in support of or in opposition to full citizenship for women. With the political stakes of historical interpretation clearer than ever, the genre exploded. Sarah Josepha Hale and Elizabeth Ellet, harboring political agendas of their own, expanded the ideas of differentiated citizenship for women that had been promoted in the eighteenth century; in the process, they shaped powerful narratives of nationalism. With these efforts under way, it becomes clear why Higginson was so excited that Caroline Dall began to experiment with competing histories of women's citizenship that supported demands for universal rights.[4]

This book is an attempt to understand and explicate Higginson's excitement. It traces the evolution of women's history from the late eighteenth century to the time of the Civil War. And it pays particular attention to how competing ideas of women's citizenship were central to the ways in which those histories were constructed. As woman's rights activists recognized, citizenship encompassed activities that ranged far beyond specific

legal rights for women to their broader terms of inclusion in society, the economy, and government. Earlier histories that criticized the economic practices, intellectual abilities, and political behavior of women in the past created a narrative of exclusion that legitimated the differentiated citizenship considered suitable for women. Moreover, because citizenship was at the heart of these histories, they were never just about women, but also about the larger polity in which women lived. Women's history was, necessarily, a history of nations.

It is not always easy to see the contours of this debate in many of the popular works that were created during this time. Women's histories also were created as entertainment for women, especially in the newly emerging literary market of the late eighteenth century. Eventually played out in the popular press of the nineteenth century, and sometimes in lyceums or other public forums, women's histories were not an academic pursuit. Of course, the same was true of the more general histories written throughout most of the nineteenth century. History was not institutionalized as a discipline until the end of the nineteenth century. Most of the great historians of the nineteenth century, men such as George Bancroft and Francis Parkman, were men of letters who wrote for a general audience. But they did, at least, have some formal training. The female authors who began to write histories of women during this time period—Lydia Maria Child, Sarah Josepha Hale, Elizabeth Ellet, and Caroline Dall, for example—did not. Many of these nineteenth-century female authors also wrote to support themselves, so their work was produced quickly and was not always as polished as the histories produced by their male counterparts. Making the contours of debate even harder to discern were their tendencies to copy from the writings of each other, or of earlier writers, and to reshape the material with slight inflections to create differences of interpretation. In doing so, they adopted the practices of eighteenth-century European writers of women's histories such as Thomas, Russell, Alexander, and Adams. To readers today, those subtle differences may be difficult to detect, particularly because such borrowings were almost never acknowledged.

New meanings, however, were slowly created. The women's histories that were produced in the late eighteenth century promoted an ideal of domestic citizenship for women that was valued as a break from a less advanced past, and hence a sign of modernity, as well as a distinguishing characteristic of national virtue at a time when a market economy and new forms of political organization were reshaping the countries of Europe and

the New World.[5] Any attempts to interrogate the past for alternative models
of more direct female citizenship were easily dismissed as examples of savagery and a danger to governments that were already viewed as fragile in the
revolutionary period. It is not surprising that Mary Wollstonecraft simply
dismissed history as worthless for her project of critiquing the condition of
women and that Judith Sargent Murray's few historical essays that tried to
create an alternative history of female citizenship were quickly forgotten.
What was crucial for a re-visioning of women's history was the sustained
assault on the limitations of women's status as citizens that began in the
1830s. The involvement of women in political activities, particularly the
radical antislavery movement, inspired much of Lydia Maria Child's argument in her *History of the Condition of Women*. But radical activism also
inspired women such as Sarah Grimké and Margaret Fuller to expand on
Child's insights and other writers' work in order to push the boundaries of
women's history to include a few African American women.

The new ideas about female citizenship that began to infuse the writing
of women's history in the 1850s engaged those questions on a terrain that
was as broad as that of eighteenth-century histories, yet also different. Concerns about the market and the structure of national government were key
components in eighteenth-century histories of women, while concerns
about industrialization, expansion, and sectional tensions suffused the writing of women's history by the middle of the nineteenth century. In response
to these changes, the nature of nationalism had begun to shift from a civic
emphasis on political commitment to a more personalized emphasis on
ethnic belonging. As scholars such as David Waldstreicher have noted, nationalism in the very early years of the republic was often focused on a kind
of civic nationalism that celebrated the political values of the movement
for independence. Describing nationalist rhetoric as a "political strategy"
deployed in different ways by different groups, Waldstreicher argues that
"the invention of modern democracy in the late eighteenth century was
inextricably tied to the creation of newly coherent national peoplehoods
whose will, it was believed, ought to be expressed in national political institutions."[6] By the 1850s, however, this form of nationalism was sharing
ground with (if not being replaced by) a more culturally and ethnically
based nationalism oriented around place and home. In this latter form of
nationalism, motherhood and gender hierarchy did not simply facilitate the
civic debates that formed the nation, they also represented an embodied
form of the nation. This was an ideological transformation that domestic

writers such as Hale and Ellet, with their versions of women's history, not only engaged, but also helped to create. It was also a transformation that made it all the more difficult for woman's rights activists to create an alternative history of citizenship that critiqued the economic and political disabilities women had faced historically. As numerous scholars have noted, nations require histories, but what kinds of histories would they be?[7]

Since the emergence of the academic field of women's history in tandem with the late twentieth-century movement for women's rights, scholars have tried to establish a historiography for the field. Julie des Jardins, for example, has carefully analyzed the ways in which women from the end of the nineteenth century to the middle of the twentieth century crafted challenges to the dominant historical narrative at the same time that they themselves faced professional challenges. Creating that historiography for the earlier part of the nineteenth century is more difficult, however, because women's history at that time was a popular genre rather than a professional endeavor. As Kathryn Sklar pointed out in one of the earliest essays on this topic, the context in which women wrote during the late eighteenth and early nineteenth centuries mattered. She suggested that women wrote by drawing on family and community connections and later, in the context of a Victorian literary world, women were as likely to produce novels and poetry as they were to produce history.[8] Understanding this earlier social context, however, does not lead necessarily to an understanding of the political significance of the work.

Indeed, one of the most important studies of nineteenth-century women's history argues that it involved no political engagement. Nina Baym, analyzing the prodigious amount of history writing produced by women in early America, has argued that both the reading and writing of mainstream political history were important ways in which women could join debates about larger political issues. She has dismissed women's growing interest in their own history, however, as a domestic retreat from the analysis of more important political issues of their times. It was a long slide downward, she argues, from Mercy Otis Warren's *History of the Rise, Progress, and Termination of the American Revolution*, written at the end of the eighteenth century, to Lydia Maria Child's *History of the Condition of Women*, published in the 1830s.[9]

As Baym has searched for the political implications of women's history written in the nineteenth century, she has focused particularly on how authors constructed their subjects as historical agents. She has found

expressions of female agency in the historical narratives of Elizabeth Ellet and Sarah Josepha Hale, both authors who were unsympathetic to the woman's rights movement. Indeed, Baym has noted the tolerance Hale displayed for both the sexual and political activities of women in earlier centuries whom she profiled in *Woman's Record*. By way of contrast, Baym argues, even though Lydia Maria Child was active in antislavery reform and more supportive of woman's rights than either Hale or Ellet, there were no female agents in Child's work.[10]

Baym has thought hard about the women's histories that emerged during this period. But in the end, she is forced to throw up her hands on the political ramifications of these books. She concludes that what united these authors instead of politics were shared beliefs about the innate spirituality of women and women's intellectual as well as biological differences from men. The new genre of writing about women in history was a distressing kind of spiritual identity politics in which their authors ceded their right to broader political commentary. No wonder she sees the overall genre as an intellectual decline from the political engagement of writers such as Warren.[11]

By examining women's history from the standpoint of debates about citizenship, this book attempts to understand the politics that Baym could not find. It begins with the argument that ideals of domesticity and gender differences that ran through the genre of women's history were always a part of a larger political debate. The stage theory that used domesticity to celebrate the superiority of European cultures over other cultures imbued domestic practices with an elaborate set of political associations that began in the eighteenth century and continued into the nineteenth. Thus, one of the contentions of this book is that the depiction of domesticity always had political implications, and sometimes those implications were quite overt.

Moreover, the political implications of depicting female agency are not as straightforward as they might seem. The issue is an important one, as various scholars have demonstrated. Writing about women's patriotism at the time of the Revolution, Linda Kerber argued in *Women of the Republic* that women conceived of their patriotism in active terms while male leaders tended to view women's patriotism as more passive. As Peter Messer has pointed out, a major turning point came after the Revolution, when women began to be written into the history of the United States as active historical agents, and this changed how they were imagined as part of the nation.[12] But it is important to note that, during the nineteenth century, growing

debates about female citizenship raised questions about the precise nature of female agency. Under what historical conditions had it been possible? How was it exercised? Was it desirable or dangerous? When Sarah Josepha Hale singled out some of the political activities of women in the past, for example, she did so within a larger framework in which she used their behavior to demonstrate that the past was less advanced than the present. Lydia Maria Child, by contrast, focused not so much on particular heroines from the past, but on a larger set of questions about the historical conditions that allowed women to exercise their agency. Concerns about citizenship necessarily raised questions about the terms by which women were included in the polity. Thus, the construction of female agency in historical writing carried with it important political attitudes that cannot be determined by simply looking for the presence of female agents.

Ironically, nineteenth-century concerns about citizenship also led to an interest in queens and other elite women in the past. This interest in monarchs and other "great women" on the part of nineteenth-century authors who were hardly monarchists themselves, has not gone unnoticed by scholars. Bonnie Smith, for example, has argued that women who focused on elites rather than the more common folk in their writings were producing a literature of trauma. These female authors faced a variety of traumas in their own lives, including poverty and emotional insecurity, not to mention physical and even sexual abuse. They were caught between two contradictory discourses of the early nineteenth century: one that promoted equal rights and the other that legally subjected women economically and politically. Their focus on powerful women such as queens allowed writers to avoid conscious recognition of their victimization. Thus, they had little interest in writing about women who were poor, powerless, or exploited.[13] What the debates about citizenship make clear, though, is that queens and other elite women in the past were being analyzed for their abilities to exercise political power. There were no assemblies of female citizens from the past to be analyzed in this debate, only monarchs. Evaluating how those female rulers and their countries had fared thus became an important proxy in debates about whether more common women had the abilities necessary to enter the political arena.

For a similar reason, educated women in the past were equally fascinating. Learned women had exercised power and influence far beyond what was normally expected of their sex. As Mary Kelley has argued recently in her important study of female learning in the early republic, access to

education gave women access to civil society, and civil society was a key component in the emerging political life of the United States. Elite women organized civil society around their salons in the late eighteenth century, but by the nineteenth century, large numbers of educated women had expanded the boundaries of civil society to encompass a range of voluntary organizations that were reshaping the political world that continued to exclude them. When authors such as Sarah Josepha Hale wrote extensively about learned women in the pages of *Woman's Record*, she celebrated their role as leaders in civil society and she provided her readers with important role models.[14]

Kelley has stressed the importance of viewing learned women in relation to civil society as a way of breaking down the binary that associates women with the household and men with the state. Civil society, she rightly points out, connected the two spheres. But as Kelley also notes, civil society could be seen as the feminine other to the masculine state.[15] This is one point that becomes clear in the debates about women's history that erupted at the time of the first movement for woman's rights. As Thomas Wentworth Higginson bluntly argued in 1853, the question was no longer whether women should be educated, but what women would be allowed to do with their educations.[16] Citizenship was a contested issue in the writing of women's history, and those questions of citizenship ranged far beyond the participation of women in civil society.

In order to fully understand these issues of citizenship, it is necessary to return to the eighteenth century. Part I of this book analyzes how the discourse of women, history, and nation was created and contested in the late eighteenth and early nineteenth centuries, particularly around the notion of what might best be called domestic citizenship, though that particular term was not used in the eighteenth century. In the United States, it would coalesce around the idea of republican womanhood. The discourse unfolded in works such as Antoine-Léonard Thomas's stinging critique of French women, which was translated by William Russell, and William Alexander's more laudatory (if no less constricting) history; both of these works quickly made their way from the European continent to major cities across the Atlantic such as Philadelphia, New York, and Boston. These histories of women were close cousins to the conjectural histories of civilization being written at the same time: histories that used the status and condition of women as an index of progress. Focused more on specific historical societies rather than the general relationships between economic conditions and culture, women's histories simultaneously tied contemporary nations to the

past and differentiated them from one another in the present. They were thus an important part of the move from the universalistic tendencies of Enlightenment history into the more nationally focused concerns of romantic history.

Part I concludes with a discussion of Lydia Maria Child's *History of the Condition of Women*. Child's work, hastily written and confusing though it may be, took deadly aim at many of the assumptions that had structured the discourse of domestic citizenship in the commonly read histories of women. Because of her engagement with that literature, some of its assumptions about the cultural superiority of modern western civilization carry through in her analysis. But what many of Child's contemporaries recognized then, and what we need to recognize now, was the way in which she challenged so much of the literature's common wisdom whether in undermining notions about domesticity or in disrupting a narrative of national progress. Thus, it is little wonder that Sarah Grimké and Margaret Fuller found Child's work to be such a powerful resource as they launched their critiques of gender inequality in the 1830s and 1840s and began to forge new definitions of female citizenship with new interpretations of women's histories.

Part II focuses on the ways in which women's history was used more overtly in debates about women's citizenship as woman's rights activism began to take hold in the 1830s. It examines how women's history was invoked and elaborated repeatedly in verbal duels focused on competing visions of female citizenship in venues that ranged from debates in Congress over female petitions to conventions to rewrite state constitutions to national woman's rights meetings and local lyceum presentations. Although none of the history that was created in these contexts was very coherent, its uses were powerful, and it sparked a new wave of women's history writing.

Sarah Josepha Hale and Elizabeth Ellet created a compelling and popular variation of this genre by elaborating histories of domestic citizenship that promoted ideals of nationalism rooted in the defense of home and family. Their domestic histories thus crossed boundaries into the politics of nationalism at the same time that they argued for the importance of the personal and familial ties that women tended. Their heroines not only promoted civilization and Christianity, but also created a people and a nation that were the essence of democracy.

Woman's rights activists such as Caroline Dall responded by producing histories that centered on a very different vision of female citizenship. Dall wrote with a growing conviction that women's history had contributed to

a public discourse that debilitated women. With an unapologetic and confrontational style, she created historical sketches of women meant to validate the activities and claims of woman's rights activists. As the 1850s came to an end, Dall became one of the first popular historians to begin experimenting with the data-driven analysis promoted by the new social science associations in Europe and the United States. Dall, unlike the professional historians who would follow her in later decades, still aimed for a popular audience and wrote unabashedly in defense of her reform ideals. Ultimately, her focus shifted to contemporary issues, leaving the past behind. But as would be clear in the historical writings of scholars who followed her, she and other activists had laid the groundwork for rewriting women's history in a way that championed full citizenship. Dall had begun to work out a historical perspective that could be used in advancing a more progressive agenda for woman's rights.

I

Women, History, and Nation

Chapter 1

Domestic Citizenship and National Progress

In the spring of 1774, Robert Aitken took out large ads in both the *Pennsylvania Gazette* and the *Pennsylvania Packet* to advertise his latest product, the *Essay on the Character, Manners, and Genius of Women, in Different Ages*. The book had been written by Antoine-Léonard Thomas and published in Paris in 1772, then translated (and expanded) by William Russell, who published it in Edinburgh in 1773. With no copyright laws to hold him back, Aitken printed and sold his own copies of Russell's translation the following year at his Philadelphia bookstore. By that summer, the printer Samuel Loudon was advertising the book in his New York shop.[1]

Aitken was a successful printer and bookseller in the eighteenth century, part of a thriving world of new commercial goods that were widely available in the colonial cities of the New World. And as his advertising made clear, this was a product that was directed at, as well as about, a key segment of his market: women. In line after line, Aitken laid out the topics covered by his new product: "the great and virtuous activities of women . . . the effects of Christianity on the manners of women . . . the books written in honour of women. . . ." Every detail addressed the importance of women, suggesting a narrative that female readers might find interesting and even inspirational. As a way of enticing potential buyers, Aitken drew a connection between this new book and the very popular novel, *Telemachus*, written almost a century earlier by François Fénelon. Aitken reminded his audience that Fénelon had also written about the education of women, suggesting that those who loved *Telemachus* might find a similar delight in Thomas's new offering, which was "indisputably the most elegant, and most philosophical treatise, on the female mind."[2]

Aitken's venture into women's history was only the beginning. Two years later, his friend and rival, Robert Bell, was advertising Lord Kames's

Six Sketches on the History of Man for a price of ten shillings. Like Aitken, Bell carefully laid out a list of the contents, which indicated that Section VI was devoted to "The Progress of the Female Sex." By the 1780s, bookstores from the mid-Atlantic states were promoting another popular entry in the field, William Alexander's *The History of Women: From Earliest Antiquity to the Present*. Booksellers had found, and were eager to sell, a new product: women's history.[3]

They promoted this new product in part because reading was becoming more widespread in eighteenth-century colonial culture, and women, in particular, were learning to read. Literacy rates were uneven; men were more likely to be literate than women, whites were more likely to be literate than blacks, and New Englanders more likely to be literate than southerners. But having said that, it is also clear that literacy at many levels was increasing during the eighteenth century and that in New England, at least, the majority of women could read by the time of the Revolution. In Philadelphia, not only were there women who could read books, but also there were four subscription libraries that circulated books among those who could not purchase them. The records of one of those libraries suggest that 40 percent of the patrons in the early 1770s were women.[4]

Booksellers such as Aitken and Bell were also recent immigrants to Philadelphia from Scotland and they continued to have strong intellectual ties to their homeland. Bell settled in Philadelphia in 1767; Aitken, in 1771. Both men are well known for their association with political supporters of the American Revolution, who ranged from Thomas Paine to Thomas Jefferson; indeed, it was Bell who first published *Common Sense*.[5] But part of their success was rooted in their ability to channel ideas circulating in Scotland into the intellectual discourse of the colonies, and that included the Scottish discourse on women.

The Scottish Enlightenment, which fostered this discourse, was not concerned with women per se but rather with the world of commerce that had emerged in Britain. Theorists who contemplated this new order fretted about the ties that would hold it together and emphasized the role of sentiment as well as contract, an approach that necessarily involved women. As they interrogated the role of commerce and consumption in the advance of civilization, they argued that women were key participants. Socially conservative by inclination, these theorists were hardly complacent about what they observed around them as they watched older distinctions of rank crumble from the onslaught of this new commercial order. They found new

forms of social stability in gender differences. Women, not men, they argued, were the great civilizers, and gender complementarity was critical to the creation of both civilization and society.⁶ Women's histories that were created in Britain and sold in the colonies drew heavily on the Scottish Enlightenment; as such, they not only were products that were marketed in this new world of commerce, but also were a commentary on the entire process.

In addition to reflecting on a new commercial order, however, these books also engaged the new world of nations. Women's histories were written as the British colonies in North America began to distinguish themselves from the metropole, and as those in countries such as Britain and France began to think about what it meant to be French or British. Britain had only been created at the beginning of the eighteenth century with the Act of Union. The British empire of the eighteenth century was built on trade and wars that England had fought with France and Spain in order to protect that empire of goods, thus fostering a growing sense of British national identity. No longer simply kingdoms or colonial outposts, these new countries confronted questions about what it meant to be a nation. If nations were rooted in a sense of common belonging, how did that belonging occur? Did women belong in the same way that men did? Were women capable of nationalism?⁷

These were also fundamentally questions of citizenship because, as questions of belonging, they asked on what terms women would participate in the nation. Commerce and national identity coalesced at this time around what some have called consumer citizenship. While many scholars have argued that consumer citizenship is something of an oxymoron, in which citizen passivity about important social and political issues is bought with material goods, others have pointed out that it is far more multivalent. Timothy Breen and Lawrence Glickman have made a strong case for the way in which residents of the British colonies were pulled out of their local community ties and into contact with more distant regions through their purchase of market goods. Most important, beginning in the middle of the 1760s, many in the colonies rallied politically around consumer boycotts of British goods. Through these protests, colonists began to adopt a growing sense of being American, as distinct from British, and the very nature of their activities meant that they also came together as citizens.⁸

Because women were central to the processes of both buying and selling, this was a transformation in which they were deeply involved. But not all

citizen consumers were equal, and the participation of women in the market revolution caused concern on both sides of the Atlantic. Their independent relationships to the economy might be seen as a threat to the status hierarchies of the family. They could be viewed as purveyors of luxurious degeneracy in a new world of goods. And their very act of reading could catapult them into public discussions in which their opinions had dangerous social consequences.[9] All of these fears surfaced and were contained in the women's histories that began to circulate at the end of the eighteenth century. These histories examined the threats of women in the past and offered a prescription for containment: domesticity. Women, conceived as domestic citizens, emerged as the apex of a historical narrative of progress that was embraced in Europe, the colonies, and the new United States.

Problems and Possibilities of the Consumer Revolution

If a citizen had to be virtuous, economically independent, and able to represent himself in public, there can be no doubt that the activities of women in the eighteenth century raised some questions. Although we think of the commercial world as one dominated by men, from the merchants who owned ships and large trading companies to the artisans who turned out a growing number of products, in fact, women were both crucial and visible participants in this market revolution. In Philadelphia, for example, almost half of all retailers were women. They presided over taverns, grocery stores, and tobacco shops. A few worked as rope-makers, chandlers, and booksellers, and many more worked as milliners. The same was true in Boston, where women constituted 40 to 50 percent of the licensed retailers in the city or surrounding area. As Ellen Hartigan-O'Connor has pointed out with respect to Newport, Rhode Island, and Charleston, South Carolina, whether women worked independently of male family members or with them, they were integral to the urban economies in which they were enmeshed. Their activities, moreover, echoed those of urban women in England. Some English women worked with their husbands, others worked independently of them, and still others were unmarried. Middling women continued to take part in a large range of trades throughout the eighteenth century. Just because a woman worked in a trade did not mean, of course, that she was economically independent. She might still be part of a family system in which she deferred (economically and socially) to a father or brother or

husband. She certainly would not have had the same access to resources as many men, a disability that would have confined her activities to small-scale operations rather than large ones. But she would have been a visible, distinctive presence in new trades as well as old.[10]

The meaning of women's participation in commerce was further shaped by the fact that in many colonial cities, an increasing number of women were heading their own households or living independently of their families. About one-third of the adult women living in Philadelphia during the 1770s either headed their own households or lived as boarders, servants, or slaves in the homes of others. In Boston and the surrounding towns, the story was much the same. Over the course of the eighteenth century, the percentage of female-headed households there tripled, reaching as high as 20 percent.[11]

Related to the issue of female-headed households was the structure of marriage and divorce as well as the rise in the number of illegitimate births. Informal marriages were common in the colonies (as they had been in the Old World). Whether it was to avoid paying for the costs of a legal marriage or because there were few officials to even conduct a marriage ceremony, many couples simply lived together as husbands and wives. While this practice was more common among the poor than among the wealthy, prominent citizens also engaged in the practice. Informal marriage had the benefit of allowing for an easy divorce, in which couples could simply declare an end to their relationship. In Philadelphia, as in England, casual (and not so casual) sexual encounters also led to a large number of illegitimate children. Parents were seldom punished for their conduct, but city fathers did make sure that proper child support was arranged. In New England, a growing number of young women who married were already pregnant at the time of the ceremony. Indeed, by the time of the Revolution, the percentage of pregnant brides there was approaching one-third.[12]

Scholars have debated exactly what this demographic profile might mean. While it could suggest that urban women experienced significant forms of independence in the late eighteenth century, the poverty of single women and the larger social structure in which they acted probably limited this possibility. They were limited in their access to capital, and they were still expected to work within a patriarchal system in which men were heads of households. Servants and slaves might not be living with their birth families, but in most cases they were living with a family and the head of that household was probably a man. Thus, the idea that women were operating

independently during this period needs to be approached with some caution.[13] On the other hand, their behavior, whether economic or social, might have been perceived as an increasing form of independence, regardless of the reality.

Further complicating this picture of economic participation is the role that women played as consumers and champions of new commercial goods. From shopkeepers such as Bell, they purchased books as well as silks and linens, sugar and tea, cutlery, ceramics, glassware, and domestic furniture that included beds, tables, and chairs. With these goods, women fostered a culture of sociability within their families and neighborhoods that powerfully affected social relationships, particularly between men and women. The world of commerce that replaced feudal loyalties with business contracts was also a world in which friendship assumed a growing importance, and the proper use of new consumer items affected one's social status. More often than not, women led the way in using new items, an activity that might be seen as civilizing on the one hand, but destabilizing and even corrupting on the other.[14]

As women transformed relationships of sociability in their households through the use of these items, they also created new social relationships with the world beyond. New consumer goods allowed individuals to experiment with their identities. Those who bought items previously reserved for the rich could begin to imagine themselves as having a higher social station, or they could distinguish themselves within their own social milieu. Because it was often women who learned the rules of consumption and trained their families in polite behavior, so it was also women who were key to manipulating social position through consumption. The woman who knew how to pour tea and promote conversation around her tea table transformed a fancy tea service into an item of social distinction.[15] Her sense of fashion could also create a sense of cosmopolitanism as she dressed her family in a way that mirrored styles in London. Moreover, the consumption of imported fabrics and tea services also connected these consumers to a larger world of transatlantic trade, binding buyers and sellers into a new kind of community. Thus, the new ties created by commerce that scholars such as Breen and Glickman have noted were connections that women facilitated in very visible ways.[16]

While women's engagement with the world of consumer items opened up new social possibilities for themselves and their families, it also created instability. They might be celebrated as the civilizers of their societies, but

these changes also created anxieties. With respect to consumption, these anxieties focused particularly on concerns about decadence and luxury, of unnecessary spending on useless items of fashion that drew people away from more useful pursuits of production. Women, and femininity in general, had long been associated with decadence. Considered too weak to control their passions, women were assumed to be more liable than men to fall prey to sensual pleasure. Thus, their interest in fashion and their knowledge of consumer items could easily be interpreted as dangerous proclivities that needed to be controlled. While their activities might be fashioning a new world, their influence and the world they were creating might be deemed undesirable.[17]

These concerns were particularly clear with respect to the tea table and the salons some elite women began to promote. Tea was a wildly popular new item of consumption in the eighteenth century, favored by women over men. Teatime, however, was often associated with the idle gossip of women. Women who organized salons instead attempted to turn tea drinking into more intellectually elevating occasions, where men and women might discuss literature, art, and even politics in polite settings. Annis Boudinot Stockton, an eighteenth-century poet, established a literary salon in her home in southern New Jersey shortly after her marriage in 1758. Elizabeth Magawley engaged in a similar venture in Philadelphia. These salons provided important connections between the intellectual worlds on either side of the Atlantic. But the very power that women exercised in salon culture meant that it could also be morally suspect.[18]

Their promotion of polite conversation also required learning, so that elite women were encouraged to familiarize themselves with the classical world that formed the basis of educated discourse in the eighteenth century. Women had to be careful not to go too far; actually learning Greek and Latin was seen as a pedantic conceit for them. But acquiring a knowledge of classical personages and history was another matter. In that way, women would understand what men had to say without actually knowing enough to start taking control of the conversations themselves. Of course, this ability to promote invigorating conversation also made the proper education of women a form of cultural capital. Such an education was an important item of consumption, particularly when paired with tea and a salon.[19]

Ideally, though, elite women were not flashing another item of consumption, they were fostering the creation of a civil society, a space apart from the government where enlightened citizens and subjects could freely

discuss and debate issues of importance. Men had other spots in which to engage in these debates, such as taverns and coffee shops, but these spaces were often off-limits to women. Salons demonstrated the ways in which women could be deeply involved in the creation of civil society and appreciated for it. Civil society, as numerous authors have pointed out, was a major component of democratic governments in emerging nation-states. It allowed a space for the expression of ideas independent of government, a space where critiques (as opposed to official ideologies) could be expressed: a public sphere. Thus, salons could be regarded with suspicion precisely because they offered women the opportunity to construct a key element of the emerging world of citizenship: a forum where participants might represent their ideas to a community beyond their households.[20]

These concerns surfaced repeatedly as women walked a fine line in their attempts to host respectable salons. England, in particular, provided a model for women in the colonies. Elizabeth Montagu of London, for example, not only sponsored an important salon, but also used her considerable wealth to provide financial support to writers such as Elizabeth Carter. These "bluestockings" brought British men and women together for intellectual conversations on literary subjects. Their efforts were quite successful and respectable until the 1790s, when they began to take up political issues as well.[21]

The French, however, were another matter. Elite women in France were famous for the salons they had created in the seventeenth and eighteenth centuries to promote Enlightenment thought. Women such as Ninon de l'Enclos, Suzanne Necker, Julie de Lespinasse, and Marie Thérèse Geoffrin introduced leading members of the intelligentsia to the nobility as part of a powerful intellectual exchange that they both stimulated and controlled. With strict rules of politeness and conversation, these women carefully mixed commoners with nobles, and they facilitated debate on points of disagreement. Their patronage was important, so important, in fact, that their power was viewed with suspicion. François Fénelon, whose name Robert Aitken had invoked to sell his new women's history, had critiqued the women of both the salon and of the court a century before in his *Treatise on the Education of Girls*. Tying their political power to the decadence of an insatiable demand for luxury, Fénelon had urged that the education of girls be redirected toward domestic skills rather than belletristic learning. Reinforcing the critique of the power of intellectual women was a parallel critique of their sexual morals. The French court was famous for its mistresses.

Some salonnières had taken lovers from their salons so their manners were considered both polite and seductive. Their behavior would be held up as a warning to women in both Britain and its colonies.[22]

The situation of salonnières paralleled that of other women in the new market economy. They ran their salons as other women ran their businesses. And their promotion of sociability, while on a grander scale than what was offered around the dinner table, carried similar contradictions. Women could promote civilization and culture, but they might also promote decadence. They could connect the men around them to a larger world of ideas and goods. Although they deferred to men intellectually, they had the learning and the means to represent their own ideas as well. And through the world of sociability that they promoted, their ideas could circulate, just as the goods produced and sold by other women did.

Women and the Progress of Civilization

All of these concerns about women surfaced within the debates of Enlightenment thinkers, particularly those of the Scottish Enlightenment school of thought, including Adam Smith, John Millar, Adam Ferguson, and Henry Home, Lord Kames. The Common Sense school, as it also was known, was the British answer to the Enlightenment culture of Paris. French thinkers such as Condorcet had also stressed the importance of women in the evolution of society, but it was men such as Millar and Kames who most thoroughly integrated women into theoretical debates about the evolution of a new commercial economy as well as the society and government that would grow up with it. They viewed commercial society as the apex of economic development, but they also argued that commercial society was not without its problems. Women, they felt, were both a source of concern and key components of the solution. Thus, the Scottish Enlightenment idealized a role for women in society that was significantly at odds with the role that many women were playing, particularly in urban centers. Common Sense thinkers such as Kames and Millar created a historical narrative of economic and cultural progress that both naturalized their own ideals and served to critique contemporary behavior.[23] Rather than focus on the role of women in commerce, the Scottish Enlightenment idealized the evolution of a domestic role for women that was both publicly performed and of broad social significance.

Gender relations and the activities of women were essential for understanding the relationship of economic organization to culture in the stage theory espoused by Common Sense thinkers. From hunting and gathering to pastoral shepherding to agriculture, then manufacturing, then trade, a division of labor arose that facilitated the growth of civilization. One of the most important divisions of labor occurred with respect to women. Women, Common Sense thinkers argued, had fundamentally different natures from men, which suited them for different activities. Civilizations advanced when these differences were recognized and valued in social, political, and economic organization. Indeed, the most advanced societies were those that had the greatest understanding and appreciation of gender differences, creating a system of gender complementarity in which men and women were responsible for different aspects of society, complementing one another perfectly in their different roles.[24] History was conceived as a narrative of societies that passed through stages of economic and political development in which differentiated gender roles gradually evolved toward the state of complementarity best suited to the natures of each sex. Because these works tended to focus on the importance of manners and civilization, they were also deemed an appropriate kind of history for women to read. Traditional histories might focus on political events and dates that were presumed to be of little interest to women, but histories of civilization spoke to their concerns and provided them with direction on how to live.[25]

Women were incorporated into this narrative most extensively by John Millar in his *The Origin of the Distinction of Ranks*, which was first published in 1771, and by Henry Home, Lord Kames, in his *Sketches on the History of Man*, published first in 1774.[26] While the sixth part of Kames's work was devoted to women, Millar actually began his book with a long section titled "The Rank and Condition of Women in Different Ages." Their narrative strategies led them to include most non-Western societies in the same "savage" category they used to categorize the distant past. And while Millar and Kames differed on some details, they were quite clear that not only did women's participation in society have to be different from that of men, but the terms of their participation had to be organized around the control of women's labor and sexuality. As men such as Millar and Kames took up issues of courtship, marriage, and family, they not only narrated an evolution over time, they also indirectly criticized those who failed to live up to the standards of domestic life they associated with the highest levels of civilization. Similarly, their narrative of the evolution of women's work carried a strong class bias that challenged the behavior of many

women who were involved in market activities. History, in their hands, was an important tool in naturalizing the terms by which women would be allowed to participate in their rapidly changing societies.[27]

Chastity was probably a woman's most important possession in modern society. Far more than simply a state of sexual abstinence, however, it was also a condition of marriage. Monogamous relationships between men and women, in which mothers focused on the nurture of their children and the promotion of companionship between the sexes, were the key responsibilities of women. Without that commitment, the social intercourse that was crucial to the success of commercial society and the virtue that was crucial to the success of the state were both impossible. Female chastity thus emerged as a key component in evolving ideas of differentiated citizenship.

Promiscuity characterized savagery. The lack of differentiation in labor and politics was sustained by indiscriminate sexual encounters. Millar described the way in which ancient Romans married through "use," by simply living together for a year. In Native American societies, women had sex with men as they chose. Such behavior, Millar concluded, damaged both the rank and dignity of women. Kames turned the discussion into a more explicit comment on conditions nearer to home when he argued that in both Scotland and Wales it was considered acceptable for young women to have sex before marriage and that they seldom expressed shame at having bastard children.[28] Indeed, with respect to chastity, one would be hard-pressed not to think of the informal marriages and high rates of illegitimate births on both sides of the Atlantic while reading descriptions of sexual relationships among those considered less advanced. Kames and Millar were issuing warnings about how women's sexuality needed to be controlled for the benefit of both the economy and the nation.

Not only did promiscuity threaten the foundations of society, they argued, but so, too, did passion, a problem that played out in the medieval period when men (particularly knights and nobles) began to appreciate women more and began to worship them to the point of fighting for them.[29] Without a commitment to chastity, passions were unchecked and further destabilized society. Again, this view of history was a warning about contemporary sexual relationships as well as an argument about the past; it indicated fears about women who ranged from the mistresses of the French court to those who deserted one husband for another.

Both Millar and Kames argued that the growth of the state and the control of female sexuality went hand in hand. As local tribes engaged in commerce, they not only stopped fighting, but also set up governments that

allowed men and women the opportunities to converse in congenial settings. This improved state of society allowed women to escape their earlier
status as slaves and then idols of men to become their companions. This
was one of the chief responsibilities of an evolving notion of domesticity.
Millar argued of such women that their "consideration and rank . . . came
to be chiefly determined by the importance of those departments which
they occupied, in carrying on the business, and maintaining the intercourse
of society."[30] Kames agreed that as the moral senses were developed, and in
particular as chastity developed among women, refinement increased, and
women could be "trusted with their own conduct . . . they make delicious
companions, and incorruptible friends."[31] Both authors created a view of
eighteenth-century domesticity that had a powerful social meaning. By
publicly constructing themselves as devoted wives, women could facilitate
sociability among men, thus providing a sound foundation for commerce
and government. The chastity that made possible the friendship between
men and women was predicated on an ideal of monogamous marriage.
Kames was particularly clear that sexual indiscretions of married people
were far more serious than sexual indiscretions of unmarried people, and
affairs were most serious if committed by married women.[32]

Women who focused their energies on their families and polite conversation had evolved from performing other forms of labor. According to
writers such as Kames and Millar, companionship was the highest form of
labor that women could undertake. Manual labor, even domestic activities
such as spinning, characterized less advanced societies. The labor of
women, along with their sexuality, needed to be controlled. Many of the
laboring activities that gave women a direct relationship to the economic
world around them undermined the ability of their societies to progress.

Kames and Millar also made it clear that the domesticity of women in
some ancient societies was only a partial step in their elevation. Millar argued that women of the Old Testament or ancient Greece garnered more
respect for these skills than savage women received for theirs but that they
nonetheless lived secluded in their homes, sewing, spinning, and cooking.
Society suffered as a result because women who experienced domesticity as
this form of manual labor failed to interact with men.[33] Domestic work that
did not have a broader component of social participation and performance
outside the home was ultimately a problem for the functioning of society.

Commercial labor had been similarly problematic. Women who entered
the market place to engage in trade challenged the gender roles that were

more suited to their natures. Egypt, in particular, demonstrated the problems of this sort of development in the evolution from savagery. As Millar explained in a later edition of his work, women who had been used to laboring in their savage state, took over businesses as they developed, while men took over domestic activities such as spinning and weaving.[34]

Millar and Kames both agreed, however, that women reached their highest level of labor, and society reached its pinnacle, when women could "put aside the spindle" and take responsibility for facilitating conversation. It was at this point that men could find the companionship that would soften their rough manners.[35] Thus, the promotion of sociability both within and beyond the home was the height of female accomplishment in commercial society.

Nothing was said, or even implied, in these historical narratives that suggested the value to society of women who ran shops or who worked with their hands in the eighteenth century. There were certainly class implications here because Millar and Kames ignored the activities of poor women in order to emphasize the activities of the elite in creating culture. Indeed, the poor, by implication, were consigned to the same unevolved status as hunters from thousands of years ago or modern-day "savages" in Asia and Africa.[36] For women in the middle who might face some choice about their activities, the decision was starkly laid out. They could participate in the economy by running a shop or pursuing a trade, but they would not be advancing the interests of their society; indeed, they might be undermining it. Domesticity, by way of contrast, offered a form of participation, and thus a form of citizenship, that would help their society advance.

It was with respect to companionship that the education of women became important. Kames and Millar agreed that if women were lacking in an adequate education, they could not be proper companions for men. They would either corrupt the men they knew with their idle chatter or, even worse, men would turn to more educated courtesans for companionship, leading to a decline in chastity. Kames bemoaned the fact that young women were educated to be agreeable, but little else. He advocated an expanded system of education for women that would allow them to inspire men in the public world as well as the private so that "the two sexes, instead of corrupting each other, would be rivals in the race for virtue."[37]

Kames's concerns about female education were particularly aimed at the society that he encountered in Britain. Women in a republic might not need much of an education because men were so busy participating in

government that they spent little time with women. But in a constitutional monarchy, where the nobility and gentry had more time on their hands so that men and women were more likely to mingle, decadent behavior would emerge if women had little more to do than gossip and chase the latest fashion. Consumption would become the downfall of such a society rather than the basis for advanced civilization.[38]

Kames's analysis had both important social implications and political implications for gender relations. Kames recognized the power of female intellectual abilities at the same time that he circumscribed them. Like many other Enlightenment thinkers, Kames championed the intellect of women and argued that a society only reached its apex when men and women were of the same rank, something he saw occurring in Britain, if not elsewhere. In making this argument, however, Kames was far from advocating anything like an equality or sameness of the sexes. He did assert that men and women were fundamentally the same in outlines, "whether of internal disposition or of external figure." However, their differences were significant: their complementary abilities balanced one another in the creation of a stable social order. These were distinctions of nature, which, if transgressed, signaled a decline in progress.[39]

Kames elaborated these distinctions in a very important set of "natural" contrasts between men and women that echoed similar analyses on the Continent. These distinctions were of critical importance in circumscribing women's activities within a domestic/civil sphere and legitimating men's activities only in the world of economy and politics. Men and women had to participate in society and government in very different ways for the common good.

Kames made four main points. First, men were strong and vigorous while women were delicate and timid. This difference meant men were suited for strenuous labor while women were better suited for child care. It also meant that men had to protect women, a position of enormous consequence because Kames argued that the power to protect was the basis for the power to rule. Kames felt that this distribution of power was particularly appropriate in light of a second set of important differences. Men, according to nature, had the intellectual judgment to govern whereas women only had sufficient intellectual abilities to obey. This was just as well in Kames's view, because a more equal distribution of political ability would "excite dangerous rivalship." Even in the realm of culture, women were limited in significant ways. Kames felt they were naturally more imaginative than men and that they became civilized faster than men. On the

other hand, "none of them have made an eminent figure in any of the fine arts," Kames asserted. One would look in vain for an outstanding female sculptor or painter or poet. Imagination was a way of expressing sensibility. Women "felt" more than men and thus were more closely tied to many of the activities of civilization. But their sensibility did not lead them to the kind of creativity that resulted in true genius. Finally, men were more patriotic than women because of their connection to the state. Women, because they were related to the state only through their husbands and fathers, felt less commitment to the government and less hatred of its enemies. Their relationships were personal, not political, and they could only derive their political beliefs through their personal experiences.[40] In making this last point, Kames advanced a particular notion of patriotism that was rooted in the very male world of political beliefs and associations.

It is difficult to overstate the intellectual power of these histories of civilization. In these analyses, the condition of civil society was the key to progress. The state might be an important agent of power, but its nature, its very success, depended on the social relationships of the civil society that underlay it. Real change was effected in this realm. Thus, female chastity, family, and motherhood (among other things) were extremely important for creating and maintaining the well-being of the state and civilization. Domesticity was construed as the center of civil society with broad political consequences. Domestic activities, therefore, became the basis for a particular form of citizenship appropriate to women.

In this discourse, women were not simply dismissed as inferior to men. That sort of thinking characterized less advanced societies. Rather women were different from men, better suited to some tasks than others. Most important, their intellectual capabilities were celebrated. Authors such as Kames and Millar were quite clear about the need to improve and expand female education. Women might not need the same education as men (this wasn't really addressed), but they needed better education. The development of these female capabilities had important consequences not only for the home but also for the state. Men needed the companionship and advice of well-educated spouses.[41]

Thus, although these histories were analytical, they were also strongly normative. These historical theories about women and civilization used nature in a powerful way to suggest psychological and physical differences between men and women. The mind might not have any sex, as Poullain de la Barre had argued in the seventeenth century, but the way in which the mind came to understand the world occurred through sexualized bodies

that experienced the world in different ways. Some societies (particularly primitive ones) failed to recognize this. They might create different norms of gender relations, but these were not optimal because they were not "natural." If one needed any evidence of this, one need only observe that society's lack of advancement in other arenas. Thus, while these histories celebrated the intellectual abilities of women and argued that women should be better educated, they did not argue that women and men possessed equal intellects. Indeed, they suggested just the opposite. The physical differences between men and women resulted in important differences in their abilities to think and understand. These differences of "nature" made a huge difference in calculating the different terms of participation in society for men and women. In a very important way, the natural distinctions we associate with nineteenth-century thinking were laid out in the eighteenth century.[42]

Women, History, and Nation

It was within this context that the first women's histories came to be written. The assumptions about female chastity, domestic companionship, educated women, and the dangers of luxury in a consumer society did not just inform the writings of Common Sense thinkers such as Millar and Kames. These issues also came to structure what might be most appropriately called the first wave of women's history, written in the late eighteenth century. Less interested in the social and economic analyses of civilization that had animated stage theory, these works focused on specific female figures and the conditions under which they had lived. More important, and this is what makes them more recognizable as a modern form of history, they articulated how women, and the condition of women, were tied to the creation of nations and particular kinds of "peoples." Rather than simply being commentaries on female abilities or celebrations of the lives of individual women, these narratives made an argument about how gender relations had evolved through the histories of earlier nations and how they were central to defining differences among the people of contemporary nations. In this way, they used history not only to describe variation, but also to elaborate what female citizenship should be.

Two of the most influential of these histories, which originated in Europe but were widely circulated in the United States, were those by

Antoine-Léonard Thomas (translated and expanded by William Russell) and William Alexander. Authors such as these began to shape women's history out of the conjectural histories of stage theorists, though they also wrote in a tradition established by the debates about women in the *querrelle des femmes* and the exemplary biographies of Plutarch. They included portraits of famous women that had been part of the biographical tradition of celebrating female worthies and female accomplishments. They also drew on the classical writings that had circulated during the eighteenth century as a way of educating elite women in classical knowledge, books such as *Wonders of the Female World* or Madeleine de Scudéry's *The Female Orator*.[43] But they showed particular concern for the ways in which women's public activities had affected their societies and the ways in which women's domestic behavior had broad public consequences.

As these authors wove narratives that moved from the Egyptians to the Athenians to the Romans and then eventually to the modern nations of Europe, they created a sense of national identity that was rooted in both continuity and disruption. Readers could look back to an ancient past as part of their own history at the same time that they experienced a sense of progress and cultural superiority over the ancients. In fact, it is important to recognize that while many still looked to classical civilizations for inspiration (as an "exemplary" form of history), these were not "exemplary histories." To the contrary, these women's histories often emphasized the limitations and failures of ancient civilizations and stressed the ways in which modern societies had advanced over earlier ones.[44] Moreover, as these authors moved their narratives into the more recent past, they emphasized the cultural distinctiveness of specific nations and peoples, elaborating the qualities that made each nation different from the others.

Contemporary scholars have noted repeatedly that nations need a history. The construction of a shared history (whether accurate or not) provides people with a shared identity, a sense of being "a people." A fictive relationship created through time can motivate collective action and legitimate government activities. A national history naturalizes the relationships of the populace. This was particularly true in an age of democratic revolutions, as new national governments were expected to express the will of the people.[45]

Women's histories purposefully engaged issues of national identity. However, in organizing their histories of nations around women and gender, these analyses of national distinctiveness took on a particular character.

Perhaps most important, these histories did not, indeed could not, focus on an assertion of sameness throughout the population. While many works of history created a sense of nation by asserting a unified past that left out minority groups, or the poor, or women, to imagine a particular kind of male citizen as embodying a nation's greatness, this really was not quite so possible with the genre of women's history. Women's history addressed the problem of national identity through the lens of gender difference. These histories, in fact, made it clear that national identity was rooted in gender differences. What was shared, presumably, was an agreement on what the differences should be in a particular society.[46]

As nation and history became intertwined in the late eighteenth century, women's history became significant in several ways. It not only emphasized the importance of women in the creation of nations, but also tied the current health and future progress of the nation to the public and private behavior of women. While this kind of narrative gave women a place of significance in national history, the genre was not without its drawbacks. Most important, the histories that circulated created a narrative of the ways in which a common descent was organized around taming the most dangerous impulses or behaviors of women and the need of modern nations to control the behavior of women. Thus, certain kinds of female citizenship that involved direct public activities were dismissed as corrupting, while a more domestic version of female citizenship was championed.[47]

Authors drew on each other's work so completely that today we would say they plagiarized one another, but they also reworked each other's material to introduce significant differences of perspective, particularly with respect to nation. In the end, however, their agreements about the importance of domestic citizenship may be more important than their differences about national identity. Antoine-Léonard Thomas wrote as a Frenchman who was dismayed by the intellectual and political power that educated women were exercising in France. But his critique was broad, and it attacked women across historical periods. When William Russell translated Thomas, he added extensive material about the contrasting intellectual accomplishments and manners of British women. Thus, his edition became a British statement that associated dangerous women more specifically with the French (rather than characterizing women generally) and provided a somewhat more admirable version of British women. Russell did, however, use the French example to warn that Britain faced similar dangers as elite women increasingly ignored their domestic responsibilities.

Finally, William Alexander, unlike Thomas and Russell, worried that women in Britain did not exercise enough influence in civil society. He wrote more in defense of women than in attack, stressing the responsibility of men in corrupting women and celebrating the inherent abilities of women more clearly. But like Thomas and Russell, Alexander championed domesticity for women as their most important civic responsibility.[48]

In creating histories that culminated in a celebration of domesticity, these authors devoted particular attention to the dangers of educated women who exercised their influence on society directly, rather than circulating their ideas through their husbands and other trusted male friends. That sort of direct participation in public debate and intellectual life resulted in nothing but chaos and harm. Antoine-Léonard Thomas laid out a devastating critique that began with Greece and moved relentlessly through the Middle Ages to his own society in France, an argument that William Russell very faithfully translated. Thus, while it was Russell's translation that generally circulated in Britain and the colonies, and we refer to it as Russell's *Essay*, it is important to remember that these ideas were also those of Thomas.

Russell's translation of Thomas made clear that the French had allowed women to corrupt society by giving them too much sexual freedom and unwarranted praise for their intellectual accomplishments. The problem began when women were allowed to be in the French court of the sixteenth century, but it had spread to the bourgeoisie in the seventeenth century as impoverished nobles intermarried with wealthy commoners to replenish their coffers. Thus, the *Essay* focused attention on the way the morals of "the people" had been corrupted. The *Essay* attacked the women of the court as well as those who ran salons where nobility and the bourgeoisie intermingled, branding them as sexually immoral troublemakers who used their intelligence and power to create political intrigue and mediocre literature. The salons and court life of the seventeenth century, which were characterized as having "little learning; many accomplishments," had degenerated in the eighteenth century into an unabashed embrace of vice and sensuality, dominated by women whose licentious natures had been cultivated and set loose as they took the independence that belonged to men by nature.[49]

This attack on the learned women of France and their corruption of the nation was a culmination of a history of women that began with the ancient Greeks, a people whom the *Essay* argued, had experienced problems similar to those of the French. The Greeks, however, had created their problems

by failing to invest the domestic activities of their wives with civic significance. The education of women had been detached from their household responsibilities. As a result, the Athenians had left their wives ignorant and sequestered them deep within their households to protect their virtue, resulting in a form of domesticity that was entirely private, while their husbands sought the companionship of beautiful and educated courtesans such as Aspasia (the mistress of Pericles), and Phrine, who served as a model for Praxiteles' statue of Venus. Lest anyone miss the connection with French salon culture, the *Essay* pointed out that the "house of Aspasia was the resort of Socrates and Pericles, as that of Ninon was of St. Evremont and Condé" (*Essay*, I: 28).

Roman women, by contrast, offered a model of learning properly harnessed by domesticity, at least in the period of the republic. Hortensia embodied that combination of education and virtue in her powerful speech before the corrupt triumvirs who unjustly wanted to tax women to support their unpopular war. This virtuous combination, however, had collapsed, as the wealth of empire corrupted the virtue of the republic. When women became more concerned with their talent than their virtue, the Roman Empire collapsed in ruin (*Essay*, I: 38–49). The broad, public consequences of learned women influencing society without a sense of domestic citizenship could not be clearer.

In the anarchy of the Middle Ages, a new imbalance in gender relations occurred as women gave their domestic relations a competitive edge. They not only accompanied their husbands into battle but also, having demanded equality in military matters, then turned their attention to similar demands for participation in intellectual debate. The *Essay* dutifully described the accomplishments of women such as Modesta di Pozzo di Zorzi, Cassandra Fidele, Isotta Nagarolla, and Vittoria Colonna. But the *Essay* framed the discussion by noting that some of the most accomplished women were known to "harangue in Latin before the popes" or were found "pathetically exhorting the Holy Father and Christian princes to declare war against the Turks" (*Essay*, I: 96–102).

The direct participation of women in political matters had clearly been problematic throughout history because women had different natures from men. In terms that were very similar to those used by Kames, the *Essay* pointed out that a clear recognition of the differences between men and women was necessary if women's intellectual abilities were to be used for the good of society. Women, for example, were more insightful in understanding a problem, but they were less patient than men in working it out

with "cool reason." Women were more imaginative than men but also were more delicate and thus in need of protection from turbulent sensations (which in men resulted in great art). As a result of these differences, women could shine in certain contexts, but that did not mean that they were superior to men or even that the exercise of their abilities in public was always desirable. The Athenians had clearly been carried away by their worship of beauty, imagination, and sentiment, ignoring the more manly expression of reason. "More guided by sentiment than reason, and having laws rather than principles," the *Essay* dolefully concluded, "they banished their great men, honoured their courtesans, murdered Socrates, permitted themselves to be governed by Aspasia, preserved inviolate the marriage bed, and placed Phrine in the temple of Apollo" (*Essay*, I: 4–6, 32).

Women of the medieval period, meanwhile, had wreaked havoc on intellectual culture, where "they were ambitious to prove they had as much genius as courage." Drawn more to the "sentimental" thinking of Plato than the reasoned arguments of Aristotle, women also promoted theology and poetry, areas of learning closer to their strengths of imagination and sentiment. The intellectual culture they fostered was suited to their abilities, but it was, unfortunately, a confused arena in which Roman laws were "disfigured" by new ideas and poetry that celebrated love as conquest (*Essay*, I: 93–96).

The *Essay* thus presented a history of women for emerging European nations and states that suggested the difficulties of creating a properly calibrated form of domestic citizenship for women, but that stressed the importance of doing so and the dangers of failure. Educated women could benefit their nation and their government when their participation was valued but also circumscribed within a world of domestic values. This did not mean that women should stay sequestered within their homes, but it did mean that they should internalize a commitment to domesticity that they carried with them into their broader social relationships. In essence, this required that women recognize their differences from men and structure both their learning and their civic participation accordingly. Neither learning nor public participation was an individual right so much as it was a social responsibility that had to be exercised for the good of society.

Thomas's attack on learned women did not go unnoticed among French intellectuals. Thomas was not only a well-known author in France, but also a participant in salon culture. Thus, his criticism of the role that women might play in promoting intellectual discourse was particularly stinging. He had described most intellectual women in both the present and

the past as lacking in virtue and intellectual talent. Diderot, in particular, denounced Thomas as something of an ingrate for failing to recognize the significance of salonnières in helping him to define his thinking and his work.[50] However, Diderot also accepted many of Thomas's assumptions about the differences in the intellectual abilities of men and women. Only Mme. d'Epinay, in a private letter, put up a spirited defense of the intellectual equality that existed between men and women. Arguing that women needed to be better educated, rather than circumscribed by domesticity, d'Epinay set forth the kind of argument that would characterize the demands for woman's rights in future decades.[51]

While Thomas's attack focused particularly on the dangers of learned women to politics, Russell and Alexander shifted attention to the problem of commerce. Russell was reasonably careful in his translation of the *Essay*, but he added materials from Common Sense thinkers such as Ferguson and Millar throughout the text and appended a long chapter on British women at the end. He argued that British history differed from that on the Continent because chivalry had been weaker during the Middle Ages, and as a result, women had retained their modesty and virtue for a longer time. It was only with the growth of commerce in the fifteenth century that learning and the arts began to flourish, and only in the sixteenth and seventeenth centuries that elite women had become more educated. As Russell summed up, "Unless manners take a turn, there is reason to believe that our British ladies, once so remarkable for modesty, chastity, and conjugal fidelity, will soon equal their sisters of France" (*Essay*, I: 73–75; II: 107–112).

Russell believed that the domestic impulse was still strong enough among enough women in Britain to carry the nation forward. Women, however, had to temper their education with concern for the poor and devotion to their families (*Essay*, II: 113–116). Thus, Russell gave his translation of Thomas some important national twists: stressing the dangers to women of commerce more than politics and expressing a confidence in British women to triumph in the realm of virtue where French women had not.

William Alexander also expressed his confidence in the women of Britain. Drawing almost verbatim from Kames's work about the distinctions between men and women, Alexander celebrated the qualities of female nature.[52] He also defended women in a way that the *Essay* did not by emphasizing that if women engaged in corrupt behavior it was not because of their own natures but because of the influence of men. "Almost every man

is full of complaints against the sex," he argued. "Without examining how
far these complaints are well or ill founded, we shall only observe, that in
cases where they are well founded, when we trace them to their source, we
generally find that source to be ourselves" (*HW* I: ii). The history of nations was one in which the virtue, and most specifically the chastity, of
women had been under assault. But although Alexander tended to blame
men more than women for their problems in remaining virtuous, he still
focused his attention on protecting the chastity of women and promoting
their domestic citizenship.

Like Thomas and Russell, Alexander idealized a civil society in which
chaste women were engaged in child-rearing rather than manual labor and
were educated enough to share in intellectual conversations with men
rather than idle chatter as they gossiped and played cards. In an extended
chapter, "Of the Influence of Female Society," Alexander stressed the importance of male-female sociability in order to promote compromise in
male disputes. Women could be peacemakers. The challenge of the present
was for men to encourage this development by acknowledging and cultivating women's talents. Women with a proper sense of domestic citizenship
were needed in the civil society that was forming in Britain (*HW* I: 466–
467, 475–506).

The Early Circulation of Women's History

As these histories began to circulate throughout Europe and the United
States, they were both reprinted and repackaged. Jemima Kindersley published her own translation of Thomas's *Essay* in 1781, adding two of her
own essays on women to the volume. Even better known in the United
States, however, was the work of John Adams, a British clergyman. Writing
anonymously in 1790 as "A Friend of the Fair Sex," he copied large portions of Alexander's history and drew even more extensively on Kindersley's
translation of Thomas, as he compiled the two works into *Sketches of the
History, Genius, Disposition, Accomplishments, Employments, Customs, Virtues, and Vices of the Fair Sex in All Parts of the World Interspersed with
Many Singular and Entertaining Anecdotes*. Beginning with Eve, Adams
ranged through biblical, ancient, and medieval history before devoting separate chapters to the characteristics of women in different countries. He

then concluded the final half of his book with an almost random assortment of sketches about the customs and deportment of women in various times and places, from ancient Rome to Lapland. And unlike previous authors, he managed to condense his sprawling history into one volume.[53]

In England, Russell's translation of Thomas seems to have met with a more favorable reception than did Adams's compilation. *The Critical Review*, edited by Tobias Smollett, deemed Russell's *Essay* to be an even-handed and compelling treatment on the subject of women's abilities. Adams's work, however, was criticized for its confusion. *The Monthly Review* noted that Adams claimed to have drawn on the work of other writers such as Alexander, Millar, and Kindersley, but that it was nowhere clear how. Even worse, there was additional information added in, "the merit of which is of such a questionable origin as to make us rather indifferent whence they proceeded." Adams's work was deemed by literary reviewers to be less convincing than that of Russell.[54]

Still, Adams's work enjoyed wide popularity in the new United States, as did the work of Russell and Alexander. Adams's work was printed in Philadelphia in 1796 and advertised as being for sale in Salem, Massachusetts, soon after that. It was reprinted again in Boston in 1807 and in Gettysburg, Pennsylvania, in 1812. Alexander's *History of Women* began appearing in bookstores in the colonies in 1780. But it became even better known once it was published in Philadelphia in 1795 and 1796.[55]

It is also worth remembering that when Robert Aitken advertised Russell's volume in Philadelphia during the spring of 1774, he did so as the British colonies were reaching a crisis in their own identity as a nation. Colonial resistance to British taxes was at a fever pitch. Inhabitants of Boston had dumped hundreds of chests of tea into the harbor just a few months before, and within a few more months, the first Continental Congress would meet in Philadelphia. Thus, Aitken's customers would have read Russell's translation of the *Essay* with an eye to the European heritage they shared, but they also would have had questions about their differences (by and large) from the French, and even, to some extent, from the British. National identity and female history were closely related.

As newspaper editors up and down the Atlantic seaboard republished small excerpts of Alexander's *History of Women* in the 1780s, sometimes liberally rewriting Alexander's text to suit their audiences, they linked national identity and progress with female behavior. The published excerpts focused on Alexander's concern with the issues of chastity, marriage, and

courtship, suggesting the continuing importance of these issues in defining female citizenship in the years following American independence. Thus, in 1795, the *Litchfield Monitor* reprinted a small piece on the way in which "Lybian" women had engaged in warlike combat in honor of the goddess Minerva, believing that she would protect them if they were virgins—a ritual that had the benefit of encouraging chastity among young women. That same year, *The Massachusetts Magazine* published its version of Alexander's argument in an article, "On the happy Influence arising from Female Society." Although the magazine did not always use his exact words, the article it attributed to him captured the basic points of his argument. The article stressed, in particular, the importance of social intercourse between men and women and drew on many of Alexander's historical and contemporary examples to explain how societies suffered or benefited as a result of understanding that principle. In 1798, James Watters's literary journal in Philadelphia, *The Weekly Magazine of Original Essays, Fugitive Pieces, and Interesting Intelligence*, published excerpts from Alexander in both its February and March editions: the first focused on customs of courtship in different times and places, the second on chivalry.[56]

Rosemarie Zagarri has noted that the domestic ideals associated with republican womanhood in the post-Revolutionary era, which had begun to formulate among Common Sense thinkers in Scotland before the Revolution, focused more on issues of commerce than politics. Zagarri suggested in that important essay that republican motherhood had a socioeconomic component as well as a political component and that it was worth looking at the former as well as the latter. Caroline Winterer, pushing the idea a bit further, has argued that study of the classics, particularly the study of Roman matrons, offered women examples of ways to reconcile luxury with republicanism: a way of being nationalistic and cosmopolitan, a way to be both public and respectable. Both scholars have emphasized how stage theory and classics opened up possibilities for women during this period, offering them a place of importance in the creation of society. In doing so, their work complements the existing scholarship about the value of Common Sense writings for women in Britain as well. These histories of women offered a vision of female agency and public participation that was enormously powerful.[57]

Viewed in the context of women's lives, though, it seems clear that while this historical imaginary opened up some possibilities, it closed off others. If we recognize the ways in which consumption was beginning to produce

the nation rather than just being a separate part of its economic development, it also becomes clear how the domestic citizenship that was being
offered to women could be imagined as both important and as a form of
citizenship. Writers agreed that domesticity did great harm if it only existed
in the home. It was important that domestic behavior be performed in
public and that it be used to organize public interactions. But these same
histories cautioned against direct participation in the economy, not to mention politics. They demanded marriage as a basis for participation. Wom-
en's history made women important, but it did so by emphasizing their
differences from men and inscribing them into a national narrative that
demanded significant constraints on their behavior. As various scholars
have pointed out, women of the emerging middle class did begin to change
their sexual behavior by the end of the eighteenth century as their virtue
was increasingly tied to their chastity. Many also began to disappear from
the shops where their presence had been so common. These changes were
key as women faced new possibilities of citizenship with the political discussions of the American Revolution.[58]

Chapter 2

Revolutionary Responses

Abigail Adams was exhausted by the efforts she had made to support the Revolution and her new government when she wrote to her husband, John, early in the summer of 1782. Interspersing neighborhood news with her opinions on diplomatic issues, she famously observed with some resignation that "Patriotism in the female Sex is the most disinterested of all virtues."[1] William Russell and Lord Kames might doubt the capacity of women to be patriotic, but Abigail Adams did not. Thus, her comment is important precisely because it suggests the contested nature of women's political capabilities and participation on both sides of the Atlantic at this time. The Revolution that tore the British colonies from England created questions of citizenship that went beyond women's participation in the formation of a nation to engage their involvement in politics more directly. As that debate unfolded, moving from issues of patriotism to direct participation in the government and then to the role of voluntary societies, competing interpretations of women's history began to evolve. In the end, historical interpretations that defended domestic citizenship would triumph but not before alternative historical views were registered that supported the possibility of broader citizenship for women.

When women such as Abigail Adams contemplated their political role, they did so with the assistance of the same women's histories that had explored the relationship of women to commerce, nation, and civilization. Millar, Kames, Thomas, Russell, and Alexander had all used history to make arguments about the abilities of women to participate in governance, and most had expressed deep skepticism. Much of their perspective survived into the nineteenth century, attesting to the power of the discourse

with which they were engaged. Despite their dominance, however, it was a historical discourse that began to be challenged in the heat of the Revolution and its aftermath by women such as Abigail Adams, by writers such as Mary Wollstonecraft and Judith Sargent Murray, as well as by authors of scattered anonymous newspaper articles.

Women on both sides of the Atlantic closely followed the battles, diplomatic maneuvers, and political clashes that played out in the American Revolution. Their activities usually involved political discussions but could extend to the way they dressed or even, in a few cases, to rioting in the streets.[2] As they participated in the political revolutions around them, however, their activities raised questions about the nature of their citizenship. What did political citizenship for women involve and how was it different from domestic citizenship? Should women participate in politics? If so, how? What was the effect of their political activities on the public good? And beyond the arena of direct political involvement, what was the effect of the associations they had begun to create during the Revolution and that they would continue to support after it? What did these groups mean for women as citizens?

Women's histories offered some pointed answers to these questions. Men and women who read the stage theory of Kames and Millar contemplated whether the female leadership among the Amazons and North American Indians was a sign of savagery. Those who picked up the histories of William Russell, William Alexander, and others encountered debates about the abilities of famous—and infamous—queens of European history as well as the civic activities of Roman matrons and the machinations of women in the French court. Russell's volume, in particular, had stressed that the participation of women in politics was not only a sign of moral decadence but also a source of political chaos.

Not all women agreed, however. In letters, broadsides, and essays, challenges began to emerge about these historical assumptions. In bits and pieces, women's history began to be reinterpreted around a competing notion of women's political citizenship. These alternative histories celebrated both the patriotism and the political leadership that women had shown in the past. In the exchange that took place, more positive views of female political accomplishments were articulated as a challenge to the domestic citizenship that had been proposed in the original histories of women.

Female Patriotism

When Abigail Adams made her claim for female patriotism in 1782, she directly engaged and rewrote a key part of the argument in Russell's translation of Antoine-Léonard Thomas's work, *Essay on the Character . . . of Women*. The book had begun with a chapter that combined Thomas's work with that of Adam Ferguson and John Millar to suggest the ways in which women had been oppressed by men throughout history. Suggesting that Thucydides, like all ancient Greeks, thought respectable women should be locked away within their households, Thomas had created (and Russell had translated) a fictional response to the great historian from a woman who argued that her domestic duties deserved the same public recognition that men received for their very different activities. "We are the wives and mothers," she claimed. "Tis we who form the union and the cordialities of families." Going on to speak of the oppression women faced, and then the sacrifices they made in "the name of citizen," she argued, "When you offer your blood to the state, think that it is ours. In giving it our sons and husbands, we give more than ourselves. You can only die on the field of battle, but we have the misfortune to survive those whom we love most" (*Essay*, I: 10–11).

In creating this fictional monologue, the *Essay* had argued that women's domestic responsibilities needed to be publicly honored and that, in creating their families, women also created future citizens and soldiers. These were key elements in the case for domestic citizenship. The Greeks had failed because they had neglected to recognize the public significance of women's domesticity or to make that domesticity a part of their public sphere. It was an effective introduction to the questions the *Essay* wanted to pose about the capabilities of women and the laws that governed their behavior, not to mention their effect on their nations, because it began by stressing that the contributions of women to society had been overlooked (*Essay*, I: 13). Trying to create an impression of impartiality, it began by recognizing the ways that women had been oppressed and by listing women's strengths before turning to their weaknesses.

The *Essay* went on, however, to deny that women were capable of patriotism. Patriotism required qualities that were specifically non-domestic, even anti-domestic. In the *Essay*, patriotism meant a love of the state greater than a love of one's family. It was the product not so much of any inherent

intellectual or emotional ability, but of specific activities that included owning land, holding office, or serving the government in some capacity. Women were denied these rights because their core responsibilities were to their families rather than to the state.[3] As a result, the *Essay* argued,

> In almost all governments, excluded from honours, and from offices, they [women] can neither obtain, nor hope to obtain, nor attach themselves to the state, from the pride of having held a place of eminence. Possessed of little property, and restrained by the laws even in what they have, the form of legislation in all countries must make them in a great measure indifferent to public welfare.

Somewhat cynically, the *Essay* also argued, "This boasted virtue is almost always a composition of pride and selfishness," thus suggesting that women need not regret too much their lack of patriotism.

Be that as it may, because women served in neither the government nor the military "they must be less susceptible of that enthusiasm, which makes a man prefer the state to his family, and the collective body of his fellow-citizens to himself" (*Essay*, II: 34–35). This was one of the key reasons that women could not be political citizens. These views were echoed by Kames when he argued that women could not experience the same level of patriotism as men because they did not have a direct relationship to the state. "The master of a family is immediately connected with his country," Kames argued, but his family was not. "Women accordingly have less patriotism than men," Kames concluded, "and less bitterness against the enemies of their country."[4] Kames, like Russell and Thomas, accepted the eighteenth-century view of patriotism that made it a political rather than a personal virtue.

Readers, however, have some license in how they interpret what they read. Two of the *Essay*'s most famous readers, Thomas Paine and Abigail Adams, appear to have interpreted it differently. Thomas Paine ignored the attack on women's capabilities that permeated most of Russell's volume by printing only the first eleven pages of the book in the *Pennsylvania Magazine*, which, like Russell's work, was published by Robert Aitken. As Mary Catherine Moran has pointed out, Paine credited neither Thomas nor Russell when he ran the piece, so most scholars since that time have viewed the article as a statement by Paine in support of woman's rights.[5] There were

no hints in the authorship to suggest that Paine's piece came from a tract that argued just the opposite.

In fact, the pages that Paine printed contained no suggestion of any rights that women deserved; instead, there was a long list of the ways in which women had been oppressed by men and a plea that their domestic activities be publicly honored. However, because of the lengthy discussion of female oppression throughout history and in different societies, and because the reprint stopped just before the *Essay* began to challenge the abilities and activities of women, the article in the *Pennsylvania Magazine* took on a different meaning. Published in August of 1775, soon after the Battle of Bunker Hill and immediately after the Second Continental Congress had gone into recess, the piece might well have been taken as an attempt to include the oppression of women in the larger discourse about the political oppression of the colonies. It might also have been read more allegorically, to suggest that the colonies, like women, had been oppressed and unappreciated. Either way, it did not convey the deep reservations about women and politics that came through in the rest of the *Essay* and it might have been read as a demand that the needs of women had to be addressed along with those of men.

More than Paine, however, Abigail Adams began to turn the *Essay* on its head not simply by omitting sections, but by rewriting the text. Her letter to her husband in 1782 demonstrated quite clearly that she had read Russell's work (because she drew on parts that Paine had not published in his newspaper); however, it also demonstrated that she had not swallowed the argument that only men were capable of patriotism. Her husband had been in Europe for over two years, attempting to gain financial support and political recognition for the newly emerging country. Much as she missed him, she framed her comments with a direct assessment of political conditions in the American states. Hoping for "an Honorable peace," Abigail informed John that there was tremendous frustration with Britain's diplomatic maneuvers so that the "different States are instructing their delegates to consider every offer as an insult from Britain (which should give a new edge to their Swords) if Independance is not made the Basis." She made it clear that her political concerns trumped her personal ones as she wrote, "Ardently as I long for the return of my dearest Friend, I cannot feel the least inclination to a peace but upon the most liberal foundation."[6]

This preface allowed Abigail to challenge the assumptions of Russell and Thomas. Having demonstrated both her knowledge of politics and her

devotion to the state over her family, Adams had no doubts about her patriotism, even on the terms of political commitment laid out in the *Essay*. Her letters to her husband, however, alternated between information about friends and family, on the one hand, and political information on the other. She repeatedly made known to John how much she missed him, but she also recognized the importance of his mission. For Abigail Adams, declarations of patriotism combined personal ties with political commitment. Rather than focusing simply on a commitment to the state, as the more masculinist interpretation of patriotism dictated, Adams offered a feminine interpretation that combined her domestic role with her political commitment. It was an understanding of patriotism that Kate Davies has identified among elite women in New England during this period and that Harriet Guest has analyzed in England. As Davies points out, particularly with respect to Mercy Otis Warren, women who were part of the political elite often mixed political intelligence with information about families and friends in the letters they shared with both male and female friends, creating an epistolary style that gave shape to this particular form of patriotism that was personal as well as political.[7]

With this more feminized view of patriotism, Adams moved to turn her legal disabilities into a political virtue. Thus, while Thomas had argued that patriotism in men derived from pride and a rather selfish pursuit of recognition, Adams argued that in women patriotism was a more disinterested virtue. Even though women lacked property and were denied a place in the government, they still supported it. Thus, she rewrote Russell (and Thomas) to say, "Excluded from honours and from offices, we cannot attach ourselves to the State or Government from having held a place of Eminence. Even in the freest countrys our property is subject to the controul [and] disposal of our partners, to whome the Laws have given a sovereign Authority. Deprived of a voice in Legislation, obliged to submit to those which are imposed upon us, is it not sufficient to make us indifferent to the publick Welfare?" To buttress that perspective, she also drew on the vision of female self-sacrifice that Thomas had used to introduce his essay and that Paine had circulated, noting, "A late writer observes that as Citizens we are calld upon to exhibit our fortitude, for when you offer your Blood to the State, it is ours. In giving it our Sons and Husbands we give more than ourselves. You can only die on the field of Battle, but we have the misfortune to survive those whom we Love most."[8]

As Adams went on to defend the patriotism of women, she also reinterpreted the historical arguments put forward in the *Essay*. A key part of the argument against women's patriotism involved the dismissal of famous cases of civic virtue, particularly among Roman women. It was hard to overlook how women had collectively dressed to mourn the death of Brutus or the way that they had saved Rome from the rage of Coriolanus. Nor had women stinted when Rome needed their wealth. They had given their gold as ransom to Brennus on one occasion and had sacrificed their jewels on another. And when unjustly taxed by the corrupt triumvirs to support an unpopular war, they had bravely protested. They even provided their own speaker, Hortensia, when no man was brave enough to represent their cause (*Essay*, I: 36–39).

However, just as the *Essay* had circumscribed the intellectual accomplishments of women in history, so too did it circumscribe their patriotism. Russell's translation recounted historical examples of civic virtue, such as those exhibited by the women in Rome, as an exception to the rule, dismissing them by arguing "there are times when nature is astonished at herself; and that great virtues spring from great calamities." Women, the *Essay* assured its readers, generally did not have the capacity to love anything so abstract as their country, or even mankind. "They must have an image of what they love." Incapable of any grander passions than their feelings for a particular lover, the *Essay* argued, "A man to them, is more than a nation; and the hour in which they live, than a thousand ages after death" (*Essay*, II: 35–36).

Adams, however, drew a very different set of conclusions about what the history of women demonstrated. Adams imagined a history of women that showed a consistent commitment to the greater good rather than a long narrative of personal passions punctuated by occasional acts of patriotism. Abigail Adams saw a pattern where Thomas and Russell argued there were exceptions. Thus, she wrote to her husband, "all History and every age exhibit instances of patriotick virtue in the female Sex; which considering our situation equal the most Heroick of yours."[9] Caught up in the conflicts of the American Revolution, women such as Abigail Adams were sure not only that they loved their state, but also that women before them had as well.

Abigail Adams's style of reading history would be repeated by others in future generations, so it is worth pausing to think about what she was

doing. She certainly gave no indication in her letter to John that she was consciously reinterpreting Russell's work. She focused, however, on individual stories from the *Essay* rather than on its argument or broader perspective. Pulling out those stories, she reassembled them into her own version of history, which differed significantly from the *Essay* in its conclusions. Russell and Thomas may not have written an exemplary history, but Abigail Adams refashioned their work into one, and in doing so, she gave herself a kind of political authority. These revisions, moreover, were consistent with the ways she used history in other contexts.[10]

Adams, for example, signed her letter to John as "Portia." The pen name, which she used repeatedly during these years, was a reference to the Roman matron who had been the wife of Brutus. In her correspondence with Mercy Otis Warren, Adams not only used the name Portia, but Warren also frequently adopted the name of Marcia, probably referring to the wife of Cato the younger. As Philip Hicks has pointed out, when Adams and Warren appropriated these names they were drawing on the exemplary theory of history that encouraged readers to learn from the examples of great figures in the past. The tradition might have been one that was considered particularly appropriate for men who were expected to enter the political world, but the resources also existed for women. As Hicks also pointed out, a long list of female worthies from history had been published in *The United States Magazine* in 1779, offering women many heroines to imitate.[11]

In deciding on Portia, Adams chose someone who not only was married to a political leader revered for his opposition to tyranny, but also was a woman who demonstrated the ability to partake fully in the political activities of the rebellion. As the wife of Brutus, Portia had stabbed herself in the thigh to prove to him that he could trust her in discussing his political plans. Thus, Adams adopted a pseudonym that suggested not only her love of her husband and her willingness to support him in his political activities, but also her ability to act decisively and heroically with respect to the politics and the tyranny he opposed. Her love of her country and her love of her husband were distinct, but they did not demand different sensibilities. Here, history once again suggested a kind of patriotism that could be both personal and political.

Abigail Adams was not alone. When Esther de Berdt Reed and Sarah Franklin Bache organized women to raise money for the Continental Army, Reed authored *The Sentiments of an American Woman*, and summoned up a long list of historical examples in which women, independent of their

husbands, had demonstrated their patriotism. Arguing that their ambition was "kindled by the same of those heroines of antiquity, who have rendered their sex illustrious," she cited both collective acts of resistance and individual leaders. Without referring to a specific instance, the broadside described women in the past "building new walls, digging trenches with their feeble hands, furnishing arms to defenders, they themselves darting the missle weapons on their enemy, resigning the ornaments of their apparel, and their fortune, to fill the public treasury, and to hasten the deliverance of their country."[12] Women of the past had fully grasped the need to defend their societies and had willingly done so.

Expressions of female patriotism such as these simultaneously raised questions about women's citizenship and common interpretations of women in history. They merged women's domestic roles with public activities and political commitments in ways that moved far beyond the domestic citizenship that had been promoted by Common Sense thinkers. Those thinkers celebrated the ability of women to facilitate the political activities and patriotism of men, but they argued that most women in the past had only created trouble when attempting the same sorts of political engagement. Women such as Adams, Reed, and Bache disagreed. They created a history of independent female action and political engagement as part of their definition of women's patriotism. Their depictions of women in the past legitimated their own activities as not simply personal, but also political and patriotic.

Claims of Political Citizenship

Different interpretations about women's political activities in the past extended beyond the issue of patriotism to more directly address their abilities to rule and otherwise participate in political decision making. Few histories written during the eighteenth century suggested that women should participate in politics. In almost all cases, authors argued precisely the opposite. One writer to the *Universal Magazine* had suggested in 1753 that women had historically demonstrated their political acumen and that "their Government has been many Times preferable to that of the men."[13] However, that opinion was an outlier. More common were the historical approaches of Russell and Alexander, who used history in different ways to argue

against women's political participation. Again, the events of the Revolution had begun to provoke a reevaluation of that historical perspective.

The histories of Russell and Alexander actually disagreed about the political abilities of women in the past, though both authors suggested that contemporary women should focus their attention on domestic responsibilities rather than on political participation. Russell's volume depicted female rule as generally disastrous, while Alexander found more to admire. As a result, the details of Alexander's *History* may have inspired confidence in women's ability to participate in politics even if his conclusions did not.[14] Alexander thus had more to offer than Russell for those who read these histories selectively and looked for examples of female political leadership.

Russell's *Essay*, like Millar's *Observations*, expressed the emerging consensus in the eighteenth century that tied female political leadership to sexual disorder and a lack of properly cultivated domesticity. It was clear in the writings of both that a woman's patriotism was weaker than a man's and that a woman's attempts to govern were both unnatural and dangerous. Women in the past had combined personal feelings with political action, leading repeatedly to the weakness and corruption of their governments.[15]

Millar associated female political leadership with sexual disorder by tying both to a state of savagery in which the political allegiances of men were perverted. Native American women as well as the Amazons had risen to leadership positions because they lived in societies where marriage either did not exist or was poorly developed. As a result, he argued, children gave their allegiance to the mother rather than to the father, providing a woman with a natural power base that undermined the political prospects of her society. Her children became used to depending on her and obeying her, so they provided her with political allegiance. Millar could not imagine that such women had the necessary qualities for leadership. He was quite sure, for instance, that children had little respect for the military talents of their mothers. Nonetheless, they still valued their mothers' experience and defended them against any challenger. For this reason, the Indians of North America allowed women to participate in public councils and to choose new chiefs. Millar also felt it likely that these conditions explained the military exploits of Amazon women. Neither Native American women nor Amazons suggested to Millar that women were capable of political leadership. Their leadership was an expression of deviance derived from their failure to marry and to provide a more "civilized" basis for political organization

in which men created a barrier and a bridge between their families and the state.[16]

As Russell's *Essay* made clear, women in more civilized societies had also done political damage, particularly through their use of sexual wiles in nations where domesticity was not properly developed. The influence of Greek courtesans on the political life of Athens had been one of the failures of that society, because respectable women lived in a restricted domestic sphere and courtesans exercised political influence unrestrained by domestic purity. The *Essay* argued, "Greece was governed by eloquent men; and the celebrated courtesans having an influence over those orators, must have had an influence on public affairs. There was not one, not even the thundering, the inflexible Demosthenes, so terrible to tyrants, but was subjected to their sway." Russell's volume expressed particular dismay that "Aspasia had been consulted in deliberations of peace and war" (*Essay*, I: 28–30).

Anti-domestic women had been even more dangerous during the colorful and controversial regency of Anne of Austria in the seventeenth century. With political goals that were as venal as their sexual conquests, women had taken up all manner of issues, creating factions that undermined the ability of France to create a functioning political order. "France was a scene of anarchy," according to the *Essay*, when "All things were conducted by women." As the *Essay* went on to describe female influence in politics during this time, it argued,

> They [women in the court] had in that period all the restless agitation which is communicated by the spirit of party; a spirit which is less foreign to their character than is commonly supposed. . . . Every one according to her interest and her views caballed, wrote, and conspired. Their assemblies were at midnight. A woman in a bed, or on a sopha, was the soul of the council. There she determined to negociate, to fight, to embroil or accommodate matters with the court.

The *Essay* stressed the disastrous way in which sex and politics mixed by noting, "They conspired to ruin a lover in the affections of his mistress, and a mistress in the favour of her lover, with as much solemnity as to lay waste a city, or assassinate a prince." There were numerous examples: Madame de Montbazon's power over the Duke of Beaufort, Madame de Longueville's domination of the Duke of Rochefoucault, and Mademoiselle de

Saujon's influence on the Duke of Orléans, not to mention Madame de Chevreuse's long list of political conquests. In each case, women had damaged the political process by tainting it with their sexual wiles unhinged from domestic controls (*Essay*, I: 50–51).

The *Essay* argued that these disasters were not surprising because success in government required a very different set of skills from success in society. "The art of governing in society may therefore be said to consist in flattering vice and folly with address; and the art of administration in combating them with judgment." While women excelled at the former, men excelled in the latter. And because men lived lives of action, they were far better able than women to size up a situation quickly and render the necessary political judgment. Speaking of the innate limitations of female psychology, the *Essay* asked, "Does not their rapid imagination, which often makes sentiment precede thought, render them more susceptible of prejudice or of error in the choice of men?" (*Essay*, II: 13–14). Thus, the qualities of sentiment and imagination that rendered women civilizers of their nations disqualified them from political activities.

To prove this point, the *Essay* examined the historical record, judging the behavior of famous queens. Acknowledging that Isabella of Spain, Christina of Sweden, and Elizabeth of England had met with some success, the *Essay* qualified their political abilities, just as it did the patriotism of Roman women, by describing their accomplishments as unusual. "But, in general questions," the *Essay* argued, "we should beware of taking exceptions for rules; we ought to attend only to the ordinary course of nature." And the ordinary course of nature was not a pretty sight. "Women in general on the throne are more inclined to despotism, and more impatient of restraint than men," the *Essay* claimed. Even Elizabeth's reign was marred by the weaknesses of her sex, as she played the coquette with her favorites and cruelly executed Mary Queen of Scots out of jealousy for her beauty (*Essay*, II: 16). Nothing in the historical record suggested that women were fit for political citizenship in a modern nation.

Alexander's *History* treated the political abilities of women in a somewhat different fashion by celebrating their past accomplishments while at the same time arguing for their retreat from politics in a more modern nation. For Alexander, the question was not rooted simply in the different natures of men and women, but in the evolution of the nation. A modern nation needed differentiated types of citizenship that had not been possible in the past. That said, Alexander also used his history to suggest that women

were fully capable of assuming a more serious role in civil society than had been the case in contemporary Britain.

Thus, when Alexander described queens of the past, he did so with no caveats about their exceptional natures or their failings, but rather as part of a larger discussion about the demonstrated abilities of women. Surveying famous queens from history, Alexander noted that successful female leaders could be found on all continents in all periods. Zenobia from Africa and Semiramis from Syria were both heroic and skillful in their leadership. Queens in England and Germany had been worthy leaders. But Alexander saved his strongest praise for the Empress of Russia (Catherine) to whom he attributed both support for the sciences and support for "the natural rights of her subjects."[17]

Alexander's admiration extended beyond female sovereigns to more common women as well. In these cases, however, he cast women's political participation as firmly rooted in the bonds of familial affection, setting up a kind of gender complementarity that was political as well as social. He recounted approvingly of the way the women of Gaul were given the right to sit in council debating war and peace after they prevented two factions of their men from going to war. "The women with disheveled hair rushed between them, put a stop to the work of destruction, and had the address to reconcile them to each other" (*HW*, I: 220). Their power and status as negotiators were so widely recognized that when Hannibal made a treaty between the Gauls and the Carthaginians he stipulated that all Carthaginian complaints against the Gauls were to be addressed to their women. In contrast to the courtesans of Greece or the women of the French court, these were domestic women who acted as peacemakers rather than partisans when confronted with political problems.

Alexander also softened the criticism of Native American women that came from writers such as Millar, arguing that their political power was a sign of status. Native American men might treat women badly in other respects, but their behavior was "chequered with the appearance of softness and humanity" (*HW*, I: 271). As evidence of this point, he noted that the Huron and Iroquois let women decide the fate of war captives. "When the Iroquois have taken prisoners of war, the council of the nation dispose of them as they think proper," Alexander argued. "But such, in this particular, is the power of the mothers of families, that they may, if they please, invalidate the determination of the council, dispose of the prisoners otherwise, or become sole arbitress of the life or death of such as have been absolved

or condemned by it" (*HW*, I: 272). Alexander did not precisely articulate the family structure in which Native American women operated, but by ignoring the specifics, he created a scenario in which family ties and female political power reinforced each other in a positive fashion.

Neither the ancient Gauls nor the Iroquois were meant to provide a literal model for contemporary women. Alexander was quite clear that one of the major distinctions of modern society from the past lay in a gendered political order in which men took almost exclusive responsibility for direct participation in politics. But his historical examples did buttress his plea that women participate more broadly in civil society as domestic citizens than was currently the practice. In criticizing contemporary society in Britain for its restrictive ideas of female domesticity, Alexander noted that while women were allowed to rule their country, they weren't allowed to do much else with respect to governance. "In Britain," he noted with some irony, "we allow a woman to sway our scepter, but by law and custom we debar her from every other government but that of her own family, as if there were not a public employment between that of superintending the kingdom, and the affairs of her own kitchen, which could be managed by the genius and capacity of woman" (*HW*, II: 505).

While promoting their participation in conversation, however, Alexander was also clear that women's direct participation in political activities would be undesirable in modern Europe because they already received alternative forms of protection and power. Special laws were put in place to protect their chastity, for example, and their husbands were responsible for any debts they incurred. These differences balanced out to a rough equality for the sexes. Indeed, his long list of female privileges contrasted with "many disadvantages, which are necessary, in civil society, to put the two sexes nearly on an equal footing with each other" (*HW*, II: 504–505). Moreover, he argued, women still managed to gain power through their charms, compensating for what was denied them in other realms. Thus, although Alexander's *History* portrayed the political abilities of women in the past (or in different contemporary cultures) in a more positive light than Russell's volume did, it still came to similar conclusions. Equality in Britain was based on difference, not on similarity. The way to balance the social privileges women received was by reserving political privileges for men.

The one area in which Alexander did push for more equality between men and women was in the arena of property rights. Civil society might demand that there be legal differences to balance the social differences that

held the civil world together, but women's property rights needed attention in order to scaffold women's exercise of domestic citizenship. Without land, Alexander noted, there could be little chance of either power or authority. Women were unfairly denied control of property, and they were also denied their fair share of a family's inheritance. "As the possession of property is one of the most valuable of all political blessings," he noted, "and generally carries the possession of power and authority along with it; one of the most peculiar disadvantages in the condition of our women is, their being postponed to all males in the succession to the inheritance of landed estates, and generally allowed much smaller shares than men" (HW, II: 506). While property reform would provide women with more independence, however, it need not result in political privileges.

The historical arguments advanced by Alexander's History of Women and Russell's Essay, not to mention those of other Common Sense thinkers, had a particular salience in the final decades of the eighteenth century. As scholars of European history have demonstrated, women were participating directly in political activities in ways that challenged the ideals of domestic citizenship. Moreover, some began to suggest that they had the right to do so. Many of these demands would culminate most spectacularly in the early years of the French Revolution.[18]

In the colonies as well, women had become increasingly involved in the politics of the American Revolution so that their civic engagement had moved beyond their drawing rooms to independent and direct activities. Their status as consumers and producers put them at the center of the political boycotts of British goods that began in the 1760s, and their social exchanges sometimes became political, a point that has been made by Barbara Clark Smith, Kate Haulman, Susan Branson, and Rosemarie Zagarri. When bands of women in towns throughout the northeast forced merchants to adhere to price controls set by local councils, they entered the realm of revolutionary politics in a manner previously unknown. Elite women, more than men, found their fashions subject to political scrutiny, particularly when they wore clothes of luxurious fabrics that suggested European influence. Beyond their clothes, however, their drawing rooms also became politicized as women actively engaged in discussion about military battles, government intrigue, and the French Revolution. By the end of the Revolution, women had become much bolder about petitioning the government concerning grievances; in New Jersey, a few women even achieved the right to vote for almost two decades after the Revolution.[19]

In addition, some women in the new republic celebrated election day and attended civic events. They were present at parades and at the dinners that followed. They were toasted by the men for their patriotism and for their support for political causes. "As their happiness depends on Federal Union," one man toasted, "may their influence be exerted in its support."[20] They gave vocal support to the candidates of their choice in a wide variety of social circumstances. Indeed, as women continued to discuss politics in the increasingly polarized political world of the 1790s, some boldly called themselves "female politicians."[21]

None of these activities suggested specifically that women wanted the right to vote or that they even wanted the same political rights that men had. But these activities do indicate that many women conceived of themselves as political citizens in some sense. During a time when the exact nature of political involvement could be much less formal than it would be fifty years later, their claim to some form of political citizenship was unmistakable.[22]

It's not surprising that some might not fully accept the arguments of Alexander, Russell, or Common Sense thinkers and that they had begun to reframe their understanding of women's history in light of women's political activities. The *Sentiments of an American Woman*, for example, had held up the queens of the past as defenders of liberty. Ignoring any qualifications that women's historians had expressed about women's abilities, or the applicability of the past to the present, the broadside singled out female leaders who "Born for liberty, disdaining to bear the irons of a tyrannic government," had fought against tyranny. "The Batildas, the Elizabeths, the Maries, the Catherines, who have extended the empire of liberty, and contented to reign by sweetness and justice, have broken the chains of slavery, forged by tyrants in the times of ignorance and barbarity." In addition to the queens, there was "the Maid of Orleans who drove from the kingdom of France the ancestors of those same British, whose odious yoke we have just shaken off." These were examples for contemporary women to emulate.

As Susan Branson has noted, the print culture in places such as Philadelphia was an important vector for raising the consciousness of women about their status in society at the end of the eighteenth century. Two of the most important writers that these women read were Mary Wollstonecraft and Judith Sargent Murray.[23] Both authors not only raised important questions about women's citizenship, but also challenged the historical

assumptions of stage theorists about women and the advance of civilization. They did so in different ways, however, as Wollstonecraft attempted to dismantle the historical assumptions of Common Sense thinkers with logic while Murray attempted to actually re-craft some of the historical narrative within their terms.

Wollstonecraft was certainly familiar with stage theory, not to mention women's history. Indeed, she was one of those who had written a scathing review of *Sketches of the Fair Sex*. She objected to John Adams's poor scholarship, damning him not only for lifting the work of other scholars without the proper use of quotations, but also for the sentimentality in his portrayals of women. She claimed that "far from being a book calculated to improve women, on the contrary, it will tend in common with novels, to render women more weak and affected."[24] But rather than rewrite these histories in *A Vindication of the Rights of Woman*, she dismissed them. Although she adopted an evolutionary approach to her understanding of the condition of women, she mounted a full challenge to the historical assumptions of stage theory.

Championing the idea that the female character had been shaped by environment rather than internal nature, Wollstonecraft argued that the gender distinctions that had evolved in "civilized" life had hurt women rather than helped them and, in the process, had hurt society. Wollstonecraft valued the opportunities that civilization promised; indeed, much of her criticism of Rousseau was based on his logic that criticized current civilization and therefore promoted a state of nature.[25] But in the current state of civilization, manners led women in a direction detrimental to their fulfilling their abilities. Women were "thrown out of a useful station by the unnatural distinctions established by civilized life." As a result, women were just as much the slaves of men as they had ever been.[26] Civilization, far from refining women in a way suited to their distinct natures, had in fact corrupted them by the creation of these distinctions. "Novels, music, poetry, and gallantry, all tend to make women the creatures of sensation, and their character is thus formed in the mould of folly during the time they are acquiring accomplishments, the only improvement they are excited, by their station in society, to acquire."[27]

As Wollstonecraft raised these issues, she engaged the same concerns raised by Common Sense theorists and historians of women who had argued that commerce and luxury could corrupt learning and talent if not properly tamed. However, she completely dismissed the idea that vices

could become public virtues with a properly cultivated sense of domestic citizenship. The public performance of devotion to one's family would not give greater glory to women's learning, talents, or companionship with men. Rather, she recommended that women should have access to the same education as men and that their education should be focused on promoting the same faculties of reasoning and morality as found in men. Wollstonecraft argued that women should be able to exist independently in civil society, and that they had the ability to run a farm, a business, or to practice medicine. Women would not be able "to fulfill the peculiar duties of their sex," she argued, "till they become enlightened citizens, till they become free by being enabled to earn their own subsistence, independent of men; in the same manner, I mean, to prevent misconstruction, as one man independent of another."[28] Far from performing domestic dependence, women needed to be trained for intellectual and economic independence, two key components of citizenship.[29]

Her work became an instant sensation in the United States and France as well as in England, where it was originally published. Mathew Carey printed a huge run of 1,500 copies in Philadelphia. Isaiah Thomas began advertising subscriptions to his edition in the fall of 1792 in newspapers throughout Massachusetts, anticipating "a generous subscription, particularly from the Ladies of this Metropolis and State, who will not certainly neglect to reward, with their patronage, the zeal of the fair author in behalf of the injured rights of the sex." Both men and women did buy it, read it, and discuss it. Wollstonecraft was reprinted in newspapers and cited in diaries and letters. Everyone had an opinion and many of them were favorable.[30]

Shortly thereafter, Judith Sargent Murray elaborated on Wollstonecraft's ideas. Rather than dismiss stage theory and women's history, Murray began to rewrite it. Like Wollstonecraft, she argued that women possessed all the capabilities necessary for full political citizenship, but unlike Wollstonecraft, she legitimated her argument with a strong historical challenge to the idea that women did not have the same abilities as men by summoning up a pantheon of female worthies who demonstrated repeatedly the ability of women to exhibit all virtues necessary for political citizenship. Murray had begun an essay on that topic in 1779, finally publishing it in the *Massachusetts Magazine* in 1790. Arguing that there was no evidence of women's intellectual inferiority to men, and that differences were much more likely due to education, Murray argued the following of men and

women: "Grant that their minds are by nature equal, yet who shall wonder at the apparent superiority, if indeed custom becomes second nature; nay if it taketh place of nature, and that it doth the experience of each day will evince."[31]

Murray wrote repeatedly on issues of women's education (as well as other matters) in her essays for the *Massachusetts Magazine* from 1792 to 1794, taking up many of the concerns that had been raised by Wollstonecraft and that had become common fare in educated conversations. In 1796–1798, when she published those essays as a collection titled *The Gleaner*, Murray described her essays as a complement to *Vindication of the Rights of Woman* and framed her work in opposition to narrow ideals of domesticity that were being promoted for women, suggesting that those who opposed education for girls wanted to return young women to more narrow training in housework.[32]

It is not clear if Murray was aware of Kames's assumption that in a republic, women did not really need to be educated because their men were too busy participating in government to have much time for socializing anyway. But Murray was careful to argue just the opposite: in the infant republic created by the American Revolution, women had to know more than sewing. Thus, a more extensive education was now considered desirable and female academies were being established to service this new demand. Murray accepted the idea that this learning could be put in service to domestic bliss, pointing out that such educated young women would still remain unassuming and that they would enter marriage and motherhood with a more realistic understanding of what to expect and how to best influence their families (*G*, 704–705). But like Wollstonecraft, Murray pushed past the ideal of domestic citizenship to suggest the importance of female independence. A well-educated woman was an independent and self-sufficient woman. She would have the ability to support herself without having to find a husband. She would be able to contribute substantially to the material support of her family if for some reason her husband could not fully accomplish this task (*G*, 727–728). A woman would, therefore, have all the attributes necessary for political citizenship.

Murray addressed these issues in four essays that she added specifically for *The Gleaner*, framing them through the lens of women's history.[33] Rather than challenging civilization as having hurt women with its manners the way Wollstonecraft did, Murray accepted the argument of stage theorists that the status of women was an indicator of a nation's advance. What

she suggested as the next stage, though, was equality rather than complementarity.

> *The idea of the incapability* of women, is, we conceive, in this *enlightened age*, totally *inadmissible*; and we have concluded, that establishing the *expediency* of admitting them to share the blessings of equality, will remove every obstacle to their advancement. In proportion as nations have progressed in the arts of civilization, the value of THE SEX hath been understood, their rank in the scale of being ascertained, and their consequence in society acknowledged. (*G*, 705)

While stage theorists and women's historians had argued that nations advanced around gender difference, thus circumscribing women's access to rights, Murray argued that nations advanced to their greatest heights around a commitment to gender equality, opening the way for a broader claim to citizenship. Indeed, Murray argued that women were capable of such an education because they were "in *every respect* equal to men." She argued that women had proven themselves the equal of men in fortitude, ingenuity, bravery, patriotism, influence, eloquence, perseverance, governing, and literary accomplishment. These were precisely the same intellectual capabilities attributed to men and so often denied to women by Common Sense theorists and women's historians who argued that women's lack of such capabilities justified their exclusion from the political citizenship available to an increasing number of men.

To prove her point, Murray reshaped the historical evidence in many of the histories circulating in the eighteenth century. Such evidence, Murray argued, was far more valuable than a disquisition on properties of the mind. Moreover, given the popular audience she conceived for herself, these facts of history might be more interesting than a more abstract argument (*G*, 709–710). Murray's juxtaposition of history and "nature" in her writing was just the opposite of the stage theorists. Rather than arguing women possessed an innate nature different from men that a successful nation had to recognize and cultivate in order to advance, she used historical behavior to undermine these assumptions about female difference. As a result, Murray did not create a narrative of historical advance but rather brief biographies that challenged common assumptions that had been used to idealize different forms of citizenship for men and women.

In arguing for the broad capabilities of women, Murray noted the way Arria showed her husband how to bravely accept death by killing herself first and the way Lady Jane Gray accepted her execution with dignity. She described how Jane of Flanders led her troops and how Roman women repeatedly saved their country. In arguing that women were "capable of supporting with equal honour, the toils of government," Murray cited the way Semiramis and Zenobia successfully ruled their kingdoms. She ignored any criticisms that existed of Elizabeth, describing her reign as "glorious," and she found Christina of Sweden to both wise and prudent. She noted that Aspasia taught Socrates rhetoric and politics, and cited many examples of female writing that existed from Sappho to Catherine Macauley (G, 711–726). Murray's Aspasia was not scorned as a courtesan but admired for her political acumen. The activities of the Roman women were evidence not only of civic responsibility, but also of patriotism. "Repeatedly they saved their country," she argued (G, 717). Though Murray was clearly uncomfortable with the idea of female warriors, she emphasized their capability in this respect also. "We would have women support themselves with consistent firmness under the various exigencies of life, but we would not arm them with the weapons of death: Yet, when contending for *equality of soil*, it may be necessary to prove the *capability* of the female mind" (G, 715).

Murray did not stop with women of other countries, but began weaving women of the United States into the narrative. She saluted Isabella of Spain for her "enterprise, decision, and generosity" (G, 727) in selling her jewels to fund Columbus's voyage to the New World. In arguing for the intellectual capabilities of women, she noted Mercy Otis Warren and Sarah Wentworth Morton ("Philenia") among others. Murray, in fact, made her motives clear in moving contemporary women into her historical analysis when she introduced this group of historical essays by arguing, "I expect to see our young women forming a new era in female history" (G, 703).

Murray's work was the first sustained attempt in the new United States to craft a history of women that would legitimate any claims they might make for political citizenship. Despite her evidence, however, Murray carefully avoided any call for female participation in politics and specifically noted she was not trying to suggest that women become soldiers. What she did instead was to build a case for the viability and the importance of cultivating in women the kind of economic and intellectual independence that was necessary not only to live independently of a man if they chose (or did not), but also to participate more fully in the state (G, 726). History, in

Murray's rendition, provided examples of women's female abilities that should be allowed to flower in the future. Murray constructed a historical paradigm significantly at odds with Common Sense thinkers and women's historians. A nation's advance, in Murray's model, was one in which the equality of women with men was finally recognized, based in part on an appreciation of women's historical activities. Murray's argument was one of the strongest that found its way into print. Even as she argued that an expanded education would make women better wives and mothers, she also argued that this was not enough. They might need to live independently, something for which they had the political, intellectual, and physical capabilities.

Women's World

While Murray's work is much better known among women's historians today than the work of either Russell or Alexander, in the short term, her voice was not the one that triumphed. On both sides of the Atlantic, the increasing politicization of women provoked a backlash that began unfolding in the 1790s and continued into the nineteenth century. The patriotism of women, particularly during the American Revolution, would become recognized and written into the historical narratives that began to define the new nation. But the political character of their activities, even of their patriotism, was effaced in various ways. Instead, the logic of domestic citizenship triumphed in the creation of what scholars have called republican womanhood. As a somewhat flexible concept, it could be narrowed to focus on only the public significance of women's activities within their homes as they nurtured husbands and children or it could be expanded to include a broader domain of public activities. Women who exercised independent rights, however, increasingly did so within the framework of voluntary organizations that they began to assemble at the end of the eighteenth century rather than through direct participation in the state. The histories of women that were constructed during this period, as well as the historical references that surfaced in newspapers and speeches, legitimated this transformation.[34]

This transformation occurred as fears of female politicians were associated with the growing partisanship in the politics of the early republic. Rosemarie Zagarri has demonstrated that, by the end of the 1790s, this

partisanship meant that women's political involvement was less likely to be seen as selfless devotion to their country and more likely to be portrayed as selfish and dangerous factionalism. While men were even more partisan than women in their support of the Federalists or the Jeffersonian Republicans, the position of women in the political order was more vulnerable.[35]

Ironically, the presence of women in political events had been meant not only to swell the numbers of supporters, but also to add a kind of disinterested civic engagement to the partisan political activities men were uncomfortable embracing. Fears of female partisanship, however, were inflamed among both Federalists and Republicans as each side sought the attendance of women at their parades, or received their banners, or suggested they keep politics in mind when choosing their suitors. Rather than muting the factionalism of both sides, women were blamed for its growth. To make matters worse, gender imagery was tossed around as angry Federalists and Republicans impugned each other's masculinity by associating their opponents with feminine weakness, or tarred each other's respectability with images of whores and loutish females. It began to appear that the only way women could exert their civic influence on the political arena was to leave it, assuming a more pure and passive role that would counterbalance the wild antics of the men in their community. Indeed, as John Brooke has suggested, women during this period were limited in their ability to express themselves on a range of issues in the public sphere.[36]

With these fears of women's political involvement growing, there were no writers who attempted to elaborate the historical work on women that Murray had begun. Instead, women of the past who had directly engaged political life were depicted as having sacrificed their respectability. The view of Aspasia as a sexually wanton troublemaker, for example, continued to be a staple in political references. In the late 1780s, when Alexander Hamilton penned one of the *Federalist Papers*, he suggested that the causes for national conflicts could sometimes be found in the power of private passions, so that Pericles had been led into war by the "resentment of a prostitute" (Aspasia), and that French and British women of the court had caused similar trouble in the preceding century. In 1807, the *New-Bedford Mercury* ran a fictional exchange on the ability of women to participate in high-level intellectual discussions. One of the female participants held up Aspasia as a historical example of a woman who had been sought out by men such as Pericles and Socrates for her wit and conversation. Her male adversary, however, argued that she should check her facts because "Pericles and his

associates were allured to her house, by something beside the feast of reason." While Aspasia was dismissed as wanton, other historical female figures could be criticized for their lack of femininity. James Wilson, in his lecture on "The Study of Law" in the early 1790s, acknowledged the superior abilities of Semiramis, Zenobia, and Elizabeth, as military leaders and as rulers, but he also argued that in developing those qualities, they had surrendered the possibility of becoming "lovely and accomplished." He urged the women in his audience not to de-sex themselves as these women in the past had.[37]

In place of politically and intellectually independent women, the domesticity of women in the past was celebrated. While a few years earlier some Roman matrons had been celebrated for their engagement with political concerns, by the end of the eighteenth century, they were more likely to be represented as apolitical wives and mothers. Cornelia, for example, had sometimes been depicted not only as devoted to her family, but also as a highly educated woman who actively entered into political intrigue and who maintained a literary salon after her husband's death. By the end of the eighteenth century, however, newspaper stories focused repeatedly on a single anecdote that suggested her mutually reinforcing devotion to her children and to a life of republican simplicity. According to the story, when a wealthy matron displayed her jewels, Cornelia responded by gathering her children together and claiming that they were her jewels.[38]

In a similar vein, more than one newspaper in 1801 reprinted an article from the *Palladium* that argued that Roman and Athenian women would have rejected the rights of woman. This article was particularly striking in its admiration for the strict rules of domesticity demanded by the Greeks, and it even argued that the same had been true of the Romans. "The monstrous doctrine of the *Rights of Woman*, as understood at present, was then unknown, and, could it have been promulgated, would have been spurned, by the ladies of Athens, with becoming indignation." Philip Hicks has noted that in both England and France, the representation of the Roman matron as politically engaged had disappeared by the end of the eighteenth century (largely as a response to the excesses of the French Revolution). In her place, a more domestic representation of Roman women arose. As newspaper articles make clear, a similar revision was under way in the United States.[39]

Occasionally, random historical acts of female heroism surfaced in newspaper accounts, but with no interpretation, leaving the impression that

these were oddities rather than characteristics of female behavior. In 1798, the *General Magazine and Impartial Review of Knowledge & Entertainment* devoted a couple of paragraphs to "female heroism." One paragraph explained how the women in Dartmouth, England, had defended their town against the French, "charging them with Amazonian courage." Another paragraph described how women in the Dalmatian Islands repulsed the Turks in the early sixteenth century after their men had fled in panic. Neither incident was used to draw any conclusions. In 1804, *The Weekly Visitor, or Ladies Miscellany*, noted that while military valor was generally not "suitable" for women, there were times when their activities deserved praise. Thus, the valor of Jeanne Hatchette, who helped to save her village of Beauvais from the Duke of Burgundy in the fifteenth century rightly deserved to be commemorated. So too was the bravery of Telesilla, who armed the women of her city to fight the Spartans in the sixth century B.C. and in so doing, left the Spartans so befuddled that they abandoned their siege. In both of these instances, though, the presentation continued the arguments of eighteenth-century writers that occasionally women behaved with bravery but that such instances were exceptions. Indeed, the very manner of presentation continued to suggest just that.[40]

Women of the American Revolution were, however, remembered as patriots. In part, this represented a real change in the way historians placed women in the narrative of American history, granting them both a presence and agency that had been previously lacking. That said, they were also remembered as patriotic because they expressed their patriotism in a way that merged their love of country with their ties to their homes and communities. In 1789, the *Massachusetts Magazine* described how the women of Bristol, Pennsylvania, had "wrought a magnificent suit of colours" for their local regiment. In 1822, when Major Alexander Garden devoted a large section of his *Anecdotes of the Revolutionary War in America* to the activities of women, he followed a similar pattern. Because his book was focused on South Carolina, he confined his stories to women from that state. Garden credited the women for keeping the spirits of the men alive when Charleston was under British control. Describing a scene of desolation in which leaders had been arrested and younger men had scattered in disorder, Garden claimed "that manly spirit which alone could secure success, might have sunk, but for the cheering smiles and intrepid firmness of the fair sex, who by sharing the calamities of their suffering countrymen, taught how to oppose and subdue them." The women, according to Garden, defied the

British at every chance and sought out prisoners and the wounded among the patriots to provide them with nursing and care. Thus, Mrs. Jacob Motte allowed the patriots to burn her house, apparently telling General Lee that she would view its sacrifice with delight if it would aid her country's victory, and she then even supplied him with the arrows that would be used to convey the flames. Mrs. Rebecca Edwards had told her sons, with the sentiment of a "Spartan mother," that they were to resist giving in to the British when captured. Mary Anna Gibbs, though only a teenager, raced through bullets to her home to rescue an infant who had been left behind when the British began shelling the neighborhood.[41]

Garden's work elicited further stories in a similar vein from readers and reviewers in other states. In 1827 the *American Quarterly Review* praised Garden for devoting a large section of his *Anecdotes of the Revolutionary War in America* to the activities of women, but the review editors added a description of one woman he had overlooked. The reviewer cited the heroism of Lydia Darrah, a Quaker woman in Philadelphia, who had been forced to host meetings for General Howe's officers and who had overheard the plans being made by the British to attack Washington's troops. Darrah managed to slip across enemy lines the following day, claiming to be in search of flour, and got word to Washington's forces of the battle plans, thus foiling British plans under the cover of her domestic responsibilities. In both her bravery and her domestic simplicity, she exemplified the virtues of the new nation. Deborah Logan wrote to Garden just after the publication of the book, recounting some of her own experiences in Philadelphia. She recalled nursing the wounded and the imprisoned, the way one of her servants had misled the British to protect their house, and the houses that burned. She also recalled the story of a wealthy woman who entertained General Howe lavishly at a long breakfast, knowing that it would give Washington and his troops time to escape.[42]

Peter Messer has noted that as women of the Revolution were written into the historical narrative of the country, they were given more agency in the creation of the United States than they had been during the colonial period when, if mentioned at all, they were depicted as passive spectators. But as Linda Kerber has pointed out, it was a very particular kind of agency that tended to erase the most rambunctious and politicized activities of women. It was rather, as Logan's letter suggests, a reflection of the life elite women were living then. Spirited and patriotic, they made personal sacrifices for the good of their country. Their historical activities had public

significance, suggesting how they had acted as citizens. But it was not a history that gave them a claim on political citizenship. The history of women's participation in the Revolution was organized around their differences from men, resulting in continued differences of citizenship. Women would have to express that citizenship differently.[43]

The growing emphasis on differentiated citizenship surfaced in a variety of ways. When Priscilla Mason graduated from the Young Ladies' Academy of Philadelphia in the spring of 1793, she had been trained in public oratory and she claimed as much right to address her audience as any man. Yet, as Carolyn Eastman has pointed out, both the training of girls in public speaking and the expectation that they would undertake such addresses were beginning to decline during this period and would evaporate by the 1820s, along with so many other civic expectations for women. Girls, increasingly, would be barred from commencement speaking at their academies and would be encouraged to practice a more modest form of speaking that supported ideals of gender difference.[44]

Mason's speech exemplifies this transition in several ways. She did demonstrate her skills in public speaking. And while she did not demand equality with men, she did decry the injustices that men had perpetrated on women. "Our high and mighty Lords (thanks to their arbitrary constitutions) have denied us the means of knowledge, and then reproached us for it. Being the stronger party," she went on, "they early seized the scepter and the sword; with these they gave laws to society." She bemoaned the fact that "the Church, the Bar, and the Senate are shut against us." Asking "Who shut them?" she answered, "*Man*; despotic man, first made us incapable of the duty and then forbid the exercise."[45]

As Mason turned to history for a solution, however, she did not demand the same rights that men had. She pointed out that the Roman emperor Heliogabalus had actually created a separate senate of women to regulate dress and fashion. It's hard to know whether Mason was being intentionally satirical here or revising the commonly accepted view of Roman history, since Heliogabalus had been reviled as one of the most degenerate of the Roman emperors and his female senate had been considered one of his many activities that were evidence of his degeneracy. Still, Mason argued that the United States also needed a female senate. Such an innovation, she argued, would "give dignity, and independence to our manners; uniformity and even authority to our fashions."[46] Mason thus concluded her attack on inequality with a proposal for separate female institutions to promote the

well-being of the country. It was not the complementarity of familial relationships, but it mimicked them on an institutional level.

Mason's use of history, whatever its problems, had brought her to champion a form of citizenship that was organized around gender complementarity rather than universal rights. Mason's argument alluded to a key development in the late eighteenth century as women's political activities increasingly came under attack: women were also forming female civic associations. Just as they had done in the Revolution to raise money for the Continental Army, they were creating organizations of women that had both a public and republican spirit. Early organizations were particularly aimed at assisting poor widows and orphans. But in addition to assisting the poor, they were also organizations that were incorporated and which gave the association legal rights that were not available to them as individuals, from the right to own property to the right to bring legal suit in court.[47] In an era when the state and federal governments were both weak and new, participation in these organizations not only offered a competing arena for exercising rights, but also drew on a well-established tradition of rights theory from the eighteenth century that located rights not in individuals but in the organizations and ranks that they inhabited.[48]

Hannah Mather Crocker also incorporated that thinking in 1818 when she both drew upon and revised the writings of Russell and Alexander in her *Observations on the Real Rights of Women.* Closer to Alexander than to Russell, Crocker championed the intellectual abilities of women at the same time she condemned any suggestion that women engage in activities that were traditionally the province of men. Crocker's theory of woman's rights adapted a Christian history of dispensationalism to suggest that women had lost their original rights and duties because of Eve's sin but had then regained them with Christ's birth. She recognized that women had not always been appreciated for their spiritual virtues, citing William Alexander's discussion of the misogyny associated with the witch hunts of late medieval Europe as an example of this phenomenon. Their contemporary reputation for spiritual purity was not one they should sacrifice.[49]

Where Crocker really intervened in history was in her rewriting of Russell's *Essay,* to which she referred repeatedly. While Crocker cited Russell as an authority, she also reinterpreted the *Essay,* perhaps unintentionally. Like Abigail Adams, she gave no indication that she was turning Russell's translation on its head. There is no doubt, however, that she both reformulated his ideas and used his historical examples to draw different conclusions. At

one point in her discussion, she noted that "women may reasonably become equal with men in patriotism and disinterested love of country."
Where the *Essay* had seen female failings, Crocker saw triumph. Whether
referring to female Christian martyrs or Athenian courtesans or famous
queens, Crocker reframed the *Essay*'s descriptions as a narrative of female
abilities rather than of female limitations. "Greece was governed by eloquent men, and the influence courtezans had held in public affairs was by
the influence of the celebrated courtezans held over the orators," Crocker
blithely wrote. Elizabeth I in her version was not hampered by petty female
vindictiveness but rather singled out "for the great strength of mind she
discovered in her youth," and her reign was "one of the most shining periods of English history."[50]

Like Judith Sargent Murray, Crocker also wrote American women into
the history by citing not only Sarah Wentworth Morton and her poetry but
also Hannah Adams and Mercy Otis Warren for their historical writings in
which they did "honour to themselves, their country and sex, as faithful
compilers of history." Indeed, Crocker cast Warren as a historian who remembered such heroic ladies of the Revolution as Harriett Ackland, a wife
who followed her British husband to war, and Martha Washington, who
"shone as a bright example of female excellence."[51]

Unlike Murray, though, Crocker's argument and her history did not
support the idea of female independence. She agreed with Murray that history demonstrated that the minds of men and women were equal. And she
ignored Russell's arguments that women in history had demonstrated that
women had limited abilities when it came to engaging public or political
responsibilities. She was quite clear, however, that what women could do
was not the same thing as what women should do. Propriety and morality
dictated that men and women should do different things. Women might be
intellectually capable of studying law and even of arguing in a court of law,
but that didn't mean they should do it. Women, she suggested, were meant
to shine within their homes, creating order and providing inspiration.[52] It
was an argument that embraced the spirit of Alexander's work more than
Russell's, though she cited neither of them when she made it.

However, Crocker, like Priscilla Mason, championed the activities of
women within benevolent organizations as well as within their homes. They
were just as intelligent as men, and if their domestic lives permitted, history
demonstrated that they could make great contributions to the world of
literature. Woman's rights, therefore, lay in their ability to be educated,

their ability to be friends and companions of their husbands (rather than slaves), and their right to form and join religious and benevolent organizations. In adding the right to form and join religious and benevolent organizations, however, Crocker, like Mason, made the significant intervention of moving women beyond the household and introducing a broad ranging arena for the exercise of rights that men did not control.[53]

Given that the state itself was a relatively weak institution at this time, and that organizations conveyed important rights and privileges to their members, Crocker's emphasis on the right to participate in benevolent organizations was not insignificant. Women in the early nineteenth century had been criticized for their lack of propriety in participating in such organizations. And as members of those organizations, women might exercise rights that were not available to them in their households as they controlled their own finances and interacted with government entities to support their efforts. But the real impact of that participation, and its effect on both women and the writing of women's history, would not be seen for more than a decade.[54]

Meanwhile, the concept of domestic citizenship had triumphed over women's political activities as well as their economic ones. Neither direct political activities nor economic participation either through housework or their shops would be celebrated in the ideals of citizenship for women. Domestic citizenship could shine beyond the household in various forms of sociability and in the voluntary associations that were developing, but it could not do so in the state or economy.

Chapter 3

The Challenges of Radical Reform

Maria Stewart was angry and defiant in 1833 as she delivered a farewell address in Boston. As a follower of David Walker's, Stewart had spent two years publicly speaking to fellow African Americans around Boston, urging them to join actively in the fight against slavery. She criticized their interests in gambling and dancing, advocating instead a path of religious devotion and rigorous education. Her criticisms of the free black community as well as the boldness of her public speaking and political writings outraged some African Americans, ultimately forcing Stewart to abandon her crusade. Her activities and her behavior, however, demonstrated just how far women's benevolent activities had come in the decade since Hannah Crocker had justified their existence in the *Real Rights of Women*. Stewart was African American, she spoke in public, and she attacked slavery, which was both an economic and a political issue. Maria Stewart thus personified the way in which earlier ideas about women's domestic citizenship were being challenged in antebellum America.[1]

Interestingly, Maria Stewart also reinterpreted John Adams's *Sketches . . . of the Fair Sex* (written under the pen name of "A Friend of the Fair Sex") to justify her behavior by reminding the audience that women had a proud history of speaking out on important matters. Disregarding any of the reservations Adams had expressed about the public activities of women in the past when he incorporated the *Essay on the Character of Women* into his *Sketches*, Stewart celebrated the Renaissance women who not only had pursued higher learning, but had also taken chairs in universities. They had studied Greek, Hebrew, and Latin, she pointed out. They had preached and they had debated in public, and they "would with the sweetest countenances and the most plaintive voices, pathetically exhort the Pope and the Christian princes to declare war against the Turks." Stewart argued that

these women were an inspiration, particularly for black women. "What if such women as are here described should rise among our sable race?" she demanded to know. "And it is not impossible. For it is not the color of the skin that makes the man or the woman, but the principle formed in the soul. Brilliant wit will shine." If anyone doubted the respect that was held for women of accomplishment in the past, Stewart argued, they should consult *Sketches . . . of the Fair Sex*.[2]

Like Hannah Crocker and Abigail Adams, Stewart ignored the criticisms that Thomas, Russell, and Adams had made of Renaissance women, focusing instead on the women's accomplishments. Indeed, Stewart's women did not "harangue" the Pope (as the *Essay* and Adams's *Sketches* claimed), but "pathetically exhort[ed]." More important, however, Stewart wrote black women into a historical narrative that had been implicitly white. By not only revising the characterization of Renaissance women as it had been presented in *Sketches* but also claiming it as an example for black women as well as white women, she transformed Adams's critique of women into an exemplary history her African American contemporaries could emulate.

Stewart started an important trend. As activist women pushed the boundaries of acceptable behavior in a range of reform movements, their behavior provoked a reevaluation of both domestic citizenship and women's history. Public speaking was one of the most controversial activities undertaken by female activists during the 1830s, particularly with respect to slavery. Questions of citizenship during this time did not center only on the ability of women to represent their ideas in public; they also involved the significance of female economic activities in both the present and the past, the meaning of marriage and chastity in the construction of a stable republic, and the challenge of including race and slavery in a national narrative. Assumptions about both the civil society within which women operated, and the nation they supported, were contested far more extensively than had been the case in the early republic. Lydia Maria Child's *History of the Condition of Women*, first published in 1835, led the way in challenging the orthodoxies of women's history that had been central in constructing arguments for domestic citizenship. Sarah Grimké followed her a few years later with *Letters on the Equality of the Sexes*, reprinting some of Child's historical work to make an even more explicit critique of manners and gender oppression. In the 1840s, Margaret Fuller pushed even further with *Woman in the Nineteenth Century*. Both Grimké's and Fuller's works had been published serially in newspapers before they were printed as books,

resulting in an even larger audience for their arguments. Joined with criticisms of female subordination, a new strain of women's history began to circulate, challenging the types of gender differences in citizenship that had previously been upheld as necessary to national progress. Moreover, Stewart's challenge to the African American community was also continued as antislavery activists wove black women into the nation's history.[3]

The Troubled Boundaries of Domestic Citizenship

Lydia Maria Child expressed some of her own contradictory feelings about citizenship in 1841, as she reflected on the growing importance of the "Woman Question." Never a leader (or even much of a participant) in the woman's movement, she wrote as a reluctant supporter who would prefer to struggle for the rights of others rather than for herself and to "*take* my freedom without disputing it." Yet like others, she had felt forced to defend the public speaking of antislavery women such as Angelina Grimké and Sarah Grimké. Writing in the pages of the *Anti-Slavery Standard*, which she was editing, Child patiently explained that women had taken up the call to improve the world through their religious tract and missionary associations and had found a host of problems in need of reform. There would be no stopping them now, she claimed, as she told the story of the sorcerer's apprentice. This young assistant to a German wizard had tried to use his master's magic to bewitch a broom into doing his chores, but he faced chaos as he lost control of the cleaning process and realized that he did not know the right spell to reverse the magic. "Thus it is with those who urged women to become missionaries, and form tract societies," she concluded. "They have changed the household utensil into a living, energetic being; and they have no spell to turn it into a broom again."[4]

Brilliantly, Child's analogy suggested that women had been drawn out of a lifeless household existence filled with domestic responsibilities and into a world where their activities were disrupting social relationships, a process that was terrifying those who had previously controlled them. It was an analogy that must have resonated with readers who had watched women take on one social problem after another during the previous decades, challenging approved social norms at every turn. Gender-specific associations had given women power and rights that threatened to spill over

into new realms of political organizing. Voluntary organizations were exerting more influence than had been expected originally, creating a volatile context for female activism. Child clearly recognized that the domestic citizenship that was championed in the early republic, and funneled into voluntary organizations, had taken on new life and a new meaning. The boundaries of differentiated citizenship were changing.

As women's organizations took on prostitution and drinking, for example, women both defended the homes that were the basis for their domestic citizenship at the same time that they challenged the authority of many of the men who were supposed to represent them in the larger world of business and politics. A range of organizations developed in large and small cities on the East Coast during the 1830s to attack prostitution. Some of the most aggressive printed the names of men who visited brothels, or they wrote newspaper articles blaming men for seducing young women. Even more extensive were the temperance societies that women began joining in the late 1820s. A decade later, women would create their own organizations and focus, by and large, on the drinking habits of fathers and husbands who squandered family resources in local barrooms. By the 1840s, the most radical would be demanding that women be given the right to divorce dissolute husbands.[5]

Some women also extended their own exercise of citizenship by questioning its racial boundaries in the petitioning campaigns they developed first to protest the seizure of Indian lands and later to protest slavery. While Indian and African American women were some of the earliest leaders in these movements, middle-class white women soon followed. Catharine Beecher secretly spearheaded a female petition drive to protest Andrew Jackson's policy of Cherokee Indian Removal in 1830. Child was among the women who signed the petition, which argued that Native Americans had a right to their lands and a place within the nation. Shortly thereafter, women such as Child began to petition for the abolition of slavery. Although antiremoval and antislavery movements involved only a small proportion of women in the country, both movements pointed to the questions that were arising about who belonged in the nation and who did not, as well as the terms of inequality that were organized around race. As Angelina Grimké defended her right to attack slavery, she argued, "Are we bereft of citizenship because we are the *mothers, wives,* and *daughters* of a mighty people? Have *women* no country?"[6]

Many women who participated in these organizations saw them as an extension of domestic citizenship, in which they expanded their roles as moral guardians of their homes to police the moral behavior of their communities. There was little doubt, however, that the most radical of their activities expanded the attributes of citizenship they claimed. Far from simply conversing with men to promote their virtue and soften their rough edges, women challenged the behavior of men in public forums. They collectively demanded changes in political organization as well as in social behavior. Moreover, these organizations created a world of female sociability and political activism that had not existed in earlier decades. Women were using their membership in these organizations to collect, hold, and distribute money, as well as to take political positions and agitate for legal changes.[7]

Further complicating these challenges to the boundaries of citizenship were the activities of young working women, particularly in the northeast. While the ideology of domestic citizenship that had been promoted in the second half of the eighteenth century may have succeeded in encouraging some middle-class women to abandon their shops, a new wave of working women had emerged. With the advent of industrialization, thousands of young, single women moved into textile production and took up other forms of piecework in rapidly transforming trades. Although many of the larger mills (and their employers) tried to create the illusion that this work was fully compatible with the ideals of the domestic world the young women had left behind, it was hard to overlook the direct economic relationship of these women to their employers or their importance in the process of industrialization. And these women, like many of those who took up issues of social reform, were not afraid to protest publicly economic injustice, as was clear in their periodic labor protests over wages and hours. The same was true of seamstresses and shoebinders, who generally worked within their homes but who still protested publicly when faced with pay cuts.[8]

Wage work and female activism changed the terms by which many women participated in the world around them, but competing ideals of domestic citizenship were trumpeted even more vociferously in the mass media that exploded during this period, particularly in the form of ladies' magazines. Journals and books instructed women on how to morally educate their children, attend to the health of their families, and set a proper table. With these activities, women would not only protect their loved ones, but also contribute to the health of the nation. The eighteenth-century

belief that manners and morals were the bedrock of national progress was broken down into practical lessons for middle-class readers. The economic value of their activities within the home, meanwhile, was effaced. Whether it be taking in boarders, cooking and cleaning, making clothes, or selling preserves, the money that housewives might earn was ignored, even hidden, in order to suggest a world of respectability that had a century earlier been limited to the most genteel and elite.[9]

Lydia Maria Child participated in this world of domestic advice literature as well. Child, however, had staked out a position that more directly addressed the economic value of housework and women's labor with her best-selling *Frugal Housewife*. Child's guide appealed to a particular niche in the market for domestic advice by focusing on the economic struggles that many women might face in achieving domestic comfort. She provided advice for women whose budgets were limited and who tended their homes without the help of servants.[10] That understanding of the economic value of women's work would surface in her writing of women's history as well. So, too, would her commitments to antislavery and the right of women to fight for it. As a result, Child's history took on the larger discourse of domestic citizenship in a way that Murray had begun to contemplate but had never executed.

Lydia Maria Child and the Creation of Women's History

Lydia Maria Child's two-volume *History of the Condition of Women in Various Ages and Nations* was one of the most significant interventions in the creation of women's history during the nineteenth century, though it's not easy to see it that way. Like the broom that came to life in her telling of the story of the sorcerer's apprentice, her work careens through history, shaking out the dust that had taken hold on ideas about women in the past, upsetting assumptions about historical progress that had been set in place by stage theorists in the eighteenth century, and overturning common perceptions about non-Western nations, without necessarily setting things right at the end. It was part of the five-volume *Ladies' Family Library* that Child published between 1832 and 1835, no doubt in imitation of the successful *Harper's Family Library*. While the first three volumes focused on female biographies, Child's *History of the Condition of Women* was more ambitious, in effect rewriting the tomes that had been produced by Thomas

and Russell, Alexander, and Adams. Yet it was an ambition Child never fully acknowledged, perhaps because she was not sure of where her analysis would lead, but also because she desperately needed to sell this series to an audience of female readers who had thrived on her domestic advice and who might be alienated by a perspective that was too radical.[11]

As she struggled to publish her *Family Library*, Child was still reeling from attacks she had suffered in 1833 for her powerful abolitionist tract, *An Appeal in Favor of That Class of Americans Called Africans*. Child had built a successful career publishing domestic literature, such as *The Frugal Housewife* and *The Girl's Own Book*. But her growing commitment to the abolitionist cause, nurtured by her marriage to the fervent antislavery advocate David Child and by her opposition to Indian removal, had led her to direct her powerful writing skills to a tightly reasoned attack on slavery. Unfortunately, the public furor that resulted from *The Appeal* seriously damaged her credentials and income as a domestic writer. David had never been able to support them, so the loss of Child's publishing income was painful. The furor also had cost her the complimentary borrowing privileges at the Boston Athenaeum where she was researching her history of women. Antislavery women, led by Maria Weston Chapman, quickly raised funds to pay for her membership but the Athenaeum refused to admit her even as a paying member.[12]

Child's *History* was hastily constructed, and it shows. The narrative is choppy and her points often seem contradictory. Although Child conventionally upheld Christianity, Western civilization, and the condition of women in the United States, she repeatedly undercut those generalizations with her examples. She described extensively the manners of different countries, past and present, at the same time that she often detached them from the significance of women's work. Those contradictions and disjunctures, though, were the heart of her project. With criticisms that were often expressed as barbed asides indirectly comparing modern American society unfavorably to other civilizations and nations, Child produced a book that challenged, in significant ways, the narrative that eighteenth-century historians had created in women's history.

Like Judith Sargent Murray, Child asserted that women were as competent as men in all areas. But while Murray had written four short historical sketches that undermined the assumptions of Thomas and Russell, Alexander, and Adams about female capabilities, Child's effort was far more ambitious in scope, covering two volumes, so that her book could replace those

earlier works. More important, she not only championed the abilities of women but also engaged in a more wide-ranging analysis of the conditions under which women had lived in different times and different places, challenging the conclusions of earlier historians about the meanings inherent in women's work, domestic arrangements, and public activities. Child systematically attacked the assumptions of progress that were key to earlier women's histories; she also critiqued the ideals of domestic citizenship. She was clearly familiar with eighteenth-century women's histories, and she drew on them extensively as a "compiler" who freely added and adapted long passages from other works as the basis for her own. She had checked out Alexander's *History of Women* from the Boston Athenaeum, but her work suggests she had also read either the *Essay* by Thomas and Russell or Adams's *Sketches of the Fair Sex*.[13] Yet buried in the mass of facts was a very different interpretation of women's history from what had been produced during the eighteenth century.

Child took on domestic citizenship, as well as the tale of national progress and identity that went with it. The assumptions of cultural superiority that characterized earlier women's histories were more muted in her work. Child's book, much more than those of Thomas and Russell, or Alexander, or Adams, celebrated the cultures of earlier times and the cultures of non-Western societies. She wasn't a total relativist by any means, but Child found much more to admire about the condition of women in other cultures and was less sanguine about the condition of women in her own than were the eighteenth-century writers. She used that position to critique contemporary society by subtly suggesting the "savagery" of many modern customs, particularly those related to class privilege. And while earlier histories had culminated in praise (or criticism) of contemporary women as the key indicator of a nation's advance, Child denied that a nation could ever progress if it was organized around the enslavement of some women or if it promoted gender ideals that failed to acknowledge slavery.

Child's reframing of women's history was organized around issues that were central to ideals of citizenship: work (free labor), political and military acumen, and marriage (chastity). She celebrated the freedom that women in the past had found in economically valuable work by stressing their ability to move in public and the respect they received from the men in their society. Though she praised the moral value of women's domestic abilities as well, Child's broader perspective on women's work was a critique of eighteenth- and nineteenth-century ideals of domestic citizenship

that focused exclusively on the moral and social value of women's activities and that turned women's work with economic value into a sign of savagery. In addition, Child highlighted the significance and recognition that women had received in other cultures for their military, political, and intellectual prowess. Rather than suggesting such behavior was exceptional or undesirable, she argued that it contributed in a sustained way to the strength of societies where practiced. Finally, with respect to the evolution of chastity and marriage, which were important components of the differentiated citizenship that had been so important in eighteenth-century histories, Child raised questions about their universal value and applicability.[14]

As Child repeatedly interrogated the relationship between work and status within different nations, she depicted women's economic activities in the past as a basis for freedom rather than for slavery. For example, she recounted from the Bible how "Jacob found Rachel tending the flocks of her wealthy father." Earlier histories would have argued that Rachel's physical labor was evidence of women's (and thus society's) degraded position during this time. Child, however, hastened to point out that Rachel's work in the field was not a sign that women were badly treated but rather that this was how all people survived during an earlier period in history: "The performance of these tasks does not necessarily imply a deficiency of respect for women, for at that period kings and princes were in the habit of reaping their own grain, and slaying their own cattle." Indeed, Child even suggested that such activities might bring with them significant privileges. She concluded, "In the patriarchal ages the Jewish women must have enjoyed a large share of personal freedom; for we read of all ranks engaged in the labors of the field, and going out of the cities to draw water."[15]

Moving beyond household labor, Child also suggested that many women in ancient Egypt enjoyed a good deal of freedom and importance in their society, particularly as a result of their prominence in commerce and agriculture. She dismissed as satiric exaggeration the criticism that Egyptian women had completely reversed the gender hierarchy by forcing their husbands to do housework. Women who engaged in commerce or agriculture did not create disorder in society nor did they undermine their status by their pursuits, Child argued (*HCW*, I: 218–220).[16] Child also noted the importance of the economic activities of Burmese women, who were known to take an active role in the supervision of their husbands' businesses in addition to overseeing more traditional female activities such as

spinning. Again, Child argued that this was evidence of both the freedom and the confidence that Burmese women enjoyed (*HCW*, I: 135).

Child even praised the convents that had been established in the Middle Ages because of the good work that nuns did in nursing the sick, caring for the destitute, and educating those under their care. Although she condemned convents as perversions of Christian spirit and as oppressive institutions that parents might use to lock up their daughters, Child saw the value in these women's organizations when it came to providing health care and education. Child also pointedly noted that in the Middle Ages, and up until the time of Elizabeth, women at court also were expected to be trained in surgery and medicine (*HCW*, II: 113, 125–126).

For Child, part of her definition of freedom came through work. Whether in the commercial world or in the home, Child repeatedly put forward examples of women in the past who had more freedom and status because their work took them outside the home to the fields or markets. And she was quite clear that this work was an opportunity that showed the status and respect for women in a society, rather than an indication of some lower form of savagery. In fact, Child was unwilling to accept the idea that these women's activities suggested that these societies were savage.

Child's celebration of work had important implications for concepts of citizenship. A strong contingent of northerners increasingly tied the virtue of the republic to ideas of free labor during the antebellum period. While property holding had been a key concept at the time of the revolution, the gradual abolition of property requirements for voting in the nineteenth century had shifted attention to the free labor status of white male workers. It was this labor, rather than property per se, that gave these men the material self-reliance that was one of the necessary ingredients for the practice of virtuous citizenship.[17] Thus, as Child conjured up images of women in the past who had engaged in economically productive work that had been recognized by their societies and had resulted in freedom and status, she also alluded to a characteristic that was a key component in ideals of American citizenship.

Equally important, Child undermined the valorization of marriage and chastity that was central to the ideals of domestic citizenship advanced in eighteenth-century women's histories. Indeed, she suggested that it might be appropriate to reconsider the meaning of female modesty and monogamy in some circumstances. While she valued both, she was reluctant to dismiss societies in which customs of female behavior or marriage were

different. This was particularly clear in Child's depiction of women in ancient Athens. Like the other writers, Child deplored the treatment of married women in ancient Greece because they were denied education and forced to endure physical solitude in their homes. She accepted the conventional wisdom that this arrangement led men in ancient Athens to seek the company of courtesans instead. But Child defended the courtesans condemned by other historians for their loose morals. While she referred to courtesans as "a shameless class," she argued that they were usually captives taken in war or women stolen by Greek sailors, so they had certainly not embraced their careers out of wanton choice. Many had gone on to attain both wealth and education. Thus, Child concluded her discussion by claiming that courtesans were the brave women who "alone dared to throw off the rigorous restraints imposed upon the sex, and devote themselves to graceful accomplishments, seductive manners, and agreeable learning." The respect these women received in their societies could no doubt be traced to this assertiveness, and their lack of modesty was assumed to follow from the way they had to assert themselves for an education (*HCW*, II: 19–20).

Child particularly went to great lengths to reframe common assumptions about Aspasia. While Russell's *Essay* and Adams's *Sketches* had condemned Aspasia as a prostitute and Murray had simply ignored Aspasia's personal life, Child felt obliged to explain the extenuating circumstances Aspasia had faced. She suggested that Pericles and his first wife had mutually agreed to a divorce as was the custom of the time for two people who had grown tired of their marriage. Pericles "bestowed her upon another man, with her own free will and consent." Child claimed Aspasia was both celebrated and respected in Athens, describing how prominent men brought their wives and daughters to her home, and how Pericles had married her once he was free to do so (*HCW*, II: 20).

Although Child went out of her way to celebrate the importance of female chastity and modesty throughout her two-volume history, she did not privilege it in quite the same way that earlier women's historians did. Earlier histories associated the danger of courtesans with their unbridled passion, a lack of self-mastery that translated into irresponsible public behavior and political influence. But Child's Aspasia was a model of self-control and decorum. At another point, Child singled out both Aspasia and Sappho as women who were ahead of their time. Child defended Sappho just as she had Aspasia. She could not believe Sappho could have been as profligate as some had made her out to be. The fact that Sappho had killed

herself over her love for one individual suggested that her heart was true (*HCW*, II: 21).

Similarly, Child dismissed the same criticisms about the dangers of sexual passions that were attributed to French women. Child acknowledged that the French were careful to distinguish between love and marriage. They had a "singular code of morals," Child blithely noted, and she would thus "gladly throw a gauze veil over the subject, *à la mode Française.*" Child framed this comment, however, by describing the way in which French marriages were arranged by parents, so that the bride and groom barely knew one another and were not expected to socialize together after marriage. Once a woman was married, however, a new world of freedom opened up to her, so much so that she might receive male visitors in the morning while still in bed. Yet Child did not see French women as particularly dissolute nor did she argue that their sexual behavior in any way undermined their participation in politics; if anything, the case was just the opposite (*HCW*, II: 151–152).

Child applauded the role that French women had taken in politics and public life. While she repeatedly deplored the excesses of the French Revolution, she expressed open admiration for the women of earlier centuries whom Thomas and Russell had attacked. Child praised Francis I for bringing women to the French court and laying "the foundation of a beautiful social system by introducing the wives and daughters of his nobles at court, where none but bearded men had previously been seen." Child also spoke approvingly of the way in which French women led different political factions during the reign of Anne of Austria, "wearing scarfs that designated the party to which they belonged." Under Anne's regency, Child claimed, women had "obtained an ascendency which they have never since lost." And although Child condemned the French Revolution for both its political excesses and gross immorality, she nonetheless noted that many women had behaved with public dignity as they challenged the brutality of the Reign of Terror (*HCW*, II: 119, 124, 151–157).

Child's appreciation for the political activities and civic-mindedness of French women was only one of many such examples she included in her history, as she celebrated the public and political accomplishments of women in all phases of history, again in direct challenge to earlier writers of women's histories. Like her predecessors, she praised Roman women, whom everyone agreed had combined civic-mindedness with domestic virtue. Drawing on Alexander (almost word for word), she traced the

privileged place of women in Roman society to the leadership of Hersilia (and other women) in mediating a truce between the Sabines and the Romans. Indeed, as Child narrated the various acts of civic activity undertaken by Roman women, she made it clear that they were agents in shaping both the history of Rome and in improving their own status. When necessary, they had given the gold of their jewelry to ransom the city and at another time to pay for its defense. For both of these activities they had received new privileges. Like Alexander, Child also reprinted Hortensia's public speech before the triumvers to defend Roman women from unfair taxation, noting that as a result of that speech the number of women to be taxed was then directly reduced (*HCW*, II: 38, 62–68).

But Child went far beyond Russell and Alexander in order to focus on the political accomplishments of women in other contexts as well. From the military and religious leadership of women among the ancient Babylonians to those of early Germanic cultures to the queens of Europe, history offered important examples of the way women had led and of their successes in their endeavors. Such leadership, Child claimed, was also an indication of the high value these societies placed on women. It was also, one might conclude, a strong historical narrative in defense of women's ability to exercise the same rights of citizenship that men had.

Child argued that the successful reigns of both Semiramis and Nitocris in Babylonian society indicated that women in their culture had achieved a high status. She made this argument in spite of the fact that the Babylonians had strangled most of their women at one point, when they were battling the Persians. She concluded, however, "This was done to prevent famine; and the lot fell upon women probably because they were of less importance in carrying on the war." While some might argue that the Babylonians were lacking in gallantry, the political leadership of women such as Semiramis and Nitocris, when weighed in the balance, demonstrated the high status of Babylonian women. "Such instances as these do not indicate a degraded condition of women," Child concluded (*HCW*, I: 25–26).

In a direct swipe at the value of manners that women were supposed to convey through their domestic citizenship, Child made it clear that political power trumped manners when it came to judging the status of women in a society. She used Tacitus to pointedly dismiss the importance of dinner-table customs that eighteenth-century histories of civilization had fetishized. The fact that many women in early Germanic societies rarely ate with their husbands was insignificant, Child argued. "This custom could not

have originated in the habit of regarding women as inferior beings; for the whole history of the north proves the existence of an entirely opposite sentiment," she argued. Child concluded that the women were no doubt too busy cooking to wish to eat with their husbands. Rather than focus on the importance of manners, Child turned her readers' attention to the broader activities that women took on in early Germanic societies. It was women, she noted, who were the physicians. But even more important were their political, military, and religious activities. Women derived their status from their labor and their leadership, not from social customs and table manners (*HCW*, II: 78).

Child, like Alexander, singled out the historical moment when the women of Gaul gained their official role in mediating conflicts in their society after they had rushed into the midst of a battle and persuaded warring factions to lay down their arms. From then on, women had become central to diplomatic negotiations. Indeed, women of the North invariably followed their men into battle, so that strict rules were established to accommodate them and incorporate them into military life. "The operations of the soldiers were from time to time settled in a council, of which their wives formed a part." The ancient Britons were led into battle by their queen Boadicea, and their army was made up of thousands of women as well as men, women who fought "with the utmost bravery" (*HCW*, II: 80–81).

The terms of citizenship for women in these northern nations was manifested not only in their military participation, but also in their religious authority. Child noted that many of the gods of northern mythology were women. In Germanic cultures, women held respected places in the priesthood. This high status in religion could also result in very successful political leadership. Thus, Child noted that these women "often administered the government with a degree of ability that excited the admiration of neighboring nations. The greatest heroes were willing to fight under their banners, and be regulated by their councils; for they imagined them to be guided by oracular wisdom, derived from sources more than human." Child's depiction of female military leadership in the past thus directly challenged arguments by stage theorists that these women lacked the true qualifications necessary for military command and that men only followed women into battle out of family loyalty, not as a result of genuine respect (*HCW*, II: 81–82).

As Child went on to describe the military valor of women during the Middle Ages, she celebrated examples very much like the military leadership

exerted by women among the Gauls, Germans, and other northern groups. Philippa, the wife of Edward III, led his troops to victory at Neville Cross. Jane, Countess of Mountfort, led her husband's troops in battle while he was imprisoned. Child noted that she was a "lineal descendant of the German women described by Tacitus, [and] possessed a large share of manly courage." Child described other important female military leaders who demonstrated military prowess, such as the Countess of March, Lagertha of Sweden, Avilda of Gothland, Marguerite of France, Margaret of Anjou, and Joan of Arc. While she agreed with her predecessors that female participation in battles was due to the political chaos of the times, Child expressed genuine admiration for their accomplishments and used multiple examples to suggest the way in which such activities could be quite natural for women. Indeed, as she concluded her second volume, she returned to this theme. Arguing, on the one hand, that Christianity was beginning to limit the amount of warfare (she had no evidence for this), it was clear that Child also was impressed with the performance of women in the heat of battle. Whether it be the Phoenician women of the ancient world, the Moorish women of medieval Spain, or young women in contemporary Dalmatia, women had repeatedly proven themselves as ready as men for battle (*HCW*, II: 120–124).

Child's discussion of bravery and military service resonated beyond a mere challenge to female stereotypes. Military service, along with free labor, was a key attribute in defining political citizenship for men. It gave them a stake in the state, even if they did not have property. Moreover, it provided evidence that they possessed the self-mastery to participate in political life. Thus, Child's exhaustive list of female warriors offered clear historical proof of the ability of women to assume the responsibilities of male citizenship.[18] Like Abigail Adams, Child saw a rule where earlier historians had seen exceptions. Indeed, while Russell had suggested that female bravery was unusual by calling it surprising, Child reframed his comment when she claimed, "The personal bravery evinced by women at all periods excites surprise." In the context of Child's writing, the phrase suggested that it was the extent of female bravery (and its lack of recognition) that was surprising, not that it had occurred in a few isolated instances (*HCW*, II: 120–121, 209–210).

Child reinforced the implications that her history held for debates about female citizenship as she took on the generalizations about "natural" differences articulated by stage theorists such as Kames and historians of women

such as Russell and Thomas who felt that women simply did not have the same capacities as men. Indeed, Child reframed the conclusion in Russell's *Essay* that women's weakness led them to be more despotic than men. When it came to the ability to govern, Child argued bluntly, "There has been a comparatively greater proportion of good queens, than of good kings." Explaining this generalization, Child continued, "Perhaps it may be that women, distrustful of their own strength, pay more attention to the public voice, and their government thus acquires something of the character of elective monarchies." Child praised Elizabeth of England and Margaret of Denmark, claiming the latter was known as the Semiramis of the North because of her wide-ranging political and diplomatic skills. She also noted the "highly-gifted Isabella of Castille." Turning to Africa, Child singled out Angola's Zhinga as the bravest and most intelligent of the continent's monarchs. Catherine of Russia equaled the accomplishments of Peter the Great, Child contended, and regents such as Blanche of Castile and Caroline of England also successfully ran their governments (*HCW*, II: 206–207).

In addition to celebrating the queens' successful leadership, Child added several paragraphs on the political activities of nonroyal women, beginning with the comment that "English history presents many instances of women exercising prerogatives now denied to them." She then described various government offices held by women in the past, from governor of the house of correction to grand chamberlain to clerk of the crown. "The celebrated Anne, countess of Pembroke," Child pointed out, "held the hereditary office of sheriff of Westmoreland, and exercised it in person, sitting on the bench of the judges." Compared to the limitations placed on women in the nineteenth century, there seemed to be a downward trend in the ability of women to participate in governance (*HCW*, II: 145–146).

Child also broke with eighteenth-century historians as she celebrated the success that women had achieved in representing their ideas and talents in public. Indeed, she claimed the learning of women in the Middle Ages and the Renaissance was one of the major achievements of that period. Like Maria Stewart, Child lifted descriptions of educated women from the eighteenth-century historians but without any qualifications or concerns. Child included Russell's passage that "women preached in public, supported controversies, published and defended theses, filled the chairs of philosophy and law, harangued the popes in Latin, wrote Greek, and read Hebrew." She celebrated the poetry of Marguérite Clotilde de Surville and

Vittoria Colonna. Child ignored Hypatia's untimely death at the hands of an angry mob and argued instead that "no reproach was ever uttered against the perfect purity of her manners" so that Hypatia was actually able to lecture to large crowds of men without fear of embarrassment. And as women proved themselves intellectually, their praises were sung by male admirers such as Boccaccio, Cornelius Agrippa, and Peter Paul de Ribera, as well as by women such as Margaret of Navarre. The Middle Ages may have been marred by warfare and brutality, but women had managed to cultivate their intellectual skills and to share them in public forums (*HCW*, II: 126–131).

Child framed the continuing debate about the intellectual capabilities of women around the public application of knowledge. She admitted that there were no female figures to compare with Homer or Shakespeare or Newton, but she argued that many women in the past had nonetheless made important and enduring contributions. She did not suggest that women were in any way limited in their intellectual capacities. If some women had been pedantic in their acquisition of knowledge, the same was equally true for the men of their time, something Child attributed to the limited uses of knowledge in those earlier societies, as opposed to the influence of gender. Pedantry was not simply a vice of women, "for the correspondence between the character of the sexes is as intimate, as the affections and thoughts of the same individual." Child saw the problem of pedantry in her own time receding because knowledge was being adapted for a wide variety of uses, from the creation of new industrial products to children's toys (*HCW*, II: 207–208).

Child's evaluation of women's intellectual abilities, like her discussion of their political and military activities, took direct aim at the issue of citizenship. The problem, she suggested (with less tolerance than Murray had shown), might have more to do with male insecurities than female disabilities. "It is by no means easy to find a man so magnanimous," she noted in some disgust, "as to be perfectly willing that a woman should know more than himself, on any subject except dress and cookery." Child recognized the importance of domestic work, and she could even imagine the value of women translating their domestic knowledge into marketable products (such as toys). But women had an intellectual range that extended beyond household activities. If society was going to move forward, women would need to hone those intellectual abilities and contribute to the public good just as men did (*HCW*, II: 209).

At the same time that Child asserted new ideals of female citizenship, she used history to undercut the idea that the United States was organized around the domestic citizenship of women. While this critique would be particularly clear in her conclusion, it emerged in stealth fashion throughout her two volumes as she described the past and analyzed other cultures. Raising issues of race and slavery, class, and the general legal disabilities of women, Child repeatedly questioned an ideology that suggested modern nations reached their apex as they organized around particular forms of female behavior; indeed, she also raised the question of whether modern nations had actually broken from the past and distinguished themselves from more savage nations.

Well before her direct discussion of slavery in the United States at the end of her book, Child examined enslavement in other societies, thus indirectly raising questions about what those practices meant for narratives of national progress closer to home. When describing Burmese women, for example, Child noted they did still "share something of the degradation imposed upon all Asiatic women" because they could be sold to pay their husbands' debts. Although ostensibly critiquing the backwardness of the Burmese, careful readers might ask themselves whether a similar sort of degradation occurred when slave women were sold in the United States. Similarly, when Child defended Greek courtesans, such as Aspasia, who were unable to make a respectable marriage by suggesting they had been captured by sailors or taken as prisoners of war, she raised another concern that swirled in the antislavery literature: the inability of slaves to legally marry (*HCW*, I: 135).[19]

Child also questioned whether or not class privileges were sometimes mistaken for national character, and in doing so, she indirectly critiqued many of the emerging practices of gentility in the United States. Child tied the decadence of the harem to upper-class life rather than to the character of the Middle East. She noted the relative freedom enjoyed by women of the middling ranks as compared to those of the upper classes in a place such as Turkey. Child spent considerable time, for example, describing the restricted lives of women in the seraglios of the Turkish sultan. But this was no more indicative of how most women lived than were descriptions of European courts, Child argued. "Women of the middling classes in Turkey appear to enjoy a very considerable degree of freedom and consideration." She then went on to describe how most women were free to come and go from their homes into "the streets and bazars of Constantinople" or to the

public baths that were designated for women. Among the Persians, whom Child found very restrictive in their treatment of women, there were important differences in the way women lived. Those who worked had a better life than those who were pampered. "Women of the middling class are more occupied than the wives of grandees, and therefore unavoidably have more freedom. They spin, sew, embroider, superintend the house, keep account of expenses, pay the servant's wages, and see that proper care is taken of the horses" (*HCW*, I: 63–65, 83). Finally, the seraglios of ancient Assyrian monarchs might also be compared to the world of upper-class women in Western society. Child noted, for example, that "singing and dancing girls were selected from the most beautiful to entertain the wealthy at their meals." But as she assessed this practice, she concluded that "we have no means of knowing whether ladies of high rank considered it a degradation to dance and sing before strangers" (*HCW*, I: 24). Her comment might well have applied to the social whirl that young women of the upper classes encountered as they were presented to society in hopes of an advantageous marriage. With these characterizations, Child deflected a critique of national character toward class instead, and it was a critique that could apply to Western nations as well as Eastern ones.

Child's history of gender and nation was far more complicated than the women's histories that had been produced in the eighteenth century. She first had raised questions about whether the divisions of citizenship based on gender were warranted, and at the same time, she raised questions about precisely which notions of gender were being used to characterize particular nations. The condition of women was affected by class or slavery as much as any sort of gendered status within a nation, Child pointed out, and nations were not organized around the status of women in general but by the status of a particular class and race of women. In her final chapters, Child turned her attention specifically to the United States, though even here she discussed it as part of two nations, one slave and one free. The South was banished to the chapter on "Slave-Holding Countries," while the North came to stand for the nation as the land of free labor and equality. The distinction between savage nations and more modern ones, which had provided the basis for stage theory and eighteenth-century women's histories, was recreated within the distinction between North and South.

Child justified her chapter on slaveholding countries by arguing that "a separate article is appropriated on this subject, because slavery everywhere produces nearly the same effects on character." She characterized the white

women of slaveholding nations as lazy, and she claimed that black slave women were physically exploited and sexually violated. Taking direct aim at earlier histories, Child attacked the assumptions that came with the celebration of domestic citizenship as she argued that "women are not beasts of burden" in these societies only if you leave out "all of those whose complexions are not perfectly white" (*HCW*, II: 212–213).[20] It was not possible for slave women to live according to dominant notions of female virtue. Child had actually made this argument before in her *Appeal in Favor of That Class of Americans Called Africans*, when she argued that slavery victimized women. As Dana Nelson perceptively points out with respect to the *Appeal*, "Child's analysis takes national unity formulated through human equality as its central aim; over and again she highlights the ways in which slavery works to divide humanity *and* nation along fault lines of race, gender, class, and region."[21] The gender hierarchies that informed eighteenth-century histories of women and nation thus collapsed in Child's narrative.

To the extent that Child believed in a modern national ideal, it was to be found in the society of the North. Portrayed as a country of simple living and industry, Child's celebration of women's work led to the depiction of an idealized society that was distinctly at odds with her portrayal of Europe. In the United States, she saw neither the peasantry nor the nobility that created a class society in Europe and led to the corruption of female morals, particularly among the wealthy. Female virtue in the United States, she argued, was particularly encouraged by a society in which "nearly all the people are obliged to support themselves by their own industry." As a wealthy class developed in the United States, therefore, female virtue was increasingly threatened by the corruption that plagued Europe (*HCW*, II: 260–261).

It was in this context that Child celebrated women's labor as the centerpiece of national progress. It was something that was done both within the home and without, and it was a source of virtue rather than a source of degradation, thus connecting it to the work of women in earlier eras. Few women would be found in the fields, but schoolrooms and millinery shops were another matter. Of industrial employment, Child noted, "many are employed to tend the looms in factories, to set types in printing-offices, and fold sheets for the bookbinders." As would be the case so often in the woman's rights movement that developed in subsequent years, Child ignored the existence of female poverty or a working class, arguing instead that "by far, the largest proportion of these do not work for support, but

to gain additional luxuries, which their parents cannot afford to furnish." Thus, paid work was part of a larger system of industrious equality in the United States where working girls could dress as well as their employers, and mistresses confronted problems with domestic servants when they failed to treat them with "a friendly interest" (*HCW*, II: 266–267).[22]

The issues of citizenship that Child addressed in her *History of the Condition of Women* focused on the questions that had been raised by women in various reform movements, particularly in radical antislavery agitation. She not only removed the slave South from the national narrative, but also created a vision of the United States that celebrated the economic value of women's work in the North. Rather than focus on the social and moral aspects of domesticity as the basis for female citizenship, she touted its economic significance. Moreover, Child created a narrative that traced the activities of women who had been public intellectuals, political and military leaders, and key participants in the economic activities of their nations. In doing so, she created a history that legitimated the public speaking and political activities of women demanding radical reform in the United States.

None of this, however, was as clear as the argument she had made in *An Appeal in Favor of That Class of Americans Called Africans*. Perhaps because of conflicted feelings, and undoubtedly with an eye to her potential audience, Child repeatedly asserted her respect for the condition of American women, although, at times, the meaning of that respect was ambiguous. She noted that it was considered "unfeminine" for a woman in the United States to have an interest in politics without commenting on what she thought about that perspective. She also stated that women were, perhaps, the freest and most influential in the world when considered as "wives, sisters, and daughters," but it wasn't clear if that influence extended beyond family matters. She noted the importance of female benevolent societies, without mentioning the causes that they championed (*HCW*, II: 265, 271).

Moreover, Child made sure to distinguish herself from radicals such as Fanny Wright. Wright had stirred up both controversy and publicity with her failed experiment in interracial living in Nashoba, her attacks on marriage, and her lectures on social and political reform that demanded, among other things, legal and educational rights for women. Child's views were a long way from Wright's on topics such as marriage, chastity, and Christianity, as she made clear in a critical review of Wright's lectures a few years earlier.[23] Thus, Child qualified her conclusion in noting, "Many silly things have been written, and are now written, concerning the equality of the

sexes." Nothing could be more dangerous than men and women exchanging places in the social order: this was the thinking of infidels when "reason has run wild," so that women "might command armies and harangue senates, while men attended to domestic concerns." This was the kind of thinking that led to the excesses of the French Revolution, the kind of thinking being promoted by Fanny Wright. Child argued that she was an advocate of separate spheres, "that true and perfect companionship, which gives both man and woman complete freedom *in* their places, without a restless desire to go out of them" (*HCW*, II: 210–211). Child's radicalism, in contrast to Wright's, lay in the way she presented history, a presentation that raised the question of what, precisely, the limits of those spheres were. In her narrative, women could do almost anything that men could do. The question was: what should they do?

Child's own relationship with that world of public accomplishment was a complicated one. She had certainly assumed a male role in editing the *Anti-Slavery Standard* and she had tramped through Boston collecting signatures for antislavery petitions. But she hated the petitioning work and she retired from public life soon after, refusing to attend antislavery and woman's rights meetings, though she remained on friendly terms with many leading activists and their movements throughout her life.[24]

This ambivalence, as much as her concern with her audience, may explain why Child's *History of the Condition of Women* is so difficult to decipher. Yet *The History of the Condition of Women* effectively destabilized the celebration of domestic citizenship that had been so successfully created by eighteenth-century histories of women. Child made it clear that a nation's progress could not be measured by the domestic accomplishments and manners of women. Child undercut the triumphal march of civilization and disrupted the narrative of national progress that most of these histories contained. The overall effect of her *History* was to question assumptions of stage theory and, by questioning the absolute oppression of women in earlier periods, to open up questions about female oppression in nineteenth-century society. Thus, her data would provide important building blocks in the demands for female citizenship that followed.

Reviews of Child's *History of the Condition of Women* were mixed, suggesting the extent to which contemporaries also wrestled with decoding the significance of her work. *The Knickerbocker* recommended it as an entertaining work of general interest, implicitly suggesting it as appropriate reading for a male audience. Quoting the epigraph for the second volume, the

reviewer asked how readers could help but be interested in "the history of those who 'in youth are our idols, at a riper age our companions, in old age our nurses, and at all ages our friends.' "[25] Other journals, however, raised questions.

Sarah Josepha Hale, writing for the *American Ladies Magazine*, read Child's work more carefully and was a bit more suspicious. She cautiously lauded the "vast amount of information" Child had collected, but she raised questions about the lack of a "philosophy of history." Where was the cause and effect, the comparisons of women among different nations and in different ages? Attributing some of these problems to Child's lack of intellectual ambition as a compiler rather than being a true historian, Hale complained, "We only regret in these volumes she should have transcribed so much, and written so little." But perhaps Hale recognized that Child's narrative was not so much lacking in interpretation as actually challenging one, when she noted that "the great and blessed influence the Christian religion has exercised on the condition of the female sex, is not, in our opinion, sufficiently dwelt upon and displayed."[26] Hale had noticed that Child did not celebrate the moral influence of women in the way that Hale did in her influential publications.

The *Boston Pearl*, however, sensed the danger in Child's work and condemned it as a sneaky attempt to reintroduce her attacks on slavery to an unsuspecting and respectable audience. Beyond that, her toleration of sexual freedom in French history was appalling and her repeated comments that Moslems treated their slaves better than did Christians were little more than an outrageous defense of infidelity. "One cannot read these volumes through, incautiously, without thinking contemptuously of women; for they are represented as being lovers of finery, licentious in principle, and profligate in practice," the journal proclaimed. This was particularly worth noting because women in the United States had more freedom, status, and privileges than women anywhere else in the world, yet Child, the reviewer contended, consigned them to a few measly pages toward the end of the book.[27]

Caleb Cushing addressed the issue of political citizenship directly when he anonymously discussed Child's *History of the Condition* in the pages of the *North American Review* along with several other historical works. Entitled "The Social Condition of Women," the review addressed many of the issues raised by Child's book without actually naming her work. Rather, Cushing reiterated the traditional perspectives of stage theorists by arguing

that Christianity had elevated the condition of women over the ages to their present high status and by emphasizing that their political skills were limited. The review concluded by noting pointedly, in a direct contradiction of Child, that while queens clearly exercised political power, it did not follow that all women should participate in politics. Queens inherited political power rather than fighting for it on the battlefield or the campaign trail so that their successes said nothing about the abilities of individual women to exercise the rights of citizenship. Their position was one of "representing sovereignty, than one of actually exercising it." Thus, women were best left tending to matters of "intellect, taste, and social refinement," rather than to matters of commerce or politics.[28]

Even more telling, however, was the way in which Child's book was drawn into the growing debate about woman's rights. Child was at pains in her later editions to tamp down that association, as she claimed that her book was not meant to be "an essay on women's rights, or a philosophical investigation of what is or ought to be the relation of the sexes." Regardless of this disclaimer, though, that is precisely how it was being interpreted, at least by some. Most famously, Sarah Grimké drew on Child's book repeatedly in *Letters on the Equality of the Sexes*, but Margaret Fuller also acknowledged its significance in a review of the 1845 edition. Years later, Elizabeth Cady Stanton, Susan B. Anthony, and Matilda Gage would acknowledge its impact on the early movement for woman's rights.[29] Moreover, the issues she raised about the way in which race and slavery also affected the narrative about both women and history would also begin to be addressed in some of the antislavery literature.

New Directions in Women's History

In newspapers and pamphlets, particularly those that engaged the antislavery issue, the questions Child raised in her *History* were refashioned as part of varying activist agendas. In this highly politicized literary public sphere, attempts were made to position African American women in a narrative that had been predominantly white. Sarah Grimké, in defending the political activities of female abolitionists, refashioned Child's work into a universal history of female oppression that dismissed any celebration of female domesticity. Margaret Fuller, on the other hand, imagined a history that would legitimate a world of political and professional opportunities of

women and that would provide new forms of domestic relationships as well. Their critiques of gender inequality thus provided new frameworks for judging the past as well as many of the historical figures who had been important in debates about women's citizenship.

With respect to African American women, early biographies of Phillis Wheatley and Elizabeth Freeman were particularly important as part of a larger attempt to renarrate the nation's history for antislavery purposes. A brief biography of Phillis Wheatley had appeared in a book by Antoine Grégoire that was published in Philadelphia in 1810. Reprinted in a textbook for the African Free Schools of New York in 1826, the biography was reprinted in *The Liberator* in 1832. By 1834, Margaretta Odell had produced a longer memoir of Wheatley, which she included with a collection of Wheatley's poetry. That, too, was advertised and excerpted in *The Liberator*.[30] Complementing the stories of Wheatley's literary success was that of the political triumph of Mum Bett (Elizabeth Freeman). The story began to circulate in an antislavery speech given by Theodore Sedgwick in 1831. His sister, Catharine, elaborated it a couple of decades later in an article for *Bentley's Magazine*. By 1855, William Nell had reprinted the biography of Freeman along with one of Wheatley in his *Colored Patriots of the American Revolution* as part of his attempt to "stem the tide of prejudice against the colored race."[31]

What emerged from this antislavery literature were biographies that encoded African American women within the revolutionary struggle for rights and that recognized the ways in which they still struggled with the same disabilities of domestic citizenship as white women had. Mum Bett, as the slave woman who asked for freedom in 1781 based on the declarations of human equality in the Massachusetts Constitution, created the rights of citizenship for African Americans in her home state. Phillis Wheatley became a symbol of African American intellectual and artistic genius. But equally important, as her story was reshaped by Margaretta Odell in 1834, it became a narrative of not only how her intellectual history diverged from that of white women, but also how she was, nonetheless, oppressed as a wife by her husband. As Margot Minardi has noted, Odell clearly placed the development of Wheatley's writing in the years before the Revolution while arguing that most women in America did not have such intellectual opportunities until after the Revolution. Wheatley's success, therefore, had nothing to do with the intellectual opportunities that were offered white women in the early years of the new republic. However, Odell also reconstructed Wheatley's life in another significant way as she explored the harsh

treatment that Wheatley received from her husband. Grégoire's version had suggested that Phillis had never been trained to do housework and therefore expected to be indulged. Odell, however, suggested that Wheatley's husband had been a ne'er-do-well who had failed to support her. Left in his care, she had withered and died. In this way, Wheatley shared the legal disabilities of all U.S. women.[32]

While Child had made a strong case for the way in which slave women were excluded from the national narrative, she had not figured out how to include them. As antislavery activists promoted the stories of Mum Bett and Phillis Wheatley, new possibilities began to emerge. Bett could be placed prominently in histories of political citizenship while Wheatley could join the pantheon of literary women who demonstrated the intellectual abilities of women. Their histories did not duplicate those of white women, but the politics of antislavery pushed them into an expanded narrative of women's history.

Antislavery affected Sarah Grimké's work in a different way. Grimké's *Letters on the Equality of the Sexes* grew out of a series of newspaper articles defending the right of women to fight the inequality and oppression faced by others (especially slaves) and enjoining women to recognize it in their own lives. Taking on the criticisms of ministers who were trying to silence abolitionist protests as unchristian, Grimké argued that Christianity had been perverted into a social doctrine that restricted women to their homes and silenced their social protests. Dismissing ideals of complementarity, she argued that public opinion had been corrupted into a belief that women should be subject to the rule of men rather than their equals as God had ordained. To challenge that notion, Grimké drew on Child's *History* both to demonstrate the abilities of women and to prove that the injuries they had suffered at the hands of men were ongoing.

Grimké had no interest in distinctions between nations or theories of progress. What history demonstrated was that men, in all times and all places, had oppressed women. As she said at the beginning of Letter IV, "Woman has suffered in every age and country from her *protector*, man." The status of women in Europe and the United States might be better than it was in Asia or Africa, but it was still far from satisfactory; there was "little in her history which can yield satisfaction." As a result, Grimké took examples of female labor, some of which Child had actually admired, and used them to show how women were abused. She interpreted the labor of women in biblical times as oppression rather than as an opportunity for

freedom. Their arduous work in shepherding animals, drawing water, grinding corn, cooking, and sewing demonstrated their heavy burden. And in Persia, Grimké reported with dismay, middle-class women did "all the laborious part of the house work."[33]

Because of her emphasis on the oppression of women, Grimké did not idealize the free labor of women in the North the way that Child did. While Child's *History* suggested that women found liberation in their work, Grimké argued that they experienced exploitation. Rather than stress the value of free labor, Grimké argued that women in the United States were paid less than men for doing the same kind of work. Men made twice or three times as much as women in professions such as teaching and tailoring. Women's work was always undervalued, even when equally difficult. "A woman who goes out to wash, works as hard, in proportion as a wood sawyer, or a coal heaver, but she is not generally able to make more than half as much by a day's work." Thus, while Child's discussion of women's work suggested the way in which it was a basis for economic citizenship, Grimké's analysis focused on the inequalities of that citizenship. Child's history suggested a path to citizenship for women in the opportunities surrounding them; Grimké argued that they would have to actively intervene to create those opportunities.[34]

As Grimké went on to craft her own version of female citizenship, she expressed ambivalence and even scorn for historical figures whom Child had praised. In part, Grimké's ideals were complicated by her Quaker beliefs that challenged both the government and the military. While Child had circled around ideas of political citizenship as she celebrated the past accomplishments of women in battle and on the throne, Grimké was much more conflicted in her use of those stories. Grimké quoted Child's work at length, but she claimed that she did so only to demonstrate the equality of men and women in their capabilities. She expressed dismay that women, like men, had exercised "brute force which is as contrary to the law of God in men as in women." The political and military history of women was neither inspiring nor exemplary for Grimké and thus of more limited value.[35]

Grimké approached the military and political activities of women in the past with caution, but she was downright contemptuous of those women who had been held up as models of domestic citizenship. This was true particularly in her somewhat startling critique of the lives of Roman women, something that almost everyone else had praised. Grimké stripped

out any references to the way in which Roman women combined domestic virtue with civic consciousness and portrayed them as little more than contented housewives who ignored the world around them. Thus, when speaking of Roman women, whom Child had portrayed in the early days of the Republic as living in domestic bliss, Grimké noted that while that was fine then (as good as it could get for those women), contemporary women had a responsibility to confront the sin surrounding them, particularly the sin of slavery. "Shall she rejoice in her home, her husband, her children, and forget her brethren and sisters in bondage. . . . Shall woman disregard the situation of thousands of her fellow creatures, who are the victims of intemperance and licentiousness, and retreating to the privacy of her comfortable home, be satisfied her whole duty is performed?" As she sought to shake middle-class American women out of their complacency, Grimké demolished any attempt they might have made to emulate the example of Roman women in the past.[36] In Grimké's view of history, there were women who had been oppressed and women who ignored that oppression (as happy wives) or maybe even caused it (as military and political leaders). There were not many examples to imitate in a history that was largely corrupt, as Grimké urged her readers to move beyond the sins of the past to a more just future.

Fuller's call to action, unlike Grimké's, more firmly rooted activist women in a continuing historical tradition. While Grimké urged her readers to leave the past behind, Fuller swept them along in a tidal wave of historical progress, which she documented in *Woman in the Nineteenth Century*. She celebrated scandalous women of the past who ranged from Aspasia to Mary Wollstonecraft to George Sand as she created a historical narrative that argued for the significance of their behavior in reshaping gender relationships. Fuller argued forcefully for equality between men and women, and she just as forcefully criticized the inequalities that women faced in their society. History, in her hands, became a way to critique the weaknesses of women in earlier centuries as the product of bad training and limited social expectations rather than as the result of differences in nature. Her ideal of historical progress offered up examples of domestic relationships that ignored gender differences rather than enshrine them.[37]

In confronting some of the foibles of gender that Child and Grimké had ignored when they analyzed the political activities of women in the past, Fuller argued that a new age had begun with the reigns of Elizabeth and Isabella. Elizabeth might not have escaped all of the weaknesses that society

ingrained in women, whether it be coquetry or passion, but even "half-emancipated" she nonetheless became a strong ruler, indicating what women might expect to do moving forward. Thus, beginning in the sixteenth century, with both the European discovery of the New World, and the emergence of nation-states, a new era for women also began.[38]

Even more boldly, however, Fuller found in recent history an ideal of marriage that discarded the gender differences of domestic citizenship in place of shared responsibilities. The marriages of Madame Roland and Mary Wollstonecraft in the late eighteenth century suggested an intellectual companionship far more potent than that recommended by British champions of complementarity. Fuller ignored the criticisms of Wollstonecraft that had swirled around her character since her death, holding her up as a historical example of the way in which domestic relations were evolving. The Rolands, Fuller claimed, shared equally in their household responsibilities and in the affairs of state. They "regulated home affairs, or prepared public documents together, indifferently." Far from viewing Madame Roland as overly involved in her husband's career, Fuller celebrated her interest as a historical leap forward.[39] Fuller thus attacked the differentiation that underlay the domestic citizenship of eighteenth-century stage theorists and women's historians as she celebrated a different kind of domestic partnership as an even more advanced form of historical evolution.

Fuller also argued that as women had experimented with new and more public roles, they paved the way for even more female success in the future, so that "it is difficult to say just *where* they must stop." Madame de Stael might have suffered from some female weaknesses due to her upbringing, but her accomplishments as a writer were what shone forth, clearing a path for contemporary young women to follow. Women, encouraged to contemplate issues of virtue and morality, had, in the present time been moved to speak out, when necessary. Thus, Fuller wove Abby Kelley Foster and Angelina Grimké into the historical narrative of female citizenship in a new era. They "invariably subdue the prejudices of their hearers and excite an interest proportionate to the aversion with which it had been the purpose to regard them."[40]

As Fuller created a narrative in which women struggled against the gendered training and expectations that they lived with, she used her history to argue that claims of inherent differences between men and women were false. "History jeers at the attempts of physiologists to bind great original laws by the forms which follow from them. They make a rule; they say from

observation what can and cannot be. In vain! Nature provides exceptions to every rule," Fuller crowed.[41] Fuller discarded the very basis for differentiated ideas of citizenship as she argued that men and women shared many characteristics, though in different amounts. Women might fight in battle and men might tend to domestic matters. What history demonstrated was that both were possible and neither unnatural. Moreover, the recognition of these shared abilities was what pushed forward a new era, opening opportunity rather than destabilizing society or signaling savagery.

Fuller's book, not surprisingly, faced a hostile reception from most reviewers. Lydia Maria Child warned readers of the *Broadway Journal* that some passages of the book would offend readers because they raised issues society would rather ignore, "subjects which men do not wish to have discussed, and which women dare not approach."[42] Child might have been preparing readers for the reaction of one of her own editors at the *Journal*, Charles Briggs, for shortly thereafter, he published a scathing review, accusing Fuller of wasting the time of her readers and failing to deliver on her promised topic, "woman in the nineteenth century."[43] "We keep looking for woman of the nineteenth century, but we only find a roster of names from Panthea to Amelia Norman." The review then went on to criticize Fuller's choice of historical heroines, arguing that the women she admired were the very ones who challenged the most sacred duties of motherhood and domesticity. "Mrs. Jamieson, with true womanly feeling, said she would prefer being Mary of Scotland to Elizabeth of England; but Miss Fuller would prefer being the termagant Queen and swearing by 'God's teeth,'" the review complained. Similarly, Fuller's praise of the companionship of the Rolands was misplaced, the review argued, for Madame Roland was "no wife at all, at least to him." Continuing the criticism the following week, the review returned to the natural differences of men and women, claiming that women simply did not have the abilities to succeed in politics, literature, or art.[44]

Orestes Brownson, who ripped the book apart in his journal, complained at one point that Fuller demonstrated a benighted admiration for the status of women in the ancient world. Although Fuller was eager to promote equality in all professions and occupations, Brownson argued that Fuller "is quite sure the ancient heathens understood this matter better than we do. They had a juster appreciation of the dignity of woman." He then went on condemn lewd sexual practices of ancient times: whether of Babylon, Syria, Phoenicia, or Rome.[45]

But perhaps the most sustained historical debate with Fuller came from the *Southern Quarterly Review*, which demonstrated the continuing power of the eighteenth-century arguments of Common Sense theorists. The review prefaced its critique of Fuller with an extensive review of the relationship between gender and history, essentially recapitulating the arguments of stage theorists that distinguished civilization from savagery according to the status of women. Singling out the manual labor of women as an indicator of savagery, and the domestic power of women over home and children as an indicator of civilization, the article covered most of the phases of history that had been laid out in eighteenth-century women's history: from the Greeks, who kept their wives virtuous but uneducated, so that men turned to courtesans for companionship; to the Romans who granted women more status; to the chivalry of the Middle Ages, which led men to revere women. Ignoring the history that either criticized or celebrated the intellectual accomplishments of women during the Middle Ages, the reviewer instead held up chivalrous adoration of women as their high point and criticized Fuller for demanding a kind of equality that nature had not suited them to. Continuing to draw on the eighteenth-century tradition that had been so central to this historical narrative, the author argued that women were not suited by nature for the kind of equality Fuller demanded. Women were too excitable and passionate, focused on details rather than the big picture, and filled with sympathy. They might demonstrate courage passively in the form of fortitude, but not actively in the form of bravery. A woman in pursuit of knowledge, whether in literature or in science, quite simply denied her sex. Women were not learned, and when they were they were exceptions. Thus, in response to Fuller's demands for equality in a man's world, the article argued, woman's "whole history, her physical and moral conformations, go to show that she can have no part in the strength, the rudeness, the impenetrability that gives man his domination."[46]

However, while reviews of Fuller's book suggested the extent to which the narrative advanced by eighteenth-century women's historians still held currency, the challenges posed to that history by antislavery activists did not disappear. A growing movement for woman's rights created new debates about the history of women that would emerge in a variety of public forums, as specific demands for woman's rights fostered new variations in the way women were imagined in the past.

II

Citizenship and Women's History

Chapter 4

Women's History and Woman's Rights

In 1854, Elizabeth Cady Stanton addressed the New York legislature to claim the right to suffrage, arguing, "We have every qualification required by the constitution, necessary to the legal voter, but the one of sex." Women, she pointed out, had "governed nations, led armies, filled the professor's chair, taught philosophy and mathematics to the *savans* of our age, discovered planets, [and] piloted ships across the sea."[1] Demonstrating her knowledge of Child's and Fuller's works, Stanton also made it clear how women's history was being reframed as agitation for woman's rights gained steam in the middle decades of the nineteenth century. Women's history was being used explicitly to legitimate the demand for suffrage, as well as demands for universal rights more generally. During the 1830s and into the 1840s, the historical interpretations put forward by Child, Grimké, and Fuller had battered the ideals of domestic citizenship enshrined by eighteenth-century women's history in order to defend the activities of female reformers. But as Grimké's and Fuller's works indicated, the activism of those reformers had provoked additional questions about what it meant to be a female citizen, most specifically around the issue of universal rights: should women have the same rights as men? In the decades leading up to the Civil War, debate exploded on a wide range of issues related to these questions of women's citizenship. In public venues that ranged from debating societies and lyceums to state legislatures and state constitutional conventions, and, of course, to the woman's rights conventions themselves, questions of citizenship were raised and, when they were, women's history was invoked.

As this debate about rights exploded, the parameters of citizenship were explored and the meaning of equality was contested. Suffrage mattered, but it was only one of many concerns raised by reformers. Indeed, as Lori

Ginzberg has pointed out, activists embraced the cause because they recognized that other reforms they had supported over the past two decades were now being pursued in a political arena, and that arena itself had changed to become one more narrowly focused on voting than on a broader range of political activities. However, many other issues were also of key importance in the woman's movement that emerged. Economic questions of work and property, for example, were of major significance. Married women in most states were unable to hold property and make contracts. Women who worked for wages made less than men, and married women did not control what little they earned. As a result, women were denied the economic independence that had been a cornerstone of citizenship ideals. Related to these economic issues, educational demands moved beyond attempts to prove the intellectual ability of women or their need to be educated to discussions about how they would be able to use their education, particularly in the professional venues that were closed to them in the nineteenth century. Meaningful citizenship meant the right to participate equally in the economic and intellectual life of the nation as well as in its political world.[2]

As activists pushed their new demands, their opponents pushed back. Although the woman's rights movement was very small during this period, fears of its impact surfaced repeatedly in newspapers throughout the country. The possibility of a newly entitled female citizen had implications for both family and state. Women with economic power might try to rule over their husbands. Women with political power might undermine government. With these fears front and center, both sides scoured the historical record to either assail or buttress these worries. Women's patriotism during the Revolution had been enshrined by succeeding generations, but the nature of their patriotism was by no means settled. Had women shown an enthusiasm for politics in their activities? Had they demonstrated the kind of bravery that entitled them to claim the rights of men? Issues of property were even more complicated. While wealth traditionally had been seen as a basis for political independence among men, it often was associated with luxury and degeneration when held by women. Could historical examples be found that made wealth a basis for citizenship among women as well as men? Did historical narratives of economic progress have to end in a celebration of women's domesticity, or were other narratives possible?

Forged in the heat of different debates, the re-visioning of women's history that took place was hardly coherent, but that doesn't mean it wasn't

important. Activists clearly recognized the power of history in legitimizing (or delegitimizing) their claims. So while drawing on interpretations that were being advanced by authors such as Child, they also began to suggest new ones of their own. To a certain extent, they were able to do so because references to women in history, if not women's history itself, were becoming available in a wide variety of institutional contexts.

Institutional Contexts for Encountering Women in History

In addition to the actual histories of women that were being written, activists of every stripe encountered women in history in the schools, libraries, and lyceums that expanded as the nineteenth century unfolded. Young women, for example, increasingly read history either as preparation for entering academies or as part of their academy training. Mary Kelley has pointed out, for example, that Charles Rollin's multivolume *Ancient History* was common reading for young women tutored at home in the late eighteenth century or in some of the more advanced female seminaries in the early nineteenth century. Because Rollin believed that it was important to study the manners of different nations to understand why they rose and fell, he frequently included discussions of family structure and women's activities in his narrative. Thus he described how the women of Carthage worked with the men to make shields and arrows to fight the Romans and how elite women in ancient times were admired for performing domestic chores. Their activities were far more admirable than the "soft indolence" of women in the eighteenth century, he claimed. Like other historians, he also included classic stories from Roman history such as the rape of the Sabine women and the intercession of Veturia and Volumnia. Sarah Pierce, who created the four-volume *Sketches of Universal History* for her students, incorporated a similar perspective, though she anchored her narrative far more extensively in biblical history than Rollin had. But Pierce, like Rollin and others, recounted the story of the Sabine women preventing war before she went on to discuss the barbarity of the laws of ancient Rome with respect to women.[3]

Emma Willard's *Universal History*, a textbook that circulated far more widely than did Pierce's, also contained a few (though not many) references to women such as Elizabeth of England (who may have governed well but had promoted absolutism) and Zenobia (whom Willard argued had been

unfairly criticized by Gibbon). Willard's *Universal History* also occasionally took up the issue of morals to suggest, for example, that Rome had fallen as a result of the profligacy of its women. Similarly, Willard's *History of the United States*, which went through numerous editions subsequent to its publication in 1828, occasionally wove stories of women into the nation's history. Students who read her textbook encountered the bravery of Pocahontas as she saved John Smith, the keen mind of Ann Hutchinson as she took on the Puritan establishment, and the patriotism of women in South Carolina who urged resistance against the British military as well as the women of Philadelphia who raised money for the troops during the Revolution. Thus, even though there is no evidence that women in female seminaries were being assigned actual books that were solely devoted to women's history, they were being assigned reading that would allow them to think about the place of women in history.[4]

Lucy Larcom is a useful example here. She used money she saved from working in Lowell, Massachusetts, factories to study at the Monticello Seminary in Illinois in 1849. Although it is not clear which textbooks she used, the notes in one of her composition books clearly demonstrate that the young ladies in her class were instructed about the importance of women in history. When studying the character of the German nations, for example, she took detailed notes on the simplicity of female dress, women's mastery of medicine, and their presence on the field of battle. "Woman always wields a powerful influence," she wrote, "and according to the value at which her character is estimated, will that influence be exerted for the weal or woe of society."[5]

Other young women also revealed the ways in which they were attuned to the experiences of women or the condition of women in their schoolwork, public lectures, and readings. Mary Dyer, who attended normal school in Newton, Massachusetts, in 1851, recorded in her notes on the Amazon River that "the Amazons were said to be a race of women of extraordinary size who constructed their own laws, who went constantly armed, and who destroyed their male children, or married them, and caused them to be slaves." Lucy Chase recorded in one of her school composition books that at the time Europeans began arriving "in this country the Indian squaws dressed the food, tilled their narrow fields and performed all the drudgery connected with their household affairs." And when she attended a lecture by Major Tochman in 1842, she was thrilled not only by his story of Polish resistance in the war with Russia a decade earlier, but

also by the role that women had played in the struggle. "Ladies did their share in this great struggle & they were often rewarded with titles of honor," she wrote. "Poland is <u>proud</u> of her ladies." Caroline Barrett White, who often read history books with her husband Frank, also judged the activities of women in the past. She took particular note of De Quincey's essay on Joan of Arc, noting that although Joan might have been deluded, she was an inspiring and zealous patriot. And having finished Agnes Strickland's biography of Queen Mary, she noted with some disdain, "finished the history of 'Bloody Mary'—by Strickland who gives her anything but a <u>bloody</u> character. I think she is a flatterer of female sovereigns."[6]

It is not clear whether Caroline White and her husband owned these books or borrowed them from a local lending library. But it is clear that works specifically pertaining to women's history were available in the wide range of circulating libraries that were proliferating in the nineteenth century. Child's *History of the Condition of Women*, for example, was available in libraries as diverse as those at the University of Alabama and the College of New Jersey; the public school libraries of New Orleans, Cincinnati, Philadelphia, and Poughkeepsie; as well as the libraries of associations such as the Troy Young Men's Association and the Girls' Department of the Apprentices Library Company of Philadelphia—to name just a few places where her book circulated.[7]

Whether found within libraries, lyceums, or school classrooms, references to women in history provided a reservoir of stories that could be shared or debated as the context demanded. These historical references to women, particularly in more general works, were often fleeting and their investment in a gendered interpretation of history might be slight, but their widespread dissemination made possible their use in a wide variety of public and political contexts. These uses of history were significant not simply for pushing women's history in different directions, but for reminding audiences of what was at stake in the writing of women's history.

Women, Politics, and History

The petitioning campaigns of women against slavery, and later demands for the right to participate in government, triggered multiple questions about the political activities of women in both the recent and distant past.

With respect to the patriotism of women during the Revolution, for example, did their behavior demonstrate an understanding of politics or had patriotism come to stand for a more personal concern for one's family and neighbors? As competing interpretations of the more recent past took on new salience, judging the political activities of women in the more distant past took on a greater urgency as well.

The fault lines for interpreting the significance of female patriotism became particularly clear in 1838, when John Quincy Adams debated Benjamin Howard of Maryland over the right of women to petition against slavery. It was part of a showdown that occurred in the halls of Congress between the two men as they fought over the Gag Rule. Antislavery petitions had been automatically tabled for a couple of years when Adams staged his extended defense of the right of the people to petition against the annexation of Texas (a slave state). Adams constructed a long history of women's participation in political matters going back to the Greeks and Romans and culminating in the activities of the founding mothers, a history his opponent flatly denied. As the two men argued, the significance of their different histories became clear.

Adams hailed the usual list of great queens, from Elizabeth to Catherine to Isabella, and noted that the latter, by funding the expedition of Columbus, had become one of the discoverers of the New World. "Did she bring discredit on her sex by mingling in politics?" Adams wanted to know. Perhaps demonstrating the impact of Child's defense of Aspasia, Adams also demanded that Howard turn his attention to the history of Greece and "examine the character of Aspasia." Adams argued that history demonstrated a respectable tradition of women who had participated in politics, and he cited Aspasia's life as one of the "innumerable instances recorded by the profane historians where women distinguished, nay immortalized their names, by the part they took in the affairs of their country." Howard, like many others who opposed the participation of women in politics, condemned Aspasia as sexually promiscuous, arguing that she "was notorious for the profligacy of her life" and hardly an example for women in the United States. Adams, like Child, challenged that critique, maintaining that Aspasia was an illustrious figure from Greek history and that she had to be judged based on the context in which she lived. No doubt deeply aware of the way antislavery women had been criticized for being sexually immoral because of their public activities, Adams celebrated Aspasia for her political

interventions, and he dismissed any suggestions that the performance of domesticity was a higher form of citizenship for women.[8]

In fact, as Adams carried this historical narrative into the American Revolution, he argued that political activities were not distinct from domestic ones and that women, with great justification, had left behind domestic comforts to undertake a broad range of political activities during the struggle for independence. He spoke at length about the shirts that had been sewn and paid for by the women of Philadelphia in their attempts to aid the Continental Army. This was not the activity of women content to sit by their fireside, but rather a highly political intervention: "They entered into the hottest political controversies of the time." Citing Johnson's *Life of General Greene*, Adams argued that such an intervention into the act of supplying troops was considered controversial during the Revolution. He also pointed out that petitioning was nothing new. Ramsay's *History of the Revolution of South Carolina* described the way women of that state had petitioned to save the life of Captain Isaac Hayne. Adams portrayed them as independent, politically engaged patriots. "Politics, sir! rushing into the vortex of politics! Glorying in being called Rebel ladies!" Adams thundered. "Shall it be said here that such conduct was a national reproach, because it was the conduct of women, who left their 'domestic concerns,' and 'rushed into the vortex of politics?'" Finally, Adams reminded his audience of Deborah Gannett's courageous service in fighting for her country when she enrolled in the military while disguised as a man. In each case, as Adams recreated the history of women in the Revolution, he separated their domestic activities from their political ones. He did not deny the importance of domesticity, and he just did not root female citizenship or patriotism in those activities. Even the sewing of shirts was a political endeavor rather than a domestic one. Adams's history of women was a history of political participation and freedom fighting that began with the Greeks, moved through Europe and eventually the American Revolution, ending in the petitioning of antislavery women. This was the history of women's citizenship and one that they had a right to continue.[9]

Benjamin Howard, who debated Adams on these points, constructed an alternative version of women's participation in the Revolution that suggested personal commitments rather than political ones. "When the relatives and friends of women are in the field," he argued, it was entirely appropriate for women to sew clothing for them or use their influence in

any way possible "to alleviate the toils of their gallant defenders." Howard's view, in some ways consistent with theorists of the eighteenth century who had denied that women could be patriotic, described women's activities as motivated by concern for family members rather than by any larger ideals. Howard was willing to acknowledge that women could be patriotic, but only by defining their patriotism as personal, rooted in loyalties to their families rather than to the state. Indeed, in casting them in relationship to their "defenders," women's contribution to the national heritage lay in being defended rather than in any more direct contribution to the effort. This sort of female behavior, in Howard's argument, was a long way from petitioning against the annexation of Texas. Moreover, he claimed, Deborah Gannett was no more an acceptable model for respectable women than Aspasia was. Respectable women dressed as such and tended to their homes.[10]

Competing interpretations of women's history were invoked in debates about both the antislavery movement and labor protests. Female operatives in Massachusetts who joined working men during the 1840s to petition the state legislature for a shorter work day had encountered criticism for their unladylike behavior just as antislavery activists did. In arguments that developed, it became clear that working people also had been reading women's histories. Editors of the pro-labor *Voice of Industry* referred at various times to the histories written by both Lydia Maria Child and William Alexander. They cited a brief excerpt on American slavery from Child in 1845 and, a few weeks later, a brief excerpt from Alexander on the importance of female education.[11]

More traditional operatives who opposed labor activism used history to argue against the participation of women in politics. Harriet Farley, writing under the pen name of "Ella," made that case in one of the earliest issues of the *Lowell Offering*, a journal partially supported by the factory owners. Using a logic similar to Hannah Crocker's, Farley argued that women could be educated to understand politics, but this knowledge was best used in the home, as the excesses of the French Revolution made clear. She praised Madame Roland, not for her political engagement, but for resisting the impulse to speak publicly on political matters and remaining content to express her political opinions through writing and through her husband.[12]

More radical operatives had a different perspective. "Martha," who wrote for *Voice of Industry*, drew on history to argue for a range of rights. She claimed that she had no more desire than anyone else to detach women

from their domestic role, but she objected to the categorization of women that found them inferior to men in "mind, talent, judgement, and capacity." Queens had been more successful than kings, Martha argued, proving that women were far from inferior to men in their minds and that they "transcended" men in delicacy. She specifically cited the accomplishments of women in the past who had demonstrated their political capabilities in leading their countries. "Who in ancient times, surpassed Semiramis? or in modern Christina of Sweden? the Catherines of Russia? Elizabeth and Victoria of England?" Interestingly, while Martha went on to demand the right of women, based on their capabilities, to an expanded education, respect for their opinions, and the ability to fully participate in the economy "to buy and sell, solicit and refuse, choose and reject, as have men," she did not follow the logic of her examples to demand political rights. In part, she was writing a couple of years before suffrage became an important component of the woman's rights movement, but she was also writing as a labor activist who did not distinguish economic issues from political ones the way middle-class activists might.[13]

Women who participated in the labor movement defended themselves not only from the attacks of their employers, but also from the suspicions of male activists who were equally uncomfortable with political women. Thus, operatives also used history to soften the political edge of their petitioning and public speaking. Sarah Bagley, for example, attempted to reconcile working men to the presence of women in the labor movement by tying their activities to a vision of women in the Revolution that emphasized their subordination to men. In one public address, she claimed, "We do not expect to enter the field as soldiers in this great warfare, but we would like the heroines of the Revolution, be permitted to furnish the soldiers with a blanket or replenish their knapsacks from our pantries." She did not suggest that women in the Revolution were engaged in political behavior in the same way that Adams did; however, Bagley politicized the nurturing vision of these women by yoking it to the political activities of women who were circulating and signing petitions in the ten-hour labor movement.[14]

Once suffrage had been introduced into the debates about woman's rights at the end of the 1840s, the political activities of women in the past became an explicit justification for the right of women to vote. Stanton used history before the state legislatures and also in local speeches for woman's rights. When she addressed a group soon after the Seneca Falls

Convention in 1848, she championed the political rights of women by noting their ability to rule. Again, drawing directly on Child, she argued that there had been proportionally more good queens than kings, and she singled out Zenobia, in particular, for praise, as well as other famous leaders such as Margaret of Denmark, Elizabeth of England, and Zingha of Angola. Using other histories as well (most particularly Emma Willard's *Universal History*), Stanton summoned up a vision of Joan of Arc as both an example of women's abilities and an inspiration women should imitate.[15] Rebecca Sandford echoed Stanton when she spoke to the Woman's Rights Convention in Rochester, New York, that same year, eloquently defending the abilities of women to take the reins of political leadership by citing the historical record. "From Semiramis to Victoria we have found the Women of History equal to the emergencies before them!" she argued. Women had used their perceptions and their judgment to change and improve the world around them. Suggesting a narrative of decline in more recent years, Sandford concluded, "The world has seen woman in power; and the after history of that age tells of the abuse of power."[16] By making direct links between women from the past and women from the present, speakers such as Stanton and Sandford explicitly urged women to walk into history and to use the examples of women in the past to change the world around them.

Henry Blackwell went further and directly tied women in the past to the creation of democracy in the United States. In 1853, when he addressed the Woman's Rights convention in Ohio, he even argued that women were fitter for politics than men were. Citing the roles of political leadership held by women in Europe, Blackwell argued, "History teaches us that if there be one thing for which woman is peculiarly fitted, it is the art of Government." Although women were excluded from politics in the United States, Blackwell argued that "it is a singular fact in the annals of almost every country of Europe, that perhaps the most illustrious monarch, the one who has done the most for the aggrandizement of the nation, has been a woman." Blackwell went on to describe in detail how Elizabeth had united a nation torn by civil war and religious feuds, creating stability and a golden age for her country. Although she faced opposition from the Catholic Church, and threats of invasion from other European countries, she ably defended her nation. Tying Elizabeth to the history of democracy in the United States, Blackwell hit his punch line: "And we are here to-day, free to discuss the rights of woman, because there was a woman then upon the throne of

England, to defend religious liberty against the oppression of Catholic Europe."[17]

Further defending his assertion that women should have the right to vote, Blackwell also constructed a history of female bravery and direct leadership in narratives of national progress. He reminded his audience that Isabella had outfitted Columbus for his voyage when no king would offer him support, connecting her as well as Elizabeth to the founding of the United States. Maria Theresa, he pointed out, had saved the Hapsburg monarchy in Austria when its own nobles had abandoned her. And in Russia, two great Catherines had brought glory to Russia. The first had risen from the humble status of a slave to become the wife of Czar Peter, taming his more savage instincts. The second Catherine had consolidated the gains made by her predecessors, providing solid ground for the current czar to exercise his power. And even in France, which denied women the throne, women had consistently led the country. "Joan of Arc was really the greatest monarch who has ruled there since Charlemagne," Blackwell claimed with some hyperbole. He did not praise Madame Roland for limiting her political expression, as Harriet Farley had, but instead argued that Roland had been at the center of the Girondist party before being executed in the reign of terror. These were not women who related to the state through their husbands or as objects to be defended. These were not women who derived their status from their place in the household. These were independent women who had led their countries. "When woman has done such great deeds in the old world," Blackwell summed up, "amid almost insurmountable obstacles and a thousand disadvantages, how strange it seems, that man should be so blind to the facts of history, as to say that the women of intelligent America are unfit to go to the ballot-box, to give their voice in the selection of their rulers." Women, Blackwell demonstrated, had protected their countries and fought for political rights, some of which were being enjoyed in the United States.[18]

Lucretia Mott, well aware of the dangers of putting women on a pedestal and highlighting their differences from men, challenged part of Blackwell's historical argument. "We ought, I think to claim no more for woman than for man; we ought to put woman on a par with man, not invest her with power, or claim her superiority over her brother. If we do, she is just as likely to become a tyrant as man is." Catherine the Second, she claimed, was a good example of how female leaders could be just as immoral as their

male counterparts. That said, Mott was content to let the rest of Blackwell's historical argument stand.[19]

The historical interpretations circulating in the woman's rights conventions spilled over into other forums as well. Almost a decade later, when debating whether or not women should be allowed to vote, Rufus Fowler argued that the country owed its existence to more women than the few who swayed a scepter. He tried to convince the members of the Blackstone Literary Association that women had proven the fitness of their sex to participate in politics. There were the women who had suffered the long and difficult five-month voyage from Europe to settle the new colonies as well as the pioneer women "who struggled with the perils of the wilderness the midnight ambush of savage foes with cold, and famine, and disease." Women not only had suffered alongside men as immigrants and settlers, but also had provided support throughout the Revolution as they "administered the fatigued soldiery amid the carnage of the battle field," praying "to the God of battles for the success of American arms and the victory of American liberty." Women had repeatedly suffered for and shown courage in the process of settlement and independence, so "why should not the women of the United States be allowed to participate in the enjoyment of these blessings?"[20] Fowler raised, in particular, the issue of historical responsibility as he argued that women had sacrificed as much as men had to create the United States and that political citizenship was a just reward for that suffering.

History and Economic Citizenship

While debates about suffrage were some of the most contentious in the first woman's rights movement, debates about property were probably the most pervasive. Moreover, supporters were stretched along a political continuum that led them to different narratives. While some argued that the ability of married women to own property was simply one of many universal rights they deserved, others saw it as a way to protect family property and opposed giving additional rights to women. By the 1830s, state legislatures were being petitioned to give married women more control over their property. Wealthy women often gained such control through the laws of chancery, which allowed fathers to set up special trusts for their daughters that were beyond the control (and liabilities) of their husbands. Legislation that gave

married women control of the property they brought into marriage would provide similar protection. Neither the separate estates that were specially set up nor the legislation that was meant to replace it was necessarily intended to promote universal woman's rights.[21]

In still other cases, the question surfaced as the United States expanded and began to absorb territories that had previously been under French and Spanish control, bringing the common-law traditions of British America into conflict with the civil-law traditions of France and Spain. The British common-law tradition of coverture prevailed in most of the antebellum United States with respect to the laws of marriage, including property. As a result, the legal identity of wives was merged with that of husbands, and their property (unless specifically protected by a separate estate) became their husbands' property. Civil law, which held sway in France, Spain, and the Netherlands, presumed male domination in most arenas, but it did allow married women to hold their own property, make contracts and wills, sue or be sued, and generally make use of the courts, all legal rights that were denied women under common law. As the United States conquered and otherwise incorporated parts of the French and Spanish empires into the new nation, civil law (also known as Roman law) came into direct conflict with common law as states carved out of French and Spanish territory crafted new constitutions.[22]

The debate about the ability of married women to own property raised larger questions about the meaning of wealth. Regardless of where advocates for married women's property rights stood on the political spectrum, they had to confront the long-standing tradition that associated women with the effeminacy and degeneration that could come with wealth. The revolutionary generation saw itself as embodying the masculine virtue of republican simplicity, in contrast to the effeminate luxury corrupting the British Empire.[23] But succeeding generations had to grapple with growing wealth and the imperial reach of the new United States as well as the fears of degeneracy that went with it. Demands that married women be allowed to control their own property fueled a panicked response infused with broader apprehensions about an expanding marketplace and territorial boundaries. For those who worried that the United States had swiftly moved into a period of imperial decline, demands that married women control their own property was further evidence that the republic was endangered.

No historical trajectory was more important in confronting concerns of wealth than the fall of the Roman Empire. As Caroline Winterer has

pointed out, elite Roman matrons had long provided women in the new republic with an example of how to combine wealth with virtue. Their sacrifices at key moments in Rome's history had saved their country and brought them respect.[24] But the decadence of women had also been tied to the fall of Rome. The virtuous matrons of the republic had given way to voracious sybarites as Rome became a wealthy empire. Women of the empire gained more wealth and exercised more power than women of the republic had, so the power and wealth of the women of the empire were tied to a sexually depraved lifestyle that was frequently associated with the fall of Rome.[25] Supporters of property rights for women had to defeat this powerful image if they were to succeed in their mission.

Of lesser importance, but significant nonetheless, was the history of common law in Britain versus civil law in France and Spain. Had the civil law of France and Spain encouraged national decadence that Britain had avoided by limiting the property rights of married women? Or was Britain wedded to a form of legislation that had emerged in the brutal Middle Ages? More conservative advocates of married women's property rights, who had little interest in demands for other forms of equality, stressed the way in which legal reforms would strengthen marriages rather than undermine them. In doing so, they often marked nineteenth-century marriages organized around companionship as an important evolution from more hierarchical relationships in earlier centuries. Common law, unfortunately, had not kept up with those changes but was a throwback to a more savage state.

As early as 1828, Caleb Cushing asserted this argument in a long essay in the *North American Review*. He did so in the context of reviewing the first American edition of Peregrine Bingham's *Law of Infancy and Coverture*, a book that defended the laws of coverture as natural. Bingham had claimed that the legal disabilities married women faced were necessary for marital harmony. Human nature demanded that if two people were to live their lives together in peace, one would have to dominate the other in order to eliminate conflict. Because man was stronger than woman, not to mention better educated, it made sense for him to be the preeminent partner. Those who "from some ill-defined notion of justice or generosity, would extend to women an absolute equality, only hold out to them a dangerous snare," Bingham cautioned.[26]

Cushing was hardly a radical advocate for woman's rights. Indeed, he would dismiss demands that women participate in politics in another

review he wrote several years later. Property, however, was another matter. He challenged Bingham's assertion of the significance of male strength by framing it as an expression of male aggression, rooted in a historical period when England was governed by brute force. In making this assertion, Cushing refashioned the argument of writers such as William Russell, who had claimed that the women in Britain maintained their virtue longer than did women in France and Spain because chivalry had been weaker and commerce had come later. In Cushing's interpretation, that lack of chivalry was also an assertion of naked power. This "monstrous doctrine" of coverture, Cushing argued, was rooted in "the right of the stronger"; in Cushing's view, this strength was a vice rather than a virtue. It was a principle "whose antiquity is its only commendation, and which, in its operation, has involved the courts in continual embarrassment." Cushing dismissed the domestic tranquility that supposedly resulted from common law, arguing that the legal disabilities that a woman faced were not "designed for her benefit and protection; but for the security of her husband."[27]

What Cushing attempted to do with this argument, in a manner that suited his conservative stance on woman's rights, was to recode the association of domestic harmony and national progress onto civil law rather than common law. "In countries that derive their laws from the civil code, woman retains many valuable rights of property in the married state," he pointed out. On the other hand, in countries dominated by common law, "her legal condition during coverture is defined by the simple and comprehensive, because despotic rule, of the complete merger of her rights, whether relating to person or property, in those of her husband." Suggesting that the power relations inherent in common law were of an older patriarchal model rather than a more contemporary domestic ideal, Cushing summarized, "She is only his *feme* or wife, but he is her *baron* or lord."[28]

Similar arguments about the brutality of the Middle Ages showed up in state constitutional conventions designed to admit states from the old Spanish empire. At the California constitutional convention in 1849, for example, delegates debated whether or not to allow married women to own property, as they did under Spanish and Mexican law, or to force the adoption of common-law traditions. Francis J. Lippitt fumed that, under civil law, husband and wife would be little more than business partners, at each other's throats at the drop of a hat and more content to live apart than together, as he claimed was so often the case in France. Meanwhile, others

turned their criticisms toward the dark origins of common law. "At the time common law was introduced, woman occupied a position far inferior to that which she now occupies," Kimball Dimmick argued. "As the world has advanced in civilization, her social position has been the subject of increased consideration, and by general consent of all intelligent men, she is now regarded as entitled to many of the rights in her peculiar sphere which were formerly considered as belonging only to man. This part of the common law is one of those portions belonging to the dark ages, which has not yet been expunged by the advance of civilization."[29] James McHall Jones echoed those sentiments, asking, "What is the principle so much glorified, but that the husband shall be a despot, and the wife shall have no right but such as he chooses to award to her. It had its origin in a barbarous age, when the wife was considered in the light of a menial, and had no rights. But in this age of civilization, it has been found that the wife has certain rights."[30] Jones, like Cushing, was not advocating property laws that would lead to female independence. Rather, both men saw property rights as a way of reinforcing the power of women within their domestic world. Their revisionist approach to the condition of Britain in the Middle Ages targeted a very specific aspect of common law, but it served to challenge the vision of noncommercial simplicity and virtue that writers such as Russell had constructed.

While recasting the chivalry of the Middle Ages was important in debates over married women's property, analyzing the decline of the Roman Empire was even more crucial. Some eighteenth-century historians such as Edward Gibbon had tried to dissociate the behavior of women from the problems of the empire. Others, however, continued the arguments advanced by intellectual luminaries such as Machiavelli and Montesquieu that linked growing female wealth to a growing addiction to luxury in the imperial period that brought about the gradual collapse of Rome.[31]

Montesquieu, in particular, focused on the repeal of the Oppian Law as the point at which Rome became addicted to luxury. The Oppian Law had been passed in 215 B.C. as a temporary tax on women to fund one of the Punic Wars. It limited women to owning no more than an ounce of gold, restricted the color of garments they could wear, and forbade them from riding in horse-drawn carriages, all symbols of luxury in Rome. But the law had also come to signify the commitment of Romans to austere virtue; and its repeal in 195 B.C., which had been championed by women, had been tied to the decline of Rome. Montesquieu suggested that the Oppian Law

was passed to make sure that women remained frugal. When the women managed to have the law repealed, they used it to promote decadent luxury. Thus, the Oppian Law was not just about funding a war, but also about the ability of women to control wealth in a virtuous rather than decadent fashion. Montesquieu expressed a similar attitude about the Voconian Law, which had also been passed during the Punic Wars as a measure to limit women's inheritance rights. According to Montesquieu, Roman inheritance laws "did not sufficiently restrain the riches of women," so "a door was open to luxury." Thus between the second and third Punic Wars, Rome had passed the Voconian Law. As Rome became more corrupt, however, the law was "buried under the opulence of the city" as most parts of the law were either evaded or repealed.[32]

Cushing handled the fears associating women's wealth with the decline of Rome by ignoring them and substituting an alternative narrative that focused on the evolution of marriage laws in Rome and the growing influence of Christianity. What he attempted to show was the way in which the property holding of women in Rome was related to a particular kind of informal marriage, rather than the luxurious decadence associated with the empire. Once Christianity was accepted, he argued, marriages became more stable and women's property holding was properly contained.[33]

Thus, Cushing stressed that in Roman history there had been two kinds of marriage. The simple marriage of consent was rooted in the rude days of the Roman Republic when men and women simply joined together and parted from one another based on a simple agreement. It was this tradition that gave women the right to control their own property. The other form of marriage that developed in subsequent years gave husbands such extreme power over their wives that women resisted its use, particularly as they gained more status. Cushing acknowledged that marriages of consent, while giving women the right to control their property, also made divorce common. Yet with the advent of Christianity, Cushing argued, Roman marriages stabilized, combining sanctity with property rights for women. The luxury of the empire had nothing to do with the ability of women to control their wealth. Cushing dodged concerns about the fall of Rome by stressing the triumph of Christianity instead. He was able to do this, in part, because he was not asking for a broad array of rights for women that would affect the nature of government but was focused on the acquisition of property rights as part of an attempt to create marriage laws that were better suited to the conditions of the nineteenth century.

Those who were trying to change the position of women in the state more broadly, however, had to take on the fall of Rome. At the 1846 constitutional convention in New York, for example, Conrad Swackhamer passionately attacked the discrimination that single women faced in education, work, and politics and he argued against the abuse women faced in marriage. Swackhamer was aware of the fears associated with women owning property and, more specifically, of the association of female property holding with the fall of Rome. Swackhamer, however, refused to join the two. In Swackhamer's telling, the fact that women were able to own property in the more decadent period of the empire was not an indication of women's weaknesses, but of men's. Echoing the argument of WJF, who published "Wives and Slaves" in the October 1845 issue of the *United States Magazine and Democratic Review*, Swackhamer argued that Roman men refused to give anything to the virtuous women of the republic and that they were so taken with their mistresses in later years that they showered them with favors. Throughout history, Swackhamer claimed, men had treated their mistresses better than their wives. So as some women had become more voluptuous and decadent at the end of the Punic Wars, men had begun to reward them. It was then that "their oppressors seemed to have discovered that they had souls, and that they possessed intelligence and power; for then they began to consult them respecting matters of state, and admit them to the councils of the nation." Swackhamer suggested that the men of New York needed to break that pattern and reward virtuous women, rather than waiting to indulge those who did not deserve it.[34]

While Swackhamer's approach represented one way of trying to detach the women's ownership of property from the fall of Rome, a more powerful reinterpretation was offered by Robert Dale Owen a few years later as he debated Roman history at the Indiana Constitutional Convention of 1850, combating the assertions of Christian Nave and William Haddon that Indiana would fall, just as Rome had, if married women were allowed to hold personal property. The Indiana legislature had already given married women the right to control their real estate, but Owen's proposition would extend that right to personal property as well. It was a move that had class implications because less wealthy women were the likely beneficiaries.[35] In a historical debate that spread over days, the combatants argued about the virtue of the propertied women of Rome, particularly in the wake of the Punic Wars, laying out the issues that had simmered below the surface in so many of the historical allusions to the dangers of married women owning

property. Did history demonstrate that women with property undermined their families and the nation, or did it prove that such women supported the social institutions surrounding them?

Nave feared for the future of the country. Women who became richer than their husbands would "become insulting to them," he warned. Jefferson, he claimed, had attributed the debauched state of French society to civil law. Moreover, their demands for property rights were only the beginning. "If we establish the principle that the pecuniary interest of women is separate and distinct from that of men," he threatened, "we should establish also their right of representation, and their right of suffrage; it would be but just, and their separate interest should be represented."[36] Implicit in Nave's argument was the belief that the home provided a moral center for both the family and the nation, but only if the wife was economically dependent upon her husband, her legal identity subsumed by his. With these fears front and center, Nave raised the issue of history, urging his fellow delegates to consider "the many evils which the Roman civil law entailed upon the Romans themselves, and the effects produced thereby upon the marriage state." The "debauchery" that had afflicted Rome could be repeated in Indiana, for the past offered a way to predict the future.[37]

William Haddon and Robert Dale Owen not only debated Roman history at the convention, but also partially reenacted it as they waved their copies of Livy at one another and debated the significance of inheritance laws. Occupying center stage in their convention hall, and watched from the galleries by concerned women as well as men, Haddon and Owen not only fought over the meaning of wealth for Roman women, but also the public protests of those women in 195 B.C. when Cato the Censor attempted to continue the tax long after the war had ended.

As Haddon both defended and took on the role of Cato the Censor, he summoned up the image of venal, greedy women who fought for their right to luxury against their stern and virtuous ruler who had tried to protect democratic values. Referring to the period at the end of the Punic Wars when many women had gained sizeable fortunes (in part because the men in their families had been killed in war) Haddon read Livy's description of the conflict that had surrounded questions not only of female taxation, but also of inheritance. Roman women had been able to inherit an unlimited amount of property, giving them great wealth and power. Cato the Censor, Haddon argued, championed a law that would limit female inheritance to approximately $40,000. It was a limitation, Haddon told his audience, that

was rooted in a fear of female weakness. Women might succumb to "luxurious indulgence" because they were "fond, by nature, of dissipation, dress, and show."[38]

Haddon portrayed Cato as a war hero who "struggled to restore the simple and virtuous customs of the earlier ages of the republic, and resisted to the utmost of power the insidious advances of luxury and extravagance." Cato's military service and commitment to republican simplicity were cast in opposition to the material demands of women, so that female wealth, decadence, and the decline of Rome were joined. Haddon recounted Cato's attacks on women not only for flaunting their wealth through luxurious fashion and jewelry, but also for using their fortunes to dominate their husbands. Rich matrons, according to Cato, "retain to themselves large sums of money, which they do not entrust to the power of their husbands, but only lend to them, they send their slaves, who importunately demand repayment and treat their husbands as if they were entire strangers happening to be their debtors."[39] Thus, when men lost control over their finances, their marriages collapsed and family intimacy evaporated. In the waning days of the Republic, leaders such as Cato saw the danger and tried to prevent it, but they ultimately failed. And nowhere was this failure more evident than in the fight to repeal the Oppian Law. In Haddon's view, it was precisely this "corruption of manners" that ultimately led to the downfall of Rome. Women with wealth undermined their marriages and ultimately brought down their nation; they did not possess the requisite qualities of citizenship that would lead to a more judicious use of their resources.

Thus, Haddon dramatized Cato's attack on women's property holding, and he also used Livy to suggest the political disorder that women with wealth could cause. He read into the convention record Livy's rendition of the way women had thronged the streets leading to the Forum to lobby the Tribunes for the repeal of the Oppian Law. Complaining about the lack of control men had over their wives, Cato argued, "If, Romans, every individual among us had made it a rule to maintain the prerogative and authority of a husband, we should have less trouble with the whole sex." Haddon used Livy to take direct aim at the women in the gallery of the Indiana state convention. When he condemned the women of Rome, it was hard to miss the parallels with the women of Indiana. As they watched the proceedings, Haddon moved to the conclusion of Cato's speech by demanding, "Will you give the reins to their intractable nature, and then expect that themselves should set bounds to their licentiousness, and without interference?"

Certainly, everyone in the hall understood the comparison between Roman times and their own period, for widespread laughter erupted in the hall at Cato's final warning: "If, then, you suffer them [the women] to throw off these one by one, to tear them all asunder, and at last to be set on an equal footing with yourselves, can you imagine that they will any longer be tolerable? Suffer them once to arrive at an equality with you, and from that moment they will become your superiors."[40] As Haddon made clear, the struggle over property for married women was but one piece of a larger struggle about the ability of women to assume the responsibilities of citizenship, and that was an ability that Haddon claimed they lacked.

As Owen took the floor in response, he masterfully yoked Roman history to that of the United States, highlighting the principles that were at stake for women in Indiana and suggesting that the women of Rome offered a model of citizenship rather than decadence. In Owen's rendition, however, respectability was joined with a demand for rights, and the women who had come to the convention were used to frame the behavior of Roman women at the Forum. Acknowledging the women who were watching the convention proceedings, Owen gallantly used their presence to celebrate the Roman women who had lobbied for the repeal of the Oppian Law. "It would seem that in those days, as now, they whose rights were at stake sought the scene of debate," Owen claimed. "Whether the matrons of that day were as fair as those who, during this discussion, have graced our Hall with their presence, may well be doubted; but this we do see, that neither on that occasion nor on the present have the sex shown that indifference to their legal rights which some gentlemen have ascribed to them."[41]

Having reframed the scene in the convention hall, as well as the memory of Roman matrons outside the Forum, into one of respectable female citizenship, Owen proceeded to challenge the applicability of the Oppian Law to nineteenth-century society. Reminding his audience that the Oppian Law had been a wartime measure, Owen asked if the delegates seriously wanted to follow Roman precedent, by enacting new sumptuary laws and dressing women "from head to foot in one Quaker hue." Did they really want to force women to walk everywhere rather than ride in a carriage, "to be compelled . . . to traverse the streets on foot, no matter how great the storm, or how deep the mud may be?" Owen went on to critique Cato as a "harsh dictator" who would silence women in public as well as in their homes, a point that Haddon had failed to make. Reading parts of Cato's

diatribe that Haddon had ignored, no doubt in part because of its extremity, Owen highlighted the extreme patriarchal stance that Haddon was invoking. Cato not only had condemned Roman women for "addressing other women's husbands in public," but also had scolded the women that "it did not become you, *even at home*, to concern yourselves about any laws that might be passed or repealed here." With Owen's retelling of the story, the image of the virtuous, republican war hero was replaced by a high-handed patriarch, clearly out of step with nineteenth-century norms of even domestic companionship.[42]

Owen then moved to recast the political lobbying of Roman women into the more standard narrative that celebrated their civic virtue and self-sacrifice. He did so by reading the response of Lucius Valerius to Cato's attack on the women. Valerius, a plebeian tribune who had proposed that the Oppian Law be repealed, defended the public lobbying of Roman women by reciting their long history of civic activism beginning with their intervention in the war with the Sabines and continuing with voluntary contributions of their wealth when Rome needed it. This was the view of Roman matrons that had been so well known in the United States. As Owen read the impassioned speech by Lucius Valerius, he connected the civic virtue and political participation of Roman women to that of women in the American Revolution. Pointing out that Roman matrons had repeatedly used their own money, not for venal display but to save their country, Owen argued that the women of the American Revolution would have done the same if "instead of being deemed by the common law, unworthy of any right to property, had been, like the Roman matrons, capable of holding it."[43] Women's property holding thus became an opportunity for the display of civic responsibility rather than vanity, a chance to show strength of character rather than weakness. However, their virtuous use of property for the good of the state was not mediated by their husbands or their families in Owen's rendition. The emphasis was on the independent and direct acts of citizenship by women.

Delegates to both the New York and Indiana conventions vacillated so that some at first voted for the amendments favoring married women's property rights, but later reversed themselves. As a result, neither Swackhamer nor Owen triumphed with their rhetoric. On the other hand, their demands would triumph within a few years of their speeches as New York passed its first Married Woman's Property Act in April of 1846 and Indiana passed legislation allowing married women to own personal property in

1853.[44] Perhaps just as important, though, was the continued circulation of the historical imagery.

Owen's recasting of the struggle over the Oppian Law was powerful enough that it would continue to inspire participants in the woman's rights movement of the 1850s. In 1856, when Lucy Stone addressed the woman's rights convention in New York, she challenged male leaders by holding up the valiant example of those Roman women. With no sense that they had been reviled in the past for their venality, she proclaimed, "We shall go to your meetings, and by-and-by we shall meet with the same success that the Roman women did, who claimed the repeal of the Oppian law." Rehearsing the story for her audience, she argued that Roman women had petitioned to have the law repealed, and when that had failed, they took to the streets to demand justice. "When the Senators went to their places, they found every avenue to the forum thronged by women, who said to them as they passed, 'Do us justice.' And notwithstanding Cato, the Censor, was against them, affirming that men must have failed in their duty or women would not be clamorous for their rights, yet the obnoxious law was repealed."[45] For Lucy Stone, as for Robert Dale Owen, Roman women who demanded property rights offered a model of citizenship rather than corruption.

Industrialization and History

While demands for political rights led to strong assertions of the role of women in past political events, and demands for property rights encouraged a reevaluation of how women had used their wealth in the past, demands for expanded professional and educational opportunities inspired a broad reassessment of the historical narrative that culminated in the domestic citizenship of women. In various ways, critics of domestic citizenship began to question that narrative of progress and the celebration of the "modern" that was encapsulated in the ability of women to promote manners and sociability, forging instead a narrative of citizenship that recognized the importance of women to both economic and intellectual endeavors in the past.

Even before the woman's rights movement took off, some of the young women in Lowell, Massachusetts, who faced criticism for their unladylike protests chafed at the view of history that failed to recognize the importance

of either their work or their struggles. "Martha" not only saw little in history to justify any arguments of female inferiority, but also dismissed the role of Christianity in elevating the status of women. Her attack on Christianity may have been motivated by the frustration many factory workers felt with the clergy in Lowell who failed to support them as they struggled for better working conditions. Whatever the cause, Martha took the admiration of women's status in ancient civilizations that could be found in the work of Child and Fuller and pushed the implications further as she claimed that the heathens of ancient Egypt, Greece, and Rome had provided women with as much "elevation in the domestic and social relationship that ever they have in Christian lands." Indeed, Christianity had repeatedly enjoined women to assume an inferior position, and the heavy manual labor done by women in Christian countries such as the Netherlands, Germany, and Switzerland was further proof that Christianity, in itself, did little to raise the status of women.[46]

It was Paulina Wright Davis, however, who articulated the strongest alternative to the narrative of national progress that had been proposed by stage theorists. She did so in an address to the woman's rights convention in New York in the spring of 1853 in which she analyzed the way that women's work had become devalued as a result of the Industrial Revolution. As she addressed the widely debated question of why opportunities for women to labor were severely limited and poorly paid, she advanced a historical analysis that suggested that though women had taken on hard manual labor within their households in earlier times, their work had been appreciated in a way that it was not now. In a direct challenge to stage theorists, she also suggested that as a new industrial order had been created, women had been displaced, implying that the general industrial progress celebrated by so many did not result in progress for women.

Davis did not celebrate the "age of semibarbarism," but she did argue that women were more respected for their work in the past than they were in the nineteenth century, "the era of steam as a mechanical power." She acknowledged that the work women had done, manufacturing items for their families within their homes, was poorly paid. But she pointed out that their families and their communities recognized the importance of that work and respected it. The household manufacturing of women might not have been intellectually challenging, but it brought honor to women. "When the whole life of one-half of the race was required in the indispensable service of the other half," she argued, "such devotion had its honors as well as its uses, and

the brain and heart, ever busy in the service which occupied the hands, were not tortured with a constant sense of suffering, of vacancy, idleness, and worthlessness." Moreover, Davis argued, while women's work in household manufacture might have been drudgery, so, too, was the work of most men. A few men of wealth might have been able to pursue "learned professions," but the vast majority of men fared little better than women did. "The toils and rewards of labor were divided between women and the mass of men, and there was not much real difference between the political and civil liberties of the bulk of the two sexes. Women were then not only much and well occupied, but were honored in their functions."[47]

While women's work before industrialization may have been difficult, at least women were in control of it. As a result of industrialization, Davis claimed, women had lost those jobs, and they had also been closed out from the new opportunities that were opening up to men as work moved beyond the household. "Machinery has not only snatched the distaff and loom from her hands, but the needle," Davis argued with respect to women. "In the middle ages she was the surgeon and doctress, also, as well as the nurse of the sick. The learned profession of leech-craft has taken these from her," Davis proclaimed. The current degradation that women faced was all the worse because with newspapers they could read so much more about their decline. Thus, she concluded, "Here then we stand amid the wreck of our fortunes, amid the ruins which the years have wrought, and cry for redress. We ask that the avocations which progress and improvement have substituted for all that we have lost be fairly open to us."[48] Women deserved a shot at the occupations they had lost: at medicine and copying, which had been open to them in the Middle Ages, or in new jobs such as printing (that had replaced copying), or in other jobs that women might easily do, in telegraph or dentist offices. "The civil subjection of the past was bad enough," she argued, "but it was at least mitigated by our social, domestic, and industrial consequence." If work had shifted from households and neighborhoods to more distant locations, then women should be allowed to move beyond the household in pursuit of those jobs. As Davis made this argument, she also made it clear that the social and moral responsibilities of domesticity were not a substitute for women any more than they would be for men. What needed to be recognized was that women had an honorable tradition of working that had woven them into their communities and led to both recognition and inclusion. The new economy, by contrast, had excluded them.

Caroline Dall complemented Davis's argument with specific information about the labor of women in both the past and the present. By 1859, Dall had begun her extensive research on women's labor, integrating into her findings far more specific historical information about the economic and political significance of the labor of common women. Reporting to the woman's rights convention held in Boston that year, Dall celebrated the recent founding in England of the Institution for the Advancement of Social Science as well as the focus of its first meeting on the condition of women. She reeled off the many occupations that the British census showed women held: the shopkeepers, butchers-wives, and brewers. Dall proclaimed, "Women have been doing hard work ever since the world began. You will see by this that they are doing as much as men now."[49]

Dall then made specific connections between the economic significance of women's work and their political behavior as she recast the history of female fishmongers who had been vilified in critiques of the French Revolution. Female fishmongers, she argued, had taken over the business during the reign of Henry IV after the corporation in charge of fishmongering had collapsed in an economic shambles. The women who took over thrived both financially and politically. They "managed so well as to become very soon a political power. They became rich and their children married into good families." But this political power did not translate into murderous behavior as had been previously charged. "You will remember the atrocities generally ascribed to them during the first Revolution," she reminded her audience. "It is now known that these were committed by ruffians disguised in their dress." Rather, female fishmongers had been model citizens. As Dall continued her catalogue of the extensive work done by women, she also singled out the historical significance of women in textile manufacturing. "Cards were invented in 1361," she noted. "In less than seventy years the German manufacture was in the hands of women—Elizabeth and Margaret, at Nuremberg."[50] Implicit in Dall's catalogue of the accomplishments of laboring women was the recognition that their activities had been of key importance in the political and economic successes of their countries and, therefore, there was a need to include women in those histories.

Economic changes, however, had not only pushed women aside in many jobs but had also actually created a vacuum that was in no way filled by the activities of domestic citizenship. Theodore Parker, speaking in Boston in 1853, argued that because the domestic activities of women had

evolved, they had more leisure time that should be usefully filled. In much the same manner as the stage theorists, he pointed out that women no longer spent all their time producing cloth and food for their families. Because they bought their goods, they had time to be educated; their time needed to be used usefully.[51] Abby Price echoed this sentiment at the woman's rights convention in New York in 1853. She argued that women had progressed a little from the earliest times, having been released from manual labor in this more refined period, but they were still the slaves of men. The lack of manual labor had led to mental vacuity for some women, but to the questioning of their condition by others.[52] Thus the release from manual labor within the home was a double-edged sword. Society needed to recognize that women could no longer contribute in the ways they had in the past but that if new opportunities were not made available to them, their usefulness to society would decline. They needed education, and they needed to take stock of their situation. And although no one said so in the context of these arguments, the idea that they focus exclusively on domestic citizenship was clearly not an adequate response nor was the sense that a woman's sphere was in the home.

As a result of this shifting historical perspective, reformers argued that women needed to reclaim some of the professions that had once been theirs by right. Elizabeth Cady Stanton challenged the limited occupations open to women in 1851, in a letter she sent to the woman's rights convention in Akron, Ohio, when she demanded that women reclaim the profession of obstetrics. Citing a source (unknown, but indicated by her quotation marks) she noted, " 'It is now in this country and in England almost exclusively in the hands of the male practitioner, though from the earliest history down to 1663, it was practiced by women. The distinguished individual first to make the innovation on the ancient, time-sanctified custom, was no less a personage than a court prostitute, the Duchess of Villiers, a favorite mistress of Louis XIV, of France.' "[53] Lucretia Mott, addressing the woman's rights convention in Cleveland in 1853, shared with the audience the inspiration she found in reading about women's professional accomplishments. "Now that women are capable of reading, and beginning to be their own painters and historians, you see how much is brought out from history," she claimed. "I heard a lecture last year which astonished me with its number of remarkable women, not only in medicine, but in the Law and jurisprudence, farther back than the Twelfth century—all this is encouraging women to go forward in this movement."[54]

As Thomas Wentworth Higginson summed up the debate in 1853, "It is a point conceded that girls shall be 'educated.'" The real difference between conservatives and radicals was not "Shall a woman have schooling?—but, What shall she do with her schooling when she has it?"[55] Higginson then went on to describe the lack of opportunities for young women who did somehow manage to get an education, pointedly dismissing the option that they use their learning simply for domestic activities. The educated women of the past were not framed to demonstrate the domestic nature of educated women, but rather the kinds of professional employment they had successfully pursued in the past. Higginson noted the female professors at Salamanca and Alcala under Ferdinand and Isabella. He singled out Maria Agnezi as well, who was appointed an Apostolic Professor of mathematics at the University of Bologna in 1758. Other women who had achieved advanced learning included Vittoria Colonna and Veronica Gambara, who "ranked as the equals and friends of Benbo and Michael Angelo." All of these women operated independently as educated professionals.[56] As Higginson went on to argue that the nineteenth-century system of education provided women with "schools and not functions," he noted the important political work of women in the past. One "of the most important treaties of modern Europe—the peace of Cambray, in 1529—was negotiated by two women," he noted: "Margaret, the aunt of Charles V., and Louisa, mother of Francis I."[57]

Their professional accomplishments were all the more impressive in light of the challenges many women had faced. While only a few women had reached the heights of learning, this was not due to natural deficiencies, as stage theorists suggested, but to limited opportunities. Given the lack of opportunity, activists argued, one could hardly expect that women would have achieved as much as men in the past. When Emily Robinson addressed the woman's rights convention in Akron in 1851, she argued that traditional explanations of women's limited intellectual abilities simply were not convincing in light of the discrimination women faced when trying to pursue a higher education. "We are told that woman has never excelled in philosophy or any of the branches of mathematics—there are no female Fergusons, Newtons, or Euclids. Is that wonderful?" she demanded. "The Universities and Colleges of the world where these sciences are taught, and the passion for their culture is originated and cherished, forbid her all access to the facilities they offer."[58]

Higginson bemoaned the way in which women had historically been denied access to a quality education in his 1859 article for the *Atlantic*

Monthly. Looking to history, he argued that women who had excelled in the past had been educated like boys rather than girls. "Take any department of learning or skill," he argued. "On the great stairway at Padua stands the statue of Elena Cornaro, professor of six languages in that once renowned university. But Elena Cornaro was educated like a boy by Emanuell Aponte." Higginson went on to celebrate the philological accomplishments of Catherine II, noting that she "shared, in childhood, the instructors of her brother, Prince Frederick, and was subject to some reproach for learning, though a girl, so much more rapidly than he did." Madame Dacier learned Greek only by "contriving to do her embroidery in the room where her father was teaching her stupid brother."[59] Women who had managed to gain a superior education had usually done so with the help of indulgent family members.

With arguments such as these, advocates for woman's rights began to construct the pieces of an alternative women's history. It was one that legitimated full citizenship for women rather than the differentiated citizenship celebrated by stage theory. But as their conflicts in Congress and state constitutional conventions made clear, these views of women in history were only one side of the debate. Opponents of woman's rights were equally adept in their uses of history and were willing to contest each point. These various uses of history make it clear how important it was to frame contemporary debates about women within some broader historical framework. Historical perspectives could be used to legitimize the status quo or to support demands for change. What these fragments of women's history suggest, however, is just how charged the depiction of women in the past had become. As the stakes became clearer, authors engaged some of the new questions being raised about the status of women, and political debate led to an explosion in the genre of women's history: a genre organized around the fault lines of the emerging woman's rights movement.

Chapter 5

Domestic Histories

The Literary World reviewed another new entry into the field of women's history in 1850, and the reviewer noted that "these ladies' books about ladies are decidedly the literary fashion of the day." Whether the books were about queens, the distinguished women of France, or the women of the American Revolution, the reviewer noted, "The lady writers seem of late to have taken the potentates and magnates of their own sex under their special protection." And these forays into the past were particularly of value in demonstrating the significance of women's behavior within their sphere. "These views of history from a feminine point of observation are valuable as showing the great influence woman has exerted for good and evil in history, in her legitimate sphere, by her influence on the affections."[1]

Debates about the history of women's citizenship not only infused constitutional conventions and woman's rights meetings, but also spilled over into the popular media of the time, fueling a growing genre of literature. Elizabeth Ellet would actually give it a name in one of the widely read books she produced: "domestic history." In trying to convey the feelings of the people, Ellet hoped to capture "the social and domestic condition of the times." Domestic histories thus focused on women as well as on men but, more important, they focused on the ways in which women related to the historical events around them as wives, mothers, and daughters, effacing any notion that women had acted independently of their families or that the past could be used to legitimate demands for woman's rights. As the reviewer in *Graham's American Monthly Magazine of Literature, Art, and Fashion* suggested in a review of Ellet's *The Women of the American Revolution* in November of 1848, Ellet's work responded to the "wish that some one would sit down and show how all great efforts have their origin in woman's devotion to her duty, and all great men owe their position to their

mother's faithful service, and how society owes the advantages which it may possess to the plastic mind of women."[2] With an emphasis on women exerting influence within their sphere, as well as the exploration of sentiment and emotion in women's participation in historical events, these domestic histories operated as an important counternarrative to the historical references circulating in the growing woman's rights movement that was making demands for full citizenship.

Rather than stressing the relationship of women to the state, domestic histories emphasized the relationship of women to the nation. Or perhaps it would be more accurate to say that, rather than focusing on the nation as a state with legal obligations, these histories focused on the nation as a cultural and ethnic entity in which the Anglo-Saxon home was a sacred site where women created the character of the people through reproduction, nurture, and sentiment. Although the home was an intensely local and personal site, growing up in such homes was an experience that all Anglo-Saxon men presumably shared and were willing to defend. Thus nationalism and patriotism in these narratives were not organized so much around allegiance to a state or a particular set of political principles but around defense of one's family. The merger of personal interests with political commitments that had surfaced in the patriotism of some women during the American Revolution evolved into a patriotism that was largely personal and local, though that patriotism was not without political meaning. These domestic histories gave the United States a common history and a sense of racial and ethnic unity, but they did so around an ideal of Anglo-Saxon womanhood in which all references to woman's rights were ignored (or even explicitly challenged). If anything, gender differences were held up as a key part of a system men fought to protect. In these domestic histories, Anglo-Saxon women were placed at the center of the creation of a national culture, both in terms of values and literature, and sometimes even conquest. It was a very active role with widespread political implications, but it was dependent on a view that undercut any demands women might make for their own legal or political rights.[3]

Lucy Larcom's class notes make it clear that special attention was paid not only to the role of women, but also to the importance of their affections in family relationships. Writing of the Germanic tribes in earlier centuries, for example, Larcom tied the military success of the men to the domestic influence of their women. "It was to the sacredness of the domestic circle that the Germanic tribes owed much of their success in battle," she wrote.

"The hallowing influence of home was ever around them—it urged them to conquest and glory." Lydia Maria Child, by way of contrast, had portrayed women in those Germanic tribes as active participants in political and military activities and as being too busy to even sit down and eat with the men.[4]

In many respects, this view harkened back to the ideals of eighteenth-century historians who had argued for the significance of domesticity as a moral activity and had tied its particular forms of expression to the character of different civilizations and nations. There were important differences, though, in the domestic histories produced in the nineteenth century. First of all, the eighteenth-century histories had focused on behavior and the acquisition of culture. By teaching manners and promoting sociability, women fostered the growth of culture. Nineteenth-century histories continued to champion those activities of women, but in addition, they created another sense of culture: as something innate within a people that needed to be acknowledged and claimed. Thus, in many instances, history did not provide examples to imitate, nor did it encode a narrative that promoted distance from earlier times; rather, it created stories that demanded identification with the past. This was particularly clear in the histories of the American Revolution where founding mothers were both celebrated as models for contemporary women and also identified as sharing the same blood and the same spirit. Moreover, in the hands of nineteenth-century domestic history writers, women were assumed to be more innately virtuous than they had been in the earlier histories, and, hence, they were far more capable of exerting their agency within their homes and for the good of their nation. In this way, domestic histories were also serious revisions of eighteenth-century histories of women; women were portrayed as active participants in shaping the nation, albeit within clearly defined gender roles.[5]

Elizabeth Ellet was probably the most well-known of these historical writers. The first two volumes of *The Women of the American Revolution* were published in 1848 and a third volume followed in 1850, along with a broader narrative, based on her research, which was entitled *Domestic History of the American Revolution*. By the end of the decade she had also published other books that incorporated her historical perspective in *Family Pictures from the Bible, Pioneer Women of the West*, and *Women Artists in All Ages and Countries*. Her books were widely reviewed in the periodicals of the day, and many excerpts from those books appeared either before or

after publication. It would have been hard for a literate person in the 1850s to have not read at least some of Ellet's historical sketches.

Sarah Josepha Hale, as an editor of *Godey's Lady's Book*, was one of Ellet's most important supporters, and Hale was probably the single most important figure in promoting domestic history in the middle of the nineteenth century. From 1848 through 1850, she ran sketches from Ellet's *Women of the American Revolution* in almost every issue. Hale's support is not surprising given her growing interest in this genre. By the early 1850s, she had produced her own very important domestic history: *Woman's Record; or, Sketches of All Distinguished Women, from "The Beginning" till* A.D. 1850. Hale also championed a major movement by which women could actually enact their commitment to domestic history during the middle of the 1850s: the Mount Vernon Ladies' Association. Spearheaded by Ann Pamela Cunningham at the end of 1853, the organization raised money throughout the country to purchase and preserve the home and burial place of George Washington. In the process, the association created a historical connection between women of the revolutionary period and those of the present, organized around the commitment to the sacredness of the home.

In both historical literature and activism, women such as Ellet, Hale, and Cunningham breathed new life into ideals of domestic citizenship. In the roles of author, editor, or fund-raiser, each of these women moved far beyond the domestic roles envisioned by eighteenth-century writers. Instead of working within the informal sociability of the drawing rooms of the eighteenth century, they worked through publishing offices and conducted fund-raisers around the country. The ideal of domestic citizenship, however, infused all of their efforts. The sanctity of the home was a crucial trope in their endeavors, as they repeatedly performed their domesticity in public. Rather than simply facilitate the conversation of men on matters of nation and patriotism, however, they claimed it as their own and as part of the responsibility of women. They lived lives that embodied the nationalist role they envisioned for women in the United States. Both Hale and Ellet saw themselves as, and were, successful participants in the creation of a national literary culture. Cunningham became the guardian of a national cultural site. And they all did these things without any demands that women receive direct rights from the state. Political rights, they recognized, would undermine the legitimacy of their particular efforts. It was a particular form of cultural citizenship that rejected political rights rather than demanding them as a corollary.[6]

None of the three women ever embraced the woman's rights movement. Ellet at times offered both direct and indirect criticism of demands
for woman's rights and of some of the other more radical reform activities
that some women had embraced, such as antislavery. As she noted in one
of her books, female artists who were diligent in their studies had as much
chance for success as any man. The sphere of a female artist was wider than
ever before, "without regarding as such the so-called 'emancipation' which
would urge her into a course against nature, and contrary to the gentleness
and modesty of her sex."[7] Cunningham believed that women and men were
intellectual equals, but she stayed away from any explicit demands for legal
and political rights, choosing instead to work through her elite connections
to achieve her goals.[8]

Hale also eschewed demands for universal rights, though she cam-
paigned actively for a wide range of changes in the status of women. She
consistently argued for the importance of higher education in the pages of
Godey's, as well as the importance of female professors. She supported the
right of married women to own property. She argued that women needed
female doctors to attend to them and that they were better equipped than
men to be clerks, typesetters, and waitresses. She even suggested that
women should be allowed to lecture in public on political topics. But Hale
advanced these arguments around a notion of difference. Women should
provide medical services for other women, not for men. They might be
suited to activities such as typesetting but not to trades such as
construction.[9]

Thus Hale was quite clear that, while she might be arguing for women's
superiority within particular arenas, she was not arguing for woman's
rights. As she noted in *Woman's Record*, "I am not aiming to controvert
the authority of the husband, or the right of men to make laws for the
world they are to subdue and govern. I have no sympathy for those who
are wrangling for 'woman's rights'; nor with those who are foolishly urging
my sex to strive for equality and competition with men." Rather than any
philosophy of rights, natural or otherwise, Hale turned to revealed religion
as the only legitimate guide to gender relations. "What I seek to establish
is the Bible doctrine, as I understand it, that woman was intended as the
teacher and inspirer for man, morally speaking, of 'whatsoever things are
lovely, and pure, and of good report.' The Bible does not uphold the equality of the sexes."[10] Of course, many woman's rights activists were arguing
exactly the opposite, so Hale's engagement with the Bible was the product

of more than her evangelical piety. If woman's rights activists saw women as equal with men before God and the same in their spiritual responsibilities, Hale saw women as divinely ordained to be different. Indeed, in *Woman's Record*, Hale developed her ideas of women's innate spiritual superiority to men, arguing that history would prove that women had been spiritually superior to men throughout time.

Despite these differences from the woman's rights movement, however, champions of domestic history such as Ellet, Hale, and Cunningham used history to offer women a form of differentiated citizenship that had important political implications. At a time when sectional conflict was growing over the issue of slavery, they offered a historical narrative of women that attempted to bind North and South together. At a time when the nation was expanding rapidly as a result of both expansion and immigration, absorbing large numbers of people who were decidedly not Anglo-Saxon, they offered a historical narrative that championed a particular female ethnic identity that could structure power relations with newcomers. Indeed, Hale offered a historical narrative that legitimated world conquest through missionary activities. Household economies (not to mention the general economy) might be changing dramatically as a result of industrialization and an expanding market, but these domestic historians erased those disruptions with their historical narrative focused on the moral influence of the home. They took domesticity as a civilizing influence to new heights by making it sacred.[11] But this political work also necessarily circumscribed women and their activities within the domestic, rather than allowing them to be imagined in any more independent relationship to the world around them. Domestic histories were histories of difference. They were among the most powerful narratives of the nineteenth century, incorporating women into the history of the nation. They gave women a prominent and active place within that history by arguing for the centrality of the home in the very idea of the nation. But, as such, they were a powerful antidote to the demands for universal rights and full citizenship.

Sarah Josepha Hale and Evangelical Stage Theory

Woman's Record, filled with biographical entries about women all the way back to Eve (for whom there was quite a long entry), was organized around a new, evangelical version of stage theory. While eighteenth-century

theorists such as Kames and Millar had tied the advance of civilization to different economic stages, and while women's histories by Russell and Alexander had focused on the relationship between the manners of women and the creation of national character, Hale advanced a new theory of world progress structured around Christianity. Eighteenth-century historians of women, as well as Lydia Maria Child, had also argued for the importance of women to Christianity and of Christianity in the changing status of women. But Hale gave Christianity a far more central place in her narrative. With her focus on religion, she ignored the issues of political participation and economy that were simmering in the emerging movement for woman's rights. Instead, she created a historical narrative in which women were the agents of Protestant Christianity, merging a story of religious progress with both the racial superiority of Anglo-Saxon women as the basis for national glory and the importance of expanding the American empire throughout the world. Like the women's historians of the eighteenth century, Hale enshrined domesticity as the height of civilization's progress and the cornerstone of American identity, but Hale's version of domestic citizenship was far more powerful than what had been imagined in the eighteenth century. Hale's heroines facilitated the activities of men who defended American culture, and they also created and spread that culture. They were able to do so because domestic histories of the nineteenth century successfully merged the values of the home with the very essence of the nation.

As with stage theory, Hale divided world history into four distinct eras, the first two of which received considerably less attention than the last two. The first era was the pre-Christian era, when any of the women who achieved fame did so through the exercise of royal power. In the second era, which extended from the birth of Christ to the Protestant Reformation, queens and courtesans were joined by martyrs and some intellectuals. The third era covered all women since the Protestant Reformation who had died. And the fourth era was devoted to living women of the time, who were essentially picking up the torch of history and moving it forward. As Hale made clear, it was only in the third and fourth eras that women had an appropriate platform for their leadership through the opportunities afforded by Protestantism. Before that time, most women struggled to do their best without having the spiritual guidance that benefited women in more recent centuries. Under the benevolent influence of women, Protestant nations were rising to greatness in the nineteenth century and were dominating other parts of the world.

Hale tied her religious history to emerging theories of race as she argued that the third era was marked by "the development of genius and talent in a new race of women—the Anglo-Saxon." These women, first in Britain and later in the United States, were able to achieve greatness because of the impact of Protestantism on their countries. "No other nations have the Bible in their homes; or the preached Gospel on every Sabbath," Hale argued. Nor could other nations hope to achieve greatness until they embraced Christianity, a judgment that invited political as well as spiritual conquest. "The Chinese nation cannot advance in moral culture while their women are consigned to ignorance and imbecility," Hale contended. "[T]he nations of the East are slaves to sensuality and sin, as well as to foreign masters; and thus they must remain till Christianity, breaking the fetters of polygamy from the female sex, shall give to the mothers of men freedom, education, and influence" (*WR*, 152).

Protestantism did not create an Anglo-Saxon race, but it lifted it to greatness in Hale's mind. Protestantism gave women spiritual influence within their families. It demanded a particular kind of family life, rooted in monogamous marriage. This social and spiritual structure was the bedrock on which national independence and superiority was based. Indeed, as Hale made clear in her introduction to the fourth era of living women, the destiny of the Anglo-Saxon race to rule the world depended on its commitment to a Protestant religion, which, unlike any other, recognized the superiority of women. In fact, Hale went on to distinguish between the "Old Saxons" of Britain and the new Saxon blood of the United States by arguing that the former still held the lead in producing "learned ladies." But the United States led in fostering female educators, whether they expressed themselves through teaching or missionary work or writing instructional books. In making this argument, Hale used a racial ideology of Anglo-Saxonism to tie the United States to Great Britain, thus undermining the political boundaries that separated them while at the same time suggesting the moral superiority of the United States over England. She also effectively ignored any issues of economic trade and production or political thought that might also differentiate and define the two nations.

Part of Hale's success was due to the way she so successfully fit into the model of romantic history unfolding at the time. Like the renowned historians George Bancroft, William Prescott, Francis Parkman, and John Motley, she assumed the divine hand of Providence was shaping a narrative of progress that began in Europe and was slowly moving westward to the United

States. She shared their assumptions that the Anglo-Saxon race was the bearer of that progress, carrying liberty to the rest of the world. However, while the others wrote of the masculine character that embodied those virtues, Hale gave it a female form, and she introduced an evangelical perspective rather than the Unitarian slant of her male counterparts. But regardless of those differences, she fit into the larger discourse of popular history on growing national greatness.[12]

Hale made it clear that her vision of female superiority, and its ties to national greatness, in no way suggested that women should therefore have the same rights as men or might be better suited than men to lead the country. Quite the contrary, Hale suggested that the true greatness of the Anglo-Saxon race came not simply from the moral influence of women but from the commitment of men to protect them. Hale singled out Laura Bridgman, who was both blind and deaf, as her emblem for the fourth era because of the men who had believed in her abilities and taught her. "After all," Hale concluded, "it is not so much what women do for themselves, as what men do for them, which marks the real state of both" (*WR*, 564). It was an argument that echoed Hale's dedication of *Woman's Record* to "The Men of America, Who Show, in Their Laws and Customs, Respecting Women, Ideas More Just and Feelings More Noble than Were Ever Evinced by Men of Any Other Nation" (*WR*, v).[13] Hale's argument that men should defend women, and their female purity, was an important element in emerging ideas of patriotism. Benjamin Howard had made a similar suggestion about the nature of female patriotism when he had debated John Quincy Adams about petitioning in 1838. In contrast to an eighteenth-century focus on defending the state and political ideals, this was one of the ways in which patriotism was shifted to a defense of beliefs that were devoid of political ideals that might provoke disagreement and were more closely tied to personal relationships.

Hale invested female purity with both value and power by arguing that it was an innate quality that women had always possessed in greater measure than men. Key to making this argument was the demonstration that, throughout time, women had always been morally superior to men. Although the valorization of female purity had become a commonplace belief in middle-class society by this time, Hale's argument pushed the boundaries in several different directions. She certainly challenged those who continued to assume that the social hierarchy demanded male leadership because of the moral weaknesses of women, which could be traced back to the time

of Eve. But she also challenged those who wished to argue that because men and women had the same moral abilities, they should have the same rights. For Hale's argument, what mattered was the assertion of a certain timeless quality in women's nature, which then naturalized their place in the social and political order as those who should be vested with moral responsibility and who should be defended by men so that they could go on with their moral duties. However, Hale made her argument by creating a new kind of history of female virtue. Unlike women's historians in the eighteenth century who pointed out the moral weaknesses of women through history, at least when they ventured into areas where they did not belong, Hale claimed they had been morally superior in all cases. She argued that women might have been corrupt in the past, but history had proved that they had always been better than the men around them. Recognizing that there were plenty of counterexamples, Hale tackled some of the most troubling cases of female licentiousness.

With evangelical commitment, Hale defended Delilah, for example, by urging her readers to ignore Milton's attack on her in *Samson Agonistes* and to focus instead on what the Bible said. It was clear, Hale argued, that Samson was irresponsible and had betrayed God's trust. Delilah had no such responsibility, to either God or Samson. She was not Samson's wife, so she did not owe him obedience. Thus, "Delilah conquered Samson, and in the means she employed she was far less culpable than he." It was Samson's fault that he could not control his passions. Hale thus promoted a vision of Delilah as a woman who may have done wrong but who was far less culpable for Samson's fall than was Samson himself. The temptress who had inhabited the popular imagination disappeared in Hale's telling (*WR*, 36).

Even more boldly, Hale engaged in an extensive defense of the moral superiority of Eve over Adam. After all, Hale argued, when the serpent offered the pair spiritual knowledge, he directed his temptation toward Eve because he knew she was the partner who made spiritual decisions. Moreover, while Eve accepted the serpent's fruit out of a desire for wisdom, Hale argued that Adam was eating merely because his wife had given it to him. It was Adam who was acting like the inferior in this case, taking orders from the superior creature. Adam had further proved his lower nature when confronted by God for his sin. Instead of meekly confessing, he tried to blame his wife. Although Eve was placed under her husband's control as punishment for her sin, through her reproductive powers a redeemer would

come. Hale thus concluded triumphantly, "Does it not mark her purer spiritual nature that, even after the fall, when she was placed under her husband's control, she still held his immortal destiny, so to speak, in her keeping?" Gone was the weak and foolish woman who had been blamed for the fall of mankind (*WR*, 39).

Hale's defense of Eve did not come out of the blue. For centuries, Eve had been repeatedly cited as a reason not to trust women with the same powers given to men. Eve had been the one to lead Adam astray, Eve was responsible for original sin, and women had been put under the authority of men as punishment for Eve's sin. In addition to Delilah, Milton had portrayed Eve as both weak and immoral in *Paradise Lost*. But criticism pervaded contemporary literature and debate as well. When A. P. Leach argued to his debating society that women did not have the same capacity for intellectual improvement that men did, he noted that their weaknesses had even been known to Satan "when he tempted our Great Grandmother Eve to eat of the forbidden fruit in preference to going to old father Adam."[14]

By the end of the eighteenth century, however, Eve's defense had begun. Judith Sargent Murray had suggested that while Eve had eaten the apple in the innocent belief that an angel was offering her wisdom, Adam had known full well that he was sinning because he saw Eve's loss of innocence before he joined in. Hannah Crocker had acknowledged that women had been punished by God for Eve's transgression by being placed under the authority of men, but she argued that women had been restored to their original equality with men through Mary's birth of Jesus. Sarah Grimké had argued that Adam and Eve were equally to blame for the fall and that "there was as much weakness exhibited by Adam as by Eve." Hale expanded that defense, though she also made it clear she did not support demands of equality put forward in the woman's rights movement. She was, however, committed to elevating the position of women in spiritual terms and she was also committed to eradicating the religious reasons, in particular, that kept women down.[15]

Reviewers did not let Hale's argument pass without notice. *The New England and Yale Review* humorously recounted Hale's depiction of the Fall, noting that she had settled "the question of Original Sin." *The North American Review* called it "a novel theory." After paraphrasing her story of Eve, again with some humor, the review concluded, tongue in cheek, "We had some doubt, at first, about the correctness of the theory. But we have

now high domestic authority for saying, that it is 'very sensible doctrine indeed, and as true as the book.' "[16]

Hale challenged the common assumptions of her readers with her defense of difficult religious examples, and she did so with difficult political cases as well, particularly as she made patriotism a female virtue by tying it to the superior moral instincts of women. Women's first devotion was to their families, but they made sacrifices for their countries as well. Sometimes this selfless devotion could be rendered to both, and sometimes women had to make a choice. In many cases, they had used their domestic relations in controversial ways to promote the good of their countries. Thus, balancing love of country with personal relationships had been a challenge for women throughout history, explaining some of the most troubling cases of women's behavior in the past. In fact, Hale went out of her way to rehabilitate women who had long been considered emblems of the failures of the female sex, trying to promote sympathy for the situations of those characters, though often with mixed results. Confronting morally problematic behavior, particularly in the first two eras of history before women had found a proper scope for their abilities, Hale assured her readers that even the most corrupt women had been superior to the men around them. They understood the meaning of patriotism better than men did.

Hale thus looked past Agnès Sorel's morally compromised position as a king's mistress to defend Sorel's impact on his political behavior. Noting that Charles VII of France had fallen in love with Sorel, thus removing any suggestion that Sorel had seduced him, Hale focused on the importance of Sorel's political influence. According to Hale, Charles was so smitten, he had irresponsibly turned his back on his political responsibilities, allowing the English to encroach on his lands. Sorel goaded him into leading the French to put up a spirited defense. Although Sorel held a compromised position, she was in many ways superior to the man she influenced and showed a deep love for her country (*WR*, 68).

Similarly, Cleopatra may have had many faults, but a lack of patriotism was not one of them. She may have had a wicked temper and lavish spending habits, and she may have been ruthless in her struggles to gain and maintain power, killing her own brother (who was also her husband) when necessary. But Hale was quite clear that Cleopatra was also devoted to the interests of Egypt. She was a great ruler who brought Egypt more wealth and power than any other leader. She may have been wicked, but she was

less wicked than Marc Antony. "She was better than the men her subtle spirit subdued,—for she was true to her country" (*WR*, 32).

In describing Agrippina (the mother of Nero), Hale portrayed a woman who loved both her children and her empire. True, she had been accused of poisoning her husband, but more likely he had died of gluttony. And she did engage in intrigues to make sure that her son, Nero, became emperor of Rome. Hale hastened to point out, however, that once Agrippina realized that Nero was unstable, she worked steadily to overthrow him, a commitment that ultimately led her son to murder her. Whatever her acts of cruelty and bad judgment, however, Hale reminded her readers that Agrippina was "actuated by one all-absorbing feeling . . . *maternal love.*" And, of course, "the woman must be judged by the circumstances under which she lived, and with reference to the morality of her contemporaries; and, so judged, she rises immeasurably superior to the greatest men associated with her history" (*WR*, 21–22).[17]

Hale's strategy of sympathy, in which she attempted to create an emotional identification centered on motherhood, was not always successful. At least one reviewer took note of Hale's defense of Nero's mother and pilloried her for it. *The New England and Yale Review* called it a complete fabrication. "The account which Mrs. Hale has given of this notorious woman is inexplicable," the reviewer claimed. "To speak plainly, it is a most palpable misrepresentation of history. This memoir is so totally at variance with the accounts in our most reliable histories, that we determined to look into the ancient writers and see if there were not some grounds for the representation Mrs. Hale has given. We could find none." Outraged by Hale's defense of Agrippina as a mother, the reviewer demanded, "Was it a mother's heart that poisoned her husband?"[18]

Hale did not encounter criticism, though, for defending women who were so selfless that they abandoned their womanly sphere to take on the masculine duties of defending and ruling their people, when necessary. Although this was an argument that allowed Hale to show admiration for these women, it also allowed her to limit the political significance of their activities. Their transgression of gender boundaries was forced upon them by historical circumstances and in some cases cost them the joys of womanhood. Their patriotic and political activities were fused with a portrayal of personal self-sacrifice.

Deborah, for example, had tried to convince Barak to lead the Israelites against the Canaanites, who were holding them in subjection. When he

equivocated, Deborah took on the role herself. God had given her "superior spiritual insight and patriotism," qualities she needed when it fell to her to raise an army. Hale condemned Barak's cowardice and noted that Deborah had tried to convince him to behave appropriately as a man. But because Barak "resolved to drag a woman forward to bear the blame of the insurrection, should the patriot effort fail; the 'honour' of success would be given to a woman" (WR, 34–35).

This love of country also animated Joan of Arc, according to Hale. Rather than portray Joan as deranged because she heard voices, Hale stressed her piety, simplicity, and chastity. Joan stepped into a position of leadership at a time when the king and his advisers were sunk in despair and lethargy. Thus, in concluding her biography of Joan, Hale argued that "enthusiasm possessed her, yet it was the lofty sentiment of patriotic zeal; not a particle of selfish ambition shadowed her bright path to victory and fame" (WR, 79).

While woman's rights advocates tended to focus on the political acumen of Elizabeth I and eighteenth-century historians had focused on her female failings, Hale attempted an analysis that challenged eighteenth-century views in another way: she demanded that Elizabeth be evaluated separately as a ruler and as a woman. Elizabeth I, Hale argued, had "voluntarily relinquished the enjoyment of domestic life, where woman's nature is most truly and beautifully displayed, in order to devote herself to the cares of state and the happiness of people." Because of this act of self-sacrifice, Hale challenged those who criticized Elizabeth's ability to rule due to her "female failings." It might be that Elizabeth was vain and had a weakness for handsome men, but those were the failings of a woman and they should be used to judge her as a woman. Because Elizabeth had split her personal life from her political life by refusing to marry, she should be judged solely "as a ruler." In this capacity she triumphed. Yet, in suggesting what Elizabeth had sacrificed, Hale also made it clear that Elizabeth's commitment to her kingdom came at the expense of her domestic world (WR, 800–801).

For Hale, the domestic merged with the spiritual and the moral and was always more important than the political. Regardless of how accomplished or powerful they were, Hale judged women with respect to their relationship to family life, praising them, where appropriate, for nurturing their children or influencing their husbands for the larger good of society. No matter what their rank, women had to be judged by their ability to shape

character. And Hale singled out those women who did not measure up. She condemned Catherine de Medici, for example, for her loose morals as well as her never-ending political intrigues, but most of all, for her parenting. "Perhaps the heaviest charge against her is, the detestable principles in which she brought up her children, who she early inured to blood and perfidy, while she weakened their minds by debauchery, that she might the longer retain her power over them" (*WR*, 248–249).

By locating many of these politically powerful women in a corrupt past, where they had little choice but to take on activities of political and military leadership, Hale showed admiration for women who had been active agents of change in history at the same time that she bemoaned their need to shoulder such burdens. Thus, while she revised the worst aspects of misogyny in eighteenth-century women's history, she also challenged the demands for universal rights that were coming from activists who argued that the political and military leadership of women in the past was a justification for women's activity in that realm in the present. Rather, what Hale championed as an evangelical variation on the arguments of stage theorists was a new era in history in which Protestantism (not just Christianity) raised women to new heights by offering them the opportunity to shape the religious and cultural destiny of their nations. This differentiated spiritual and domestic citizenship was the mark of modernity and the reason for the triumph of the Anglo-Saxon race, which, Hale proclaimed, would "soon rule the world." Hale invested many of these women with agency, but they were active agents in a politically significant endeavor without having the legal and political rights of men; Hale argued that they were agents precisely because they did not have those rights. As civilization evolved, women became historical agents by fulfilling their domestic roles as women and embracing the concept of differentiated citizenship (*WR*, 563).

Thus, Ann Judson embodied for Hale the highest achievements of the third era. As the wife of missionary Adoniram Judson, she left her New England home in 1812 and traveled with him to Burma, where she spread ideas of Western culture and Christianity. When he and his coworkers were jailed, her domestic skills became particularly important as she brought them food and tended to their illnesses. Likewise, she not only nursed her family through a deadly smallpox epidemic but also used her knowledge of Western medicine to inoculate her village against the disease. Exhausted from her heroic work, Judson eventually died. But with her domestic and

spiritual powers, Hale made clear, Judson was a leader in spreading American influence (*WR*, 367–369).

Hale's biographies of Kapiolani and Queen Kamalu, both of the Sandwich (later Hawaiian) Islands, represented the other side of the story. The Sandwich Islands were a well-known destination for American missionaries. Both Kapiolani and Kamalu were converts to Christianity and their conversions helped to create a narrative that suggested that Western conquest was welcomed, structured around shared values rather than resistance or force. The women used their influence on their husbands to bring them to embrace Christianity and a range of other Western values. King Liholiho had four wives, for example, but with Kamalu's influence (and his conversion to Christianity), he was clearly moving into a more monogamous relationship with her at the time of their deaths. Kapiolani challenged not only the traditional Hawaiian god Pele, but also the islanders' "infanticide, debauchery, and drunkenness" (*WR*, 371–372).

Hale unfolded a similar historical narrative around Pocahontas, stressing the way in which the young woman had secretly (and sometimes not so secretly) helped the British settlers when they arrived in Virginia. Ignoring any political or military concerns that her father, Powhatan, might have had about the British, Pocahontas proved her superior values by ignoring those issues and tending to the care of the new arrivals. Her eventual marriage to John Rolfe not only relieved tensions between the Indians and the British but also united "the races . . . thus proving the unity of the human family through the spiritual nature of the woman." As Hale concluded, "She is another proof to the many already recorded in this work, of the intuitive moral sense of woman, and the importance of her aid in carrying forward the progress of human improvement" (*WR*, 475).

As scholars such as Anne McClintock and Amy Kaplan have pointed out, these stories of women bringing civilization to non-Anglo-Saxon peoples of the world, and the stories of savage women accepting Christian values, did important ideological work in masking the economic goals and military conquests that often accompanied such ventures. For this reason, the ideology of domesticity was one of the most potent political instruments for constructing both nationalism and imperialism. Hale, in fact, muted the memories of the French and Indian War, the American Revolution, the War of 1812, the Mexican War, and innumerable conflicts with Native Americans throughout the continent by claiming that the spiritual

values of the Anglo-Saxon race in the United States meant that "no blood has been shed on the soil of this nation, save in the sacred cause of freedom and self-defense; therefore, the blasting evils of war have scarcely been felt" (*WR*, 564). The new economic world that was being created through trade with Asia and Africa also was erased in stories that focused on spiritual goals. With this historical perspective, she could then argue that the spiritual and cultural values that Anglo-Saxon women brought with them were tied not to a new political and economic order but were coded as a cultural inheritance that they shared with those who had not been fortunate enough to experience it as part of their own cultural patrimony. The differentiated citizenship that white women had accepted provided a model for differentiated citizenship offered to and accepted by those in foreign lands who came under the influence of the United States. Women thus preserved their national culture and inheritance at the same time they spread it.[19]

Hale set great store by the idea that women created and spread national culture, and she celebrated the female missionaries who did so, as well as the women writers. It was in this context that Hale explained her own driving ambition and personal success. In the entry she made about herself, as part of the fourth era, which was subtitled "Of Living Female Writers," Hale traced her inspiration for writing to the first novel she read: Ann Radcliffe's *The Mysteries of Udolpho*. Hale noted that up until that time she had seen few books "written by Americans, and none by *women*." Hale was apparently emboldened to pick up the tradition of writing that women in Britain, such as Radcliffe, had promoted and to carry it to her own country as part of her own sense of patriotism. "The wish to promote the reputation of my own sex, and to do something for my own country, were among the earliest mental emotions I can recollect." It was her wish to exert the "mental influence of woman over her own sex" (*WR*, 687) that had prompted her to write *Woman's Record*.

As Hale went on to recount the accomplishments of other living women in her period, she evaluated them on similar terms, though this sometimes meant totally ignoring their political activities and at other times circumscribing them as unfortunate choices. Thus, she celebrated Lydia Maria Child for her domestic literature and concluded that Child's controversial and powerful antislavery tract, *An Appeal in Favor of That Class of Americans Called Africans,* was the unfortunate result of Child's overwhelming sense of benevolence. Hale dismissed Child's political work as a philanthropic effort that had ended up causing more harm than good (*WR*, 619–

620). Refusing to accept the fact that Margaret Fuller, who had died several years earlier, did not even belong in the fourth era, Hale described her as a virtuous woman whose qualities shone particularly brightly in her home. This was presumably a reference to Fuller's legendary abilities as a conversationalist. Fuller might have taken a wrong turn with her arguments in *Woman in the Nineteenth Century*, Hale suggested, but those mistakes arose from Fuller's generous spirit that aimed to improve the lot of others. And despite some problems in the book, it still contained "many useful hints and noble sentiments" (*WR*, 666). Both Child and Fuller were thus ushered into history as domestic women who sometimes strayed from their responsibilities but only because they were unable to discipline their womanly traits of benevolence.

In a similar vein, Hale praised Lucretia Mott for her philanthropy and her dutiful support of her husband. She criticized, however, her demands for equal rights as a violation of biblical doctrine. Using her critique of Mott as an opportunity to celebrate the domestic responsibilities of women, Hale concluded that Mott should be admired for her private life more than for her public one (*WR*, 752–753).

National culture was better promoted by female writers who championed moral values and steered clear of political controversy. Thus, Hale celebrated Harriet Farley, suggesting that the success of the *Lowell Offering*, which Farley had edited, proved even to the British the "intellectual progress . . . the American *people* have made." In doing so, Hale argued that it was the moral goodness of the operatives' work in the journal that really mattered. "Rejecting the fashionable isms of the day, resisting all persuasions from those who have striven to draw their journal into the arena of party, these noble-minded women have been true to their sex and their Saviour" (*WR*, 659). General expressions of morality were the basis for national unity and the proper province of women.

Frederika Bremer also more closely idealized the role of female author for Hale than did either Child or Fuller. Bremer had visited the United States in the late 1840s and had become quite inspired by the woman's rights movement, an inspiration that would begin to affect her writing in the middle of the 1850s. That transformation may not have been clear to Hale at the time she wrote her entry on Bremer; she certainly said nothing about it. Rather, she focused on Bremer's ability to evoke the Scandinavian past through her stories of everyday life. Recreating stories "hidden by the curtain of time," Bremer introduced her readers to the sanctuary of her

home, thus "awakening in our people an interest for the people of Sweden" (*WR*, 586). This was precisely the work of nationalism that Hale celebrated for women: recovering an ethnic past, rooted in family relations, that conveyed the essence of a society and promoted emotional ties with the audience.[20]

Elizabeth Ellet did the same sort of work for the United States, providing a national sense of "the people" in her writings as she transcended the geographic boundaries of North and South. Hale indirectly alluded to Ellet's ability to effect this reconciliation through her own ties to both parts of the country: she had lived first with her husband in New York and then had moved with him to South Carolina. She wrote both for the northern *North American Review* and for the *Southern Quarterly Review*. Through her history writings about the Revolution, Ellet had shown "the spirit of the period" and the "state of feeling among the people during the war." During the divisive period of the 1850s, Hale recognized, Ellet did important cultural work in weaving the nation together through the history of its women (*WR*, 644–645).

Elizabeth Ellet and the Personal Politics of the American Revolution

Hale was right. No one did a better job of weaving women into a narrative of nationalism than Elizabeth Ellet did. Continuing a tradition that had begun in works such as Garden's *Anecdotes of the Revolutionary War*, Ellet's heroines actively participated in the American Revolution at the same time that they embodied and promoted what their men sought to defend. Ellet celebrated these women's patriotism, but as was the case with Hale, it was the gendered patriotism of home and family that was distinct from, and sometimes even in opposition to, the political commitments of their husbands and fathers. Like Hale, Ellet suggested an Anglo-Saxon nationalism that both drew different parts of the United States together and bound it with Europe. Her biographical sketches included the wives of soldiers who fought for England along with the wives of patriots. As William Gilmore Simms suggested when he reviewed Ellet's history, she had created a sense of the way a "people" are created—a key component in any notion of the nation.[21]

Ellet's three-volume history of women in the Revolution was really a series of sketches of different women whose stories she had been able to piece together from earlier historical works, family papers, local archives, and interviews with descendants; in each sketch, the heroine's relationship to her family figured prominently. As reviewers noted with approval, she had begun her history with the mother of George Washington, celebrating the noble matron's well-run household and pious training of her son. "The home in which Mrs. Washington presided," Ellet declared, "was a sanctuary of the domestic virtues." She taught her son obedience so that he knew in the future how to command. She taught him high moral principles and shaped his ability to judge. She taught him religion. In all of these, she shaped a son who could lead the country. Other sketches followed of the wives of famous generals and founding fathers, from Martha Washington and Abigail Adams to Frederica de Riedesel and Harriet Ackland. Indeed, in introducing her first volume, Ellet quoted from a letter of John Adams to Abigail in which he argued that illustrious men owed much to their wives, mothers, and sisters "to whose instigation a great part of their merit is to be ascribed."[22]

As Ellet established her domestic framework for understanding the activities of women during the Revolution, she always assessed women in relationship to their families, even those who had achieved a reputation independent of their male family members. Ellet described Mercy Otis Warren as "perhaps the most remarkable woman who lived at the Revolutionary period." Given Warren's place in a prominent political family, it was not surprising that she had become interested in "political affairs," but Ellet stressed that Warren never allowed her writing "to interfere with household duties, or the attention of a mother devoted to her children" (*WAR*, I: 76).

Similarly, Deborah Sampson's story was one of a young girl who had been taken from her poverty-stricken (and debauched) parents at an early age and placed with a respectable family who fed and clothed her but gave her little education. As she became caught up in the fervor of the revolutionary struggle and contemplated joining the troops (not unlike Joan of Arc), her lack of family was a key element. "Alone in the world, there were few to inquire what had become of her, and still fewer to care for her fate." After her discharge, Ellet noted, Sampson became an exemplary wife and mother (*WAR*, II: 122–135).

For Ellet, the Revolution was a story of families rather than of economics or politics. Women had opportunities to defend their families, and they

sometimes suffered the trauma of seeing them torn apart. It was a time "when households were broken up by war in its worst form." By creating this particular kind of history, she offered a narrative of the nation's founding that both northerners and southerners could value. In making this claim, she took the gendering of patriotism to new heights. "It will be seen," she argued, "that the men and women of America . . . acted with one heart and one mind. . . . whether at the East, in the Middle States, or at the South."[23]

Thus, Behethland Moore of Virginia defended her family when British troops attempted to pillage her farm. Though she was a young girl fresh from boarding school, she stopped the soldiers from stealing apples from her house and from slaughtering sheep in the barnyard. "The determination to interfere, though at no little personal hazard," Ellet concluded, "required a degree of courage in one of her age, which can be estimated only when we consider the ferocity of the marauders who then made it their business to pillage private families" (*WAR*, II: 98).

Lydia Darrah, a Quaker in Philadelphia, protected her husband as she worked for the patriot cause. British soldiers had commandeered her house for a secret late-night meeting after her family was asleep (perhaps because her Quaker beliefs kept her from participating in war). While the soldiers met and her family slept, Lydia eavesdropped on the conversation, learning that the British planned to leave the city and launch a secret attack on the Americans at White Marsh. Rather than tell her husband, who "might be less wary and prudent than herself," she informed him early the next morning that she had to go for flour, and she obtained permission to cross British lines to shop at the local mill (which was in the hands of the patriots). Quickly finding an American officer, she informed him of the British plans and hastened back to her home. As Ellet concluded, "All who admire examples of courage and patriotism, especially those who enjoy the fruits of them, must honor the name of Lydia Darrah" (*WAR*, I: 171–177). Yet while Darrah was clearly motivated by her political commitment to the patriot cause, she was also at pains to protect her husband when she acted.

This concern for loved ones was even more central to the other dramatic acts of patriotism recounted by Ellet. She described Jane Thomas of South Carolina as "another of the patriotic females in whose breast glowed such ardent patriotism, that no personal hazard could deter from service whatever service could be rendered." When Jane Thomas overheard some loyalist women discussing an impending attack on Cedar Springs, where

some of her sons were stationed, she rode "nearly sixty miles the next day and arrived in time to bring information to her sons and friends of the impending danger. . . . The [whig] victory thus easily achieved they owed to the spirit and courage of a woman!" (*WAR*, I: 250–256). But what makes this story compelling is that Thomas went to such extraordinary lengths to save her children. This is the story of a mother, caught up in the events of a war, and thus pushed into extraordinary behavior.

Mary Slocum of North Carolina cleverly deceived the British in order to protect her husband. When they took over her house, they wanted food and also information on the location of her husband. Through a variety of sharp exchanges, she refused to provide information. However, later in the afternoon, her husband charged through the eastern portion of their plantation on horseback, accompanied by her brother and a couple of neighbors. Too late, he discovered that twenty British soldiers were waiting for them. While her husband wheeled around and headed in the other direction, Slocum thought quickly and came up with an alternative strategy: she convinced the British that they should not follow him because he was leading a large band of soldiers (*WAR*, I: 305–313). It was an act of deceit that saved American troops, but the narrative was structured around a woman's protection of her family and neighbors.

Dicey Langston was only a teenager when the Revolution occurred. Like Jane Thomas, she lived in South Carolina. Her family sided with the patriots in the conflict and on more than one occasion provided food and drink to soldiers passing through. During the course of one of these visits, the soldiers revealed their plans to steal horses from one of Langston's neighbors, who was a tory. Both Langston and her father were appalled. Local ties were apparently more important than national ones, and their neighbor was "a peaceable citizen," even if he was siding with the British. With her father's blessing, Langston secretly rode off to warn her neighbor. However, when Langston discovered that her neighbor was also going to use this information to prepare an ambush for the whig soldiers, she rode off in the other direction to carry this warning to the would-be horse thieves. With her daring and fine horsemanship, she "thus saved an enemy's property, and the lives of friends" (*WAR*, I: 289).

Dicey Langston might have been brave, but her patriotism was gendered: her goal here was to protect friends and neighbors rather than to participate in a political struggle. Indeed, the political struggle between the colonists and Britain was more an occasion to defend the local world she

knew than an occasion for political commitment. Patriotism did not involve an act of resistance or a struggle against tyranny, but rather the protection of friends and family.

Reinforcing this view of patriotism, Ellet never articulated any political differences between the colonists and the British, and she did not refer to even the vaguest political ideals that the colonists might be fighting for. These differences were effaced in her stories of family. Instead, she often stressed similarities with the British. The activities of women, in fact womanhood in general, also allowed Ellet to highlight the ties of the colonists to England, rather than the conflict in which they were engaged. She detailed the ways in which wives of European officers shared in the same experiences as the wives of colonists and the ways in which the wives of patriots sometimes expressed concerns for British soldiers as much as they did for Americans, tories as much as patriots, thus linking the warring sides as part of an Anglo-Saxon culture rather than separating them around political differences.

The construction of a shared Anglo-Saxon heritage occurred as Ellet detailed the trials and insults faced by the wives of British and Hessian soldiers as well as by the wives of patriots. In her long chapter on the Baroness Frederica de Riedesel, the wife of one of the commanders of Hessian troops, Ellet described a devoted wife and mother who followed her husband from one camp to another and joined him in captivity when he was captured. While Ellet noted that Riedesel found most Americans very accommodating, despite their political differences, she detailed the repeated slights the baroness faced from women committed to the patriot cause who refused to give her food for her children because her husband fought for the enemy. In each case, Riedesel was cast as the supplicating mother, and patriot women with strong political convictions were depicted as brutes who would let children starve. Similarly, Ellet praised Harriet Ackland, the wife of a major in the British army, for her bravery in moving behind American lines to nurse her husband after he had been wounded in battle and captured. "Her resolution, and devotion to him, touched the feelings of the Americans, and won the admiration of all who heard her story" (*WAR*, I: 127–135, 151). As Ellet evoked sympathy from her readers for the trials and the devotion of British and German wives to their families, she led her readers to look beyond the political conflicts of patriot troops who fought against England toward a unified sense of Anglo-Saxon womanhood that they could identify with.

Women were important to the revolutionary struggle precisely because they looked beyond the political conflict and urged reconciliation. Rebecca Motte of South Carolina, for example, was such an ardent supporter of the patriot cause that she allowed the Patriots to burn part of her house in their attempts to defeat and drive out the British. Both David Ramsay and Alexander Garden had mentioned this incident in their histories of the Revolution, but Ellet took it further, claiming that immediately after the battle Motte moved to reconcile the winners and losers by giving a dinner party. Somehow throwing together a "sumptuous dinner" among the smoking ruins of her home, she "endeavored to obliterate the recollection of the loss she had been called upon to sustain, and at the same time to remove from the minds of the prisoners the sense of their misfortune" (*WAR*, II: 67–76). This civility in turn inspired Francis Marion to halt the hangings of captured British soldiers whom the victorious troops were beginning to execute.[24]

In another instance, Ellet recounted an "anecdote of female compassion," about a heroine whose name she did not know. Ellet wrote approvingly of the tale of Colonel Cochran, the British soldier who was hidden and fed by a woman whose own husband was charged with capturing the soldier. Cochran was sick and malnourished when he presented himself to the woman for aid, confessing that he was the man her husband was hunting and throwing "himself entirely upon her mercy, trusting to her fidelity, for protection." The woman first concealed him in her house then took him to a hiding place a half-mile from her cabin. "He remained sometime in this place of concealment, undiscovered by anyone except this faithful Rahab of the forest, who like a good Samaritan, poured in the oil and wine, until his strength was in a measure restored, and he was able to return to his country and his home" (*WAR*, I: 152–154). Here was a woman who was not so much showing the independence of her political beliefs from those of her husband as much as she was demonstrating a lack of concern about politics.

The sense of nationalism that Ellet created in her narratives was repeatedly organized around the shared values of the colonists and the British. Women on both sides demonstrated the commitment to domesticity that was a key component of the cultural values of Anglo-Saxon culture that were being championed in the nineteenth century. The most admirable women were the ones for whom human suffering always trumped political beliefs. Indeed, the line of difference was drawn not between American and

British women or even between tory and patriot, but between political and apolitical women. The patriot women who denied Baroness Riedesel food were the ones who drew Ellet's ire.

Linda Kerber has suggested that, by placing them near the scenes of battle, Ellet placed her heroines near the site where citizenship was gained. It is an important argument that suggests the significance of women's history writing during this period. But it is also important to note that the kind of citizenship that was being promoted for women was different from that of men and that it was rooted in a different form of participation in military conflict.[25]

As numerous scholars have indicated, the sort of reconciliation that Ellet promoted had an important political value during the 1850s as tensions between North and South were on the rise. Ellet, as well as Hale for that matter, used domestic writings to promote a shared sense of family values and sympathy that extended across regional lines. This was one of the primary jobs of southern "plantation" and domestic novels in the nineteenth century as marriages between northerners and southerners were used to join the different regions together metaphorically. But that sort of agenda extended beyond novels to a wide range of writings that championed shared values of family and that evoked sentiment and sympathy for families of "the enemy" as well as those on one's own side. Indeed, Ellet's descriptions of women who participated in the Revolution provided a metacommentary on this kind of political work: it was specifically identified as female patriotism. It would strengthen the Union despite political differences over issues such as slavery, and that strength would come through an assertion of shared values of Anglo-Saxon culture rooted in an idealized home to be protected.[26]

Ellet privileged domestic ties over political beliefs not only through her stories, but also through her use of dialogue. Throughout her work, but particularly in the third volume, Ellet created extended dialogues for her heroines, in a manner reminiscent of the historical novels of Walter Scott. This use of dialogue created both sentiment and an identification between her readers and their subjects. Through these exchanges, Ellet was able to create highly charged scenes around the costs of war for particular families, and such scenes articulated the feelings of her heroines. Her characters thus displayed a kind of interiority that would encourage readers, particularly female readers, to identify with them and to imagine themselves in these historical moments. The familial nationalism that Ellet was creating in her

history became more visceral through dialogue. Political differences were effaced in the personal encounters that Ellet created.[27]

Sarah McCalla is one of the most memorable women depicted through dialogue. While her husband was held as a prisoner of war in a Camden, South Carolina, jail, McCalla repeatedly clashed with the British officers she confronted on each visit, so much so that she was barred from the prison. Ellet created a spirited dialogue between McCalla and the commanding officer, Lord Rawdon, to frame the release of McCalla's husband from prison. By casting Rawdon as haughty and McCalla as spirited, Ellet depicted a scene in which a soldier's release from prison became a very gendered story about personal insult and social snobbery. Thus Ellet described Rawdon as striding over to the gate of the prison to bully McCalla by demanding, "Did I not order you, madam, to keep out of my presence?" McCalla played the part of a woman unfairly attacked by responding, "I might turn the tables on you, sir, and ask, why did *you* come out to the gate to insult a woman? I have received from you nothing but abuse. My distresses you have made sport of, and I ceased long since to expect anything from you but ill-treatment." Ellet introduced the issue of rights into the scene, by having McCalla argue, "I am now not your supplicant; I come to *demand*, as a right, the release of my husband!" (*WAR*, III: 261–262). While McCalla's persistence and ability to confront the legal order were on display here, the context in which they were displayed undercut the more radical aspects of her behavior. In the scene that Ellet set up, McCalla's conflict with a British officer really was not so much about politics or rights, but rather about appropriate gender relations and the proper reconstitution of a family. Tyranny was social rather than political, as a valiant woman fought the British not about political principles but about how to protect her husband.

Ellet also circumscribed the political commitments of Isabella Ferguson in South Carolina through dialogue. Focusing on a scene in which Ferguson's brother-in-law tried to recruit her husband and brother to the loyalist cause, Ellet recounted a confrontation that highlighted the way families were torn apart by the war. Thus Ellet described the pride with which James Ferguson wore his rich British uniforms, and she surmised, "He could not help thinking that if his young sister-in-law could see him thus in the pomp of war, she would no longer detain her husband from a chance of a like promotion." Isabella, however, countered with a defense of her family in which she claimed "I am a rebel!" and also that her "brothers are rebels,

and the dog Trip is a rebel too!" Ridiculing his clothes, and representing a democratic spirit that celebrated more modest dress, Isabella continued, "Now James, I would rather see you with a sheep on your back, than tricked out in all those fine clothes!" (*WAR*, III: 199–201). Isabella's focus on reclaiming her brother-in-law was reinforced by the personal nature of the dialogue. His choice to become a loyalist was cast as a foolish grasp at status (rather than politics) that cost him his family relationship.

Nancy Anderson said nothing of politics when she gave her husband her support in going to war. Rather, focusing on their farm, she said simply, "I think, William, little Lizzy and I can finish the crop, and gather it in if need be, as well as take care of the stock." In the conversation that followed over the next few pages, Anderson and her husband talked about their church and their courtship, wrapped in a quiet domesticity that served as an effective build-up to the departure of Anderson's husband and his death a few pages later (*WAR*, III: 128–129).

Certainly these scenes conveyed more than domestic interactions. In McCalla's conflict with Rawdon and in Ferguson's confrontation with her brother-in-law, there is an implicit valorization of democratic as opposed to aristocratic values. But democratic in this context does not refer to political principles so much as it refers to cultural ones, principles in which family relationships trump aristocratic domination, and snobbery substitutes for politics. The nationalist narrative that women created in these dialogues was tied to their defense of their families and local worlds.

The personalization of both history and politics that occurred through these conversations was consistent with the gendered nationalism that Ellet also promoted in her writing. Dialogue allowed Ellet to explore the interior emotions and to elaborate the personal feelings of her subjects. It was this sentiment that was really at the heart of Ellet's project. As she noted in her introduction, "Attention should be directed to the source whence power was derived—to the sentiment pervading the mass of the people. The force of this sentiment, working in the public heart, cannot be measured; because, amidst the abundance of materials for the history of action, there is little for that of the feeling of those times" (*WAR*, I: 13). On the one hand, Ellet's work promoted a kind of nationalism organized around the protection and valorization of family relationships, creating a domestic image of what men fight for. On the other hand, while it was an image that put women in the center of the narrative, it was also one that limited their participation to creating the home life that was being protected. And

because these were values that Ellet imputed to British and German women as well, women were of central importance in creating a sense of nationalism that was organized around a broad Anglo-Saxon heritage, rather than a nation with the geographical boundaries of the state.

While Ellet celebrated the political value of the domestic life that women created, she disparaged more direct political action. She took a swipe at contemporary antislavery fairs sponsored by women in the North in her description of Esther Reed. Reed's campaign to raise money for the continental army during the Revolution was one of the most audacious undertaken by women at the time, because the campaign was organized independently. The antislavery fairs picked up on some of that spirit as women made and sold a large variety of goods, some quite fancy, to raise money to support the antislavery cause. Ellet undercut any attempts those women might have made to claim the revolutionary mantle by arguing that the work of Reed's association "was charity in its genuine form and from its purest source—the voluntary outpouring of the heart. It was not stimulated by the excitements of our day—neither fancy fairs nor bazaars; but the American women met, and seeing the necessity, that asked for interposition, relieved it" (*WAR*, I: 53).[28]

Critics, by and large, hailed Ellet's innovation in history writing, praising the way in which she fused domesticity with the creation of a nation. The *Christian Inquirer* commended her study of "the mothers of American freedom." The *Home Journal* celebrated her work in collecting the "records of the wives, the mothers, sisters and daughters of that noble band under whose guidance and through whose sacrifices, our political independence was achieved." Their memoirs, the journal contended, were a tribute to the character of American women in portraying their "heroic and pious domestic examples." *The Independent* echoed those sentiments, noting that the Revolution "affected the fireside circle as well as the assembly in the forum or the camp" and that the women of the time, who sent their fathers, brothers, and husbands to war, had developed "new qualities of character," as they guarded the home front. Reviewers repeatedly celebrated the behavior of women in terms of personal qualities such as bravery. "They were the secret springs which fed and filled those more conspicuous streams of daring and self-devotion which poured themselves in triumph over a hundred battle-fields."[29]

While most reviewers celebrated the fusion of domesticity with nationalism, there were some important differences. *The United States Magazine*

and Democratic Review had little time for the broad Anglo-Saxon heritage that Ellet was constructing by including British and German women in her history. The political sympathies of the women mattered. Cheering the patriot women who had refused to give food to the Baroness de Riedesel, the reviewer skewered her husband for having brought ruthless Hessian mercenaries into the war. Class mattered, too, as the magazine also took Ellet to task for her focus on elite women. "We had expected to read less of the fine ladies who received company and lived in style, but more of the heroic matrons who tended the wounded, or took down the rifle from the wall to arm a son or a husband for the battle," the reviewer commented. It was great to read of Miss Mary Jackson kicking a tory down the steps, but the drawing-room romances of some of the elite young women were less appealing. Far more interesting to the *Democratic Review* were stories of humble matrons who shared the politics of their husbands, bandaged their wounds, and loaded their muskets.[30]

William Gilmore Simms, writing anonymously in the *Southern Quarterly Review* a couple of years later, challenged that viewpoint. Taking aim at the suggestion that more humble women should be included, Simms argued that because elites had spearheaded the Revolution, elite women were most involved. Displacing the criticism of the *Democratic Review* onto Ellet, and suggesting that she mistakenly attributed leadership in the Revolution to "the great mass of the people," Simms argued that elites had the education to constitute the "native intellect of the country" while more common people opposed it.[31]

These elite women, he argued, sacrificed for the Revolution by making bandages and clothing, tending the sick, and even spying. And through their activities, they exemplified and created a set of values centered on domesticity, values that could inspire patriotism at the same time that they could transcend geographical and political boundaries. Gender was fused with class privilege to create a particular vision of women's domesticity that both inspired and sustained the Revolution. Thus, Simms asked in his review "to what degree the action of the political world was influenced by the emotions of the social." "The feelings of the fireside" was what men fought for, as Simms argued that "the domestic nature informs and influences the decision, the courage, and the enterprise of the patriot." Simms thus summed up his argument: "It is the family fireside—the source of all the virtues—that the lawgiver must first learn to protect and make grateful to the affections of those who seek warmth upon its hearthstones. Hence

spring all the virtues and securities of a nation. . . . The household, in fact, is not only the source but the true guardian of the nation. From that high habitation, the race goes forth, spreads widely and becomes an empire."[32]

In Simms's view, women were at the center of a nation, creating through both physical effort and nurture "a race" that constituted the nation. And it was only through domestic histories that this understanding of a nation could be achieved. Political and military histories, focused on individual greatness, failed to recognize the people behind these leaders. As Simms made these arguments, he created an elite, and raced, notion of democracy that was counterposed against a feudal alternative on the one hand and a more inclusive republic on the other. A leader, Simms argued, must recognize "that race from whose ranks all his greatness must be evolved" and the "sympathy with his stock which is the only guarantee of its safety." "The people," rather than a king, might constitute the core of a republic, but Anglo-Saxon women were used to make this a racially restrictive core, organized around gender hierarchy. Although Simms might criticize Ellet on details, he embraced her larger argument about the way in which women's history could anchor a particular kind of American nationalism.[33]

The Mount Vernon Ladies' Association:
Memorializing Domestic History

Drawing on the ideals of domestic history promoted by Hale and Ellet, Ann Pamela Cunningham offered women the opportunity to enact their commitment to their domestic influence in history through the founding of the Mount Vernon Ladies' Association. During the 1850s, as the head of the organization, she led a national campaign to purchase the crumbling home of George Washington and to restore it as a sacred shrine. As Cunningham appealed to women across the country to join her in saving a part of history tied to the American Revolution, she said nothing of politics, which was just as well, because her ancestors had actually been tories. Rather, the association became an effort to connect women in the past to those in the present through a celebration of domestic responsibility. Their patriotism was nationalist, but it was also personal.[34]

Hale supported this effort in the pages of *Godey's*, which was not surprising because Hale had spearheaded a similar effort a decade earlier. In

1840, as progress on the Bunker Hill Monument in Boston languished for lack of money, Hale led a major fund-raising effort by local women. Over a period of seven days, they had sold food, books, and fancy items that they had sewn, among other things, and raised approximately $30,000.[35] Hale was well versed in fund-raising, and she saw this as an arena in which women could join their domestic concerns with stewardship of the country's history.

Although there was some controversy about the appropriateness of their attempts to purchase the land, the members of the Mount Vernon Ladies' Association were generally lauded. Rather than treating the ownership of property as an economic issue (as those who supported married women's property rights did), this movement stripped property holding of its economic value and invested it with the sacred duties of motherhood and protection of the home. Couching her appeal to women under the pen name of "A Southern Matron," Cunningham claimed that "manufacturing speculators" wanted the land. Divesting Mount Vernon of commercial value, Cunningham argued that it was invested with emotional significance for all Americans. For those who worried that it was unseemly for women to be purchasing land, the *Southern Literary Messenger* ran a letter that revealed the fund-raising activities of women in Virginia during the American Revolution. If George Washington's mother could raise money then, it was suggested, then surely women could engage in similar fund-raising in the 1850s in order to honor his memory. As Beverley Wellford argued, they were saving Mount Vernon from "Mammon-worshipping speculators."[36]

In his Fourth of July address delivered to (and on behalf of) their organization, Wellford connected the women of Virginia who were interested in saving Washington's house directly to the women of the Revolution not just as a matter of history but as a result of shared characteristics of "race." The women of Virginia, he claimed, were made of the same stuff as the women of the Revolution. They would send their sons off to battle if necessary just as the women of the Revolution had. Speaking of one woman who had defended the activities of her husband in the Revolutionary War, Wellford claimed, "It was characteristic however not more of the times than of the race. The women of 1855 inherit the instincts and the spirit of their mothers of 1776." The inheritance was not one of law or legal privilege; instead, it was one of shared physical characteristics. The women's connection was in a kind of ethnic nationhood rather than of shared civic citizenship.[37]

And tying them back further in history, Wellford also described the precedent for their activities in the mother of Coriolanus, whom he portrayed exclusively as a mother rather than as a civic-minded woman of Rome. Her contribution was one of emotion. She shed her tears before her son and appealed "to him by all the hallowed memories of his uncorrupted boyhood." It was the ability to convey the same kinds of sentiment that women of Virginia were called upon to deliver as they "engaged in the sacred work of reviving revolutionary associations and rekindling revolutionary feelings."[38]

As Wellford promoted the importance of the emotional and domestic work of women in history, he contrasted them to those who expressed dissatisfaction with their domestic roles. "From other sources we hear occasional clamor in unwomanly tones of a tyrant public sentiment and public law, divesting woman of her natural rights in and withholding from her an equal participation with man in the labors and burthens, the honors and rewards of active and public life. But from the daughters of Virginia come no such discordant notes."[39]

Elizabeth Varon has pointed out that the Mount Vernon Ladies' Association also had a political goal: that of promoting sectional reconciliation at a time of rising sectional conflict. It dealt in political symbols rather than in votes, but it suggested that women were more patriotic than men and thus better able to resolve the sectional tensions. Varon cites a speech from one of the orations given in support of the movement, which argued that women's patriotism involved "love of country" while male patriotism involved "love of self." But while Varon is quite right that there were political implications to these activities, it is also important to note that these activities only gained legitimacy because they did not claim to involve partisan politics or even an overt commitment to anything political. The political import lay in the nationalist vision that was conjured up, one in which women were domestic. Women thus inhabited and connected with a historical tradition that was also domestic.[40] The vision of domestic history that was promoted by Cunningham, as well as by authors such as Ellet and Hale, legitimated the differentiated citizenship of women at a time when arguments were being pushed forth demanding full citizenship.

Chapter 6

Caroline Dall's Usable Past:
Women and Equal Citizenship

As 1852 drew to a close, Caroline Dall grumbled in the pages of her journal, "Finished Miss Kavenaugh's 'Women of Christianity,' and meditate a review of that stupid book Mrs. Hale has put out 'Woman's Record.' I wish I could write it over, and consider it no small misfortune that the task fell into her hands."[1] Dall was living in Toronto at the time, where her husband was the minister to a local congregation, and she had not yet become actively involved in the movement for woman's rights, though her antislavery connections were drawing her into those debates. A month after muttering about Hale in her journal, Dall produced a review criticizing *Woman's Record* for *The Una*, Paulina Wright Davis's fledgling journal devoted to the cause of woman's rights. Over the next two decades, as Dall became more committed to the movement, she increasingly defined herself against Hale and the narrative of national progress that Hale championed. Dall took the bits and pieces of history that were scattered through the woman's rights conventions of the 1850s (some of which she had contributed) and began to expand them into an alternative vision of women's history that legitimated the demands for universal citizenship raised by woman's rights activists.

Beginning with short essays on historical figures for *The Una*, which Dall later included in her 1859 book, *Historical Pictures Retouched*, and continuing through lectures and writings in the late 1850s into the 1860s, Dall developed both a critique of history and new kinds of history writing that championed equal citizenship for women and men. It was a project that culminated in one of her most successful works, *The College, the Market, and the Court*, which she published in 1867. As she explored issues of

economic, intellectual, and political citizenship, Dall took on many of the historical arguments that preceded her writing: the corruption women brought to politics, the nature of their intellectual abilities, and the effects of their public activities on their personal morals and family life, rewriting that history to tell a different story. In doing so, she developed an extensive critique of the role of history in shaping public opinion, injecting a new kind of self-consciousness into the writing of women's history that had been absent in earlier efforts. Dall's criticisms of history, as with all of her history writing, were tied overtly to her commitment to reform and woman's rights. This meant that she not only championed equal citizenship, but also justified the need for reform with a historical trajectory that often suggested decline rather than progress. Like Hale, she sought to rehabilitate the reputations of some women in the past who had been maligned, but she did so not by promoting empathy with motherhood (as Hale did) or sympathetic identification with female patriotism (as Ellet did) but through allegories meant to justify simultaneously the activities of women who transgressed traditional gender norms in both the past and present.

Dall's history writing faltered, however, as she struggled for recognition from various factions of the woman's rights movement and failed to obtain it. Instead, she moved into the emerging world of social science. As a founding member of the American Social Science Association (ASSA) in 1865, she was one of the earliest proponents of using "scientific" data in her writing, but she never embraced the "objective" stance that professional historians would use to define their new profession. Committed to the use of data for purposes of reform, Dall moved instead in the direction of social engineering by the end of the 1860s, leaving the project of re-writing women's history to others. What she left behind, however, was a new set of questions for linking women's citizenship and women's history.

Women's History and the Dangers of Public Opinion

In one of her earliest essays on the women of Renaissance Bologna, Dall warned her readers about the insidious nature of public opinion, particularly with respect to women. "Whoever writes in the present day can hardly remain neutral with regard to the responsibleness of women towards women," Dall claimed. "Let every conscious woman beware, lest an unlucky witticism, a smart saying, or a careless slur, injure for ever a reputation of which she knows nothing with certainty. Public opinion is a mingled

stream, flowing from a thousand nameless sources." For several decades, woman's rights activists had been criticizing the role of public opinion in restricting women's behavior. But Dall's injunction that both writers and readers be more self-conscious in their historical interpretations turned that criticism in a new direction. History, Dall suggested, was part of a dynamic process in which present prejudices could create a dangerous past that then further rigidified current injustices.[2]

Dall's engagement with the dangers of public opinion and woman's rights was one that she knew from both sides. She had shied away from the movement in its early years in part because of her fear that the boisterous conventions organized for woman's rights were actually doing damage to the cause with the public at large. She openly expressed her fears on this issue in the pages of *The Liberator*, where she was an established presence due to her strong antislavery convictions. She singled out Paulina Wright Davis, one of the early leaders in the movement, as the figure most likely to shape a more palatable and respectable image for woman's rights activism. Even before they had actually met in person, Dall initiated a public correspondence with Davis criticizing the impact of contentious behavior at the conventions.

In what became a yearly occurrence between 1850 and 1853, the two women lamented the mayhem of the conventions in the pages of *The Liberator*. After the second convention in Worcester, Massachusetts, where Davis had served as president, Dall noted the "vexations" of the movement and expressed her confidence in Davis to maintain some decorum. Davis was, Dall claimed, "a person of true refinement and feminine feeling, to uphold a banner to which, beside the wise and pure, many of the restless, unhappy and mischievous will not fail to resort."[3] The 1852 convention in Syracuse, New York, where Davis had chaired the central committee, was even more contentious, however, as participants wrangled over whether to refer to the Bible and whether women who were not good speakers should be allowed to address the audience. Writing to Davis again in *The Liberator*, Dall bemoaned "the continued existence of an antagonistic tone, which, it seems to me, is not called for." Dall worried particularly about how the freewheeling debates of the conventions would be reported in the mainstream press. "Sorry would they be to be thought disappointed women, who have gone up to this meeting to pour out their gall upon absent brothers, fathers or husbands; yet this is the only construction that the popular and ignorant mind can put upon many things it sees in print."[4] Davis responded to Dall

in print a couple of weeks later, saying, "No one can regret more deeply than I do the antagonistic spirit of which you speak." Going on to describe her own approach as one that rejected confrontation (and actions such as a refusal to pay taxes) in favor of rational argument, Davis noted, "Truth is mighty, and though long restrained, it will, like the resistless mountain torrent, when it breaks forth, sweep away all barriers, and accomplish its full purpose."[5]

As Dall and Davis continued their conversation in private, they began discussions about the way in which print might begin to alter the character and the message of the woman's rights movement. Indeed, reflecting on the effect that her letter in *The Liberator* had had, Davis commented, "The last convention though defended by the friends was really a poor affair. In my letter to you, in the Liberator I said some things which have been felt by those for whom they were intended and I hope it will produce a change before an other year."[6] More important, though, Davis hoped to create a new image of the woman's rights struggle through the creation of her own newspaper. Noting that the conventions harbored "women filled with personal ambition" who "can show off in them," Davis argued that they would "hold less influence" once a newspaper was created "which will give the tone to the movement." Casting her lot with the written sphere rather than the vocal, Davis concluded by saying, "I do not wish to attend conventions, I weary of the strife, but I never weary of home labor."[7] Reflecting on the Syracuse convention later in the year, Davis wrote to Dall that she had received letters from others, calling her "to account for allowing the convention to run down in tone." But she claimed, "I am not the one to go into a convention and force my way, I could not contend against the odds in the one at Syracuse but I hope better things for the next one."[8]

As Nancy Isenberg has pointed out, a split developed early in the movement between those who favored the freewheeling oral performances of the yearly conventions and those who pushed for a more controlled written debate in the pages of a publication. Isenberg has noted that women such as Elizabeth Oakes Smith faced criticism from within the movement over their lack of oratorical skills, a criticism that Davis, in particular, found objectionable. As Isenberg further points out, oratory was just the sort of embodied performance that was difficult for women to pull off because it was so clearly associated with a masculine public sphere of political performance. Writing, by way of contrast, offered an avenue of public participation that was more comfortable for many women.[9]

When Davis moved to set up her newspaper, she saw herself as creating a literary public sphere in which advocates could rationally and effectively discuss their agenda for woman's rights. This literary endeavor, Davis hoped, would shape public opinion much more positively than the conventions had. The question, however, was who would control this literary sphere and how much power would it have in the movement at large? Davis had hoped to make her paper the official journal of the women's movement, but this move had been rebuffed at the convention at Syracuse in 1852. Perhaps because Davis had made her concerns about the boisterousness of the conventions known, some participants may have worried about the exact message she would craft in her journal. The woman's rights movement itself was aggressively anti-institutional, however. It never set up a governing structure, preferring instead to organize around the yearly meetings.[10] An official newspaper, particularly one that was controlled by someone who had openly criticized the tenor of the meetings, could have been perceived as a threat to the very essence of the movement.

Thus, the newspaper Davis set up, *The Una*, came into being as both a challenge to the more widely recognized conventions *and* as one of the most important public records of those conventions and of the woman's movement of the 1850s. Although the 1852 convention had refused to adopt *The Una* as its official paper, Davis still promoted the journal in those terms, promising to record the "correct history" of the movement for equal rights and expressing her plan to record also "the public lives" of its leaders.[11] As Davis worked to persuade Dall to become one of her chief writers, she made it clear to her that *The Una* would eschew both the passionate rhetoric of radical reform, on the one hand, and the ornamental amusements of ladies magazines on the other. "It will not be a reform paper in the sense that the Liberator is, nor a literary paper in any respect like the magazines. I shall not exclude the thought that may come to me from some pure, earnest, thoughtful heart," Davis reassured Dall.[12] As Davis promised in the first issue of *The Una*, its purpose would be "to speak clear, earnest words of truth and soberness, in a spirit of kindness. To discuss the rights, sphere, duty and destiny of woman, fully and fearlessly; and our aim will be, to secure the highest good of all."[13] What Davis envisioned was a use of print media to reshape public opinion about women and the reforms that woman's rights activists promoted. By 1855, the newspaper's importance was recognized by Elizabeth Cady Stanton, who urged those attending the Saratoga Woman's Rights

Convention to subscribe to *The Una* if they wished to fully understand the movement.[14]

Dall shared Davis's concerns, and not just because of her dismay about the nature of the woman's rights conventions. She was equally concerned about the power that Sarah Josepha Hale exercised over public opinion, particularly with respect to ideas about women. As she noted in her journal in the summer of 1853, she had been to see Mrs. D. S. Hunt "and had a vigorous talk, a good deal about Mrs. S. J. Hale's adroitness."[15] Dall was right to be concerned. Hale was far more successful at disseminating her views than Davis and Dall would ever be. Despite the eventual endorsement from Elizabeth Cady Stanton, *The Una* was never a great success. At its height, *The Una* barely had one thousand subscribers, and more than half had not paid. *Godey's Lady Book*, by way of contrast, had approximately forty thousand subscribers at the middle of the century.[16]

Dall's concern about the way in which public opinion was shaped in the literary sphere, particularly through history, extended far beyond Hale, though Dall repeatedly criticized *Woman's Record* in many of her historical sketches. In one essay after another, Dall challenged Hale's footnotes and her historical accuracy in an attempt to undermine Hale's credibility with educated readers. But Dall also went after British clergyman, Charles Kingsley. Kingsley had written a historical novel about Hypatia that portrayed the brilliant young scholar of the fourth century as a demented pagan who brought about her own destruction by rejecting marriage and the opportunities of true womanhood. Dall raked him over the coals for tarnishing Hypatia's reputation for scholarship and virtue simply so that he could write a novel about the conflict between the emerging world of Christianity and the world of paganism it would replace. The popularity of his efforts added to the problem, forever removing Hypatia as a model for young women who sought the life of the mind. Hale and Kingsley were not the only offenders. Even someone such as Lady Sydney Morgan (author of *Woman and Her Master*) thoughtlessly undermined the accomplishments of women in the past. Dall admired Lady Morgan for her "democratic" spirit, but she pointed out that even such an advocate for the underdog could easily slip into the trap of reinforcing derogatory stereotypes of women in the past as well as the present. When Morgan had carelessly ridiculed the homely visages of Isotta da Rimini and Madame Dacier, she delivered an unnecessary slap in the face to educated women. It was precisely these tainted portrayals from a range of writers that Dall sought to

correct, not simply for historical accuracy, but as her contribution to the struggle for woman's rights.[17]

Dall's writings were finding their mark, at least among the small group who read *The Una*. Thomas Wentworth Higginson believed that Dall's writings would not only push the woman's rights movement forward, but also place her in the vanguard of major revisions in the writing of history. Paulina Wright Davis also lauded the impact of Dall's work when she wrote to her, "You, who read the Languages and have always had the classics to refer to can scarcely conceive how these articles are seized upon and swallowed by our readers." Within a few years, though, Dall was beginning to think about the problem of public opinion from a more institutional point of view. By 1858 she began delivering lectures in Boston and other New England cities on how public opinion was shaped in the schools, and more specifically, the way in which that process took place in the teaching of history and the classics. Those reflections on the way educational institutions shaped public opinion coincided with her own leadership in the woman's rights movement and in direct attempts at legal reform. As she explained to William Lloyd Garrison, she closed each lecture with a promise to her audiences that she would begin to circulate petitions for them to sign demanding the right to vote. And as Garrison reported in *The Liberator*, Dall carried that campaign to the Massachusetts legislature.[18]

Dall's three lectures on public opinion, which were encompassed under the larger series title of "The College," seem to have been well received. The *Worcester Spy* reported on one of the lectures favorably in 1859, for example, saying that her presentation on "Public Opinion, as it is derived from the Study of Classics and History, General Literature, Customs, and Newspapers" had been quite successful. The newspaper took care to note that Dall had not only persuasively critiqued both scholarship and popular media, but also effectively defended historical figures maligned by others, such as Hypatia. By 1867, she had published those lectures, along with six others, in *The College, the Market, and the Court*. Here, her critique of history was most fully developed as she lambasted both the study of the classics and contemporary forays into history for purveying an image of venal and dangerous women. "The existing public opinion with regard to woman has been formed by the influence of heathen ages and institutions, kept up by a mistaken study of the classics," Dall complained in the opening to one of the chapters. At a time when the study of the classics still constituted a core requirement for both admission to and graduation from

U.S. universities, Dall's challenge was an important one. Anyone with a college education had studied the classics, and that education constituted a key component in both educated debate and educated public opinion.[19]

In line with her institutional critique, Dall criticized not only the attitudes of classical writers toward women, but also the way in which classics was currently taught in colleges: with slavish reverence rather than with a more critical spirit. Dall noted the low opinion of women that pervaded Greek literature and at one point she suggested that the study of some writers, particularly Aristophanes, be abandoned. Thus, she complained, "Athens and Rome, Aristophanes and Juvenal, are more responsible for the popular views of woman, and for the popular mistakes in regard to man's position toward her, than any thing that has been written later."[20] Compounding this problem, however, was the way in which classicists uncritically replicated the attitudes of the ancients. Through the classics, professors sustained ideals of female inferiority, offering the attitudes of ancient Greeks toward women as a model for contemporary society. "One of the most vulgar assaults ever made upon the movement to elevate woman in this country was made in a respectable quarterly by a Greek scholar," Dall pointed out. "It was sustained by quotations from Aristophanes, and concluded by copious translations from one of his liveliest plays, offered as a specimen of the 'riot and misrule' that we ambitious women were ready to inaugurate."[21] Dall did not suggest that the classics be rejected wholesale, but she did argue that both the faculty and classrooms needed to be changed. Classics should be taught by faculty who had more respect for women, "so no coarse, low-minded man should interpret Greek or Roman, but some noble soul, not indifferent to social progress, capable of discriminating, and of letting in a little Christian light upon those pagan times." Moreover, if classrooms were integrated, and young men and women were taught together, as at Antioch and Oberlin, some of the worst effects of studying classics would be ameliorated because, presumably, there would be less temptation to accept misogynistic views of women. Dall thus took her critique of the way the classics were taught and joined it to demands in the woman's rights movement for broader access to higher education.[22]

Beyond the classics that corrupted the universities, though, the popular histories that circulated in the mass media of the nineteenth century also had a devastating effect on popular opinion as they reified misogynist views about the abilities and activities of women. Because of this tendency in the popular press, the growing interest in the condition of women that had

taken hold in the nineteenth century had been subverted by the production of sensationalist histories that only contributed to the worst assumptions about women. One recent work, Dall noted, focused on women who were "assassins, parricides, and poisoners, fortune-tellers, and actresses!"[23] Men and women who looked to histories to find out about what women had achieved in the past were likely to be bombarded with colorful stories of women who were morally corrupt, dangerous, or foolish. There was little entertainment value to be found in reading about women of accomplishment. Authors as well as audiences reinforced public opinion about the weaknesses of women through their use of print. "If men start with the idea that woman is an inferior being, incapable of wide interests, and created for their pleasure alone; if they enact laws and establish customs to sustain these views . . . they will write history in accordance with such views," Dall argued. Such authors would find Cleopatra and Messalina and Catherine de Medici and Ninon de l'Enclos quite representative of their low view of women.[24]

Dall's critique of public opinion informed the way in which she imagined a history of woman's rights in one of the essays in *Historical Pictures Retouched*. Unlike the histories of the movement that would be produced a few years later by Paulina Wright Davis and Elizabeth Cady Stanton, Dall focused on the broader intellectual issues and critiques that had been raised by women ranging from Aspasia to Margaret Fuller. Indeed, her historical sketch of woman's rights culminated in a celebration of Margaret Fuller's critique of gender relations in "The Great Lawsuit." While the contemporary movement for woman's rights was important, Dall privileged the intellectual arguments and accomplishments of women who had worked to improve the status of women in issues related to education, vocation, and civil position. Here, public opinion had been challenged.

Dall argued that the cause of women was first championed around the issue of education, where "the cry of the tortured victims" emerged from those seeking to defend themselves "from the inevitable miseries of worn-out toys." Dall celebrated Mary Astell as one of the first to agitate widely for women's education. Even more important, however, was the work of Mary Wollstonecraft, who Dall claimed was "born to utter one wild, despairing cry for education." Dall noted the significance of Wollstonecraft's *Vindication of the Rights of Woman*, and she also argued that Wollstonecraft's work had been transformative for the women who read it. "Few women of the present day know how much they owe to the strength and

purpose of this one," Dall claimed. Wollstonecraft had given shape and power to the kinds of issues that Mary Astell had begun to raise a century before. "The influence of Mary Astell and her compeers had roused woman to an effort after *general* education; Mary Wollstonecraft gave *special* impetus to this common effort." Wollstonecraft had inspired a generation of women who included not only Maria Edgeworth, Lady Morgan, Harriet Martineau, and Anna Jameson in Great Britain, but also Margaret Fuller in the United States. Fuller, in turn, had pushed debate on woman's issues even further, by tying concerns about education to those of jobs and professions. "From Margaret Fuller flowed forth the first clear, uncompromising, scholarly demand for the civil rights of her sex . . . the effect of her paper was seen not only in the inspiration communicated to minds of smaller grasp . . . but in that general demand for freedom of vocation."[25]

In creating this narrative of female demands for their sex, Dall did not focus completely on individuals. She argued, for example, that the Revolution had had an important impact on women in pushing them to think about education as an accomplishment with practical merit rather than as a vain pursuit of leisure. Dall also noted the significance of the woman's rights movement of the 1850s. It might not have any "formal organization," but it was still a "'Woman's Rights Party.'" And since the convention at Seneca Falls, "the demand for civil equality has been steadily pressed in the United States." This movement, Dall pointed out, argued that women had a right to any education, to pursue the careers of their choice, and to receive equal rights in law, which included the right to vote. That said, however, Dall still felt the need for specific women to articulate a rationale for those demands. Astell and Wollstonecraft had led the way with respect to education, and Fuller had built on their work with respect to vocation, but no one had yet matched those earlier advocates in defending women's legal and political rights. "When this is fitly done," Dall claimed confidently, "it will level the last defence of the feudal Past."[26]

Witnesses of the Past: Female
Influence and Female Citizenship

Dall's critique of history and of its role in shaping public opinion framed her efforts during the 1850s and 1860s to invent a new kind of women's

history. History writing, she argued, was crucial to the success of the woman's rights movement. Early in 1855, as she assumed editorial leadership of *The Una*, Dall argued that attempts to reform the present were doomed to fail without an adequate knowledge of the past. "Without reading the past clearly, it is impossible to go to the root of present evils. Many a reform fails for want of accurate knowledge based on this, of what is needed to be done." Rather than simply editing the journal, Dall claimed that her "duty" would continue to be "ransacking the records of the past, and supplying biographical matter" to *The Una*. The history of women, she asserted, was "yet to be written." Writing several years later, Dall introduced these essays again in the collection *Historical Pictures Retouched*, making a similar argument: "No feminine jury—no *human* jury, I would rather say, constituted equally of men and women—has, thus far, summoned the witnesses of the past." Those "witnesses" would not only demonstrate the accomplishments of women, but also justify their demands for equal citizenship with men.[27]

Dall had no interest in the issues of patriotism and nationalism that Hale and Ellet had spun around their heroines from the past. Perhaps that is not surprising because, as a committed abolitionist, Dall had little interest in the project of sectional reconciliation that captured the attention of domestic writers such as Hale and Ellet. If there was to be a nation, Dall expected that it should be one that recognized and valued the political and economic activities of women in the past. Equally important, Dall's historical narrative was not one of national triumph but of decline in certain respects, in which women's work and accomplishments in previous centuries were obscured. Her histories, particularly her earlier ones, were also meant to justify and frame the activities of female reformers in the 1850s who faced ridicule and scorn in their demands for equal rights. Quite didactic, and sometimes allegorical, Dall's early sketches simultaneously recreated the past and used it as a comment on the present in an attempt to break the stranglehold of public opinion and justify the political citizenship of female activists.

Thus, Dall not only rescued Hypatia from Charles Kingsley's Christian romance, but also recast her as a woman of principle who faced angry Christian mobs when she defended the downtrodden, a portrayal that was meant to resonate with contemporary women who had taken on unpopular reforms in the middle of the nineteenth century. Hypatia, Dall argued, was a brilliant scholar who deserved her place as the leader of the Platonist school in Athens at the end of the fourth century; she was also a public

intellectual who had been brutally murdered by fanatical Christians for trying to intercede with the governor on behalf of Jews who were being persecuted by those Christians. Dall portrayed the Christians as the dupes of unscrupulous leaders, including the bishop who was jealous of Hypatia's influence and the governor who was anxious to deflect the mob's anger away from himself. The mob directed its fury toward Hypatia, based on false rumors that she was the cause of unrest in the city. Dall described in detail the brutal scene in which Hypatia was dragged by horses through the streets of Alexandria until arriving at a church where the crowd stripped "her naked, tore her flesh with broken bits of tile and shells, until she died, when her limbs were torn apart and burned in the public square."[28]

Dall was particularly clear that Hypatia was not murdered simply because she was "a heathen," as Kingsley had suggested. Rather, she had to contend with a particularly corrupt form of Christianity that was hostile to learning and led by a corrupt bishop who valued political influence more than religious principles. Taking a swipe at the ignorance of contemporary evangelicals, Dall (a Unitarian) argued that it was understandable that Hypatia had chosen neo-Platonism over Christianity. The Christians of her city had shown their contempt for learning by sacking the Serapion and destroying its library. "Day after day, as she went to the Academy, the ruins of this splendid Library stared her in the face, and gentle as she was, she must have thought with a grief that was all but anger, on the mistaken Zealots who had destroyed it." Rejecting the values of bigoted Christians, Hypatia argued for tolerance and used her powerful position as an educational leader to persuade government leaders to behave in a more noble fashion. She was murdered, Dall summed up, "because she was suspected of having an opinion and an influence in public affairs. Because she was deemed worthy to sit in the councils of Church and State!"[29]

Readers of this essay were well aware of the public criticism and violence that many women had faced in the previous decades as they had expressed radical political views. Abolitionist women, in particular, had faced angry mobs when they tried to hold conventions. But even woman's rights activists who tried to venture outside in bloomer costumes were chased and ridiculed in the street. Hypatia's martyrdom offered them an explanation, albeit a gruesome one, of the price women might have to pay for political and intellectual citizenship. Her death demonstrated the price that women paid for trying to exercise that citizenship, but it also provided the inspiration of martyrdom if it was properly understood.[30]

In her biography of Aspasia, Dall made a similar defense, drawing parallels between Aspasia and the women who had participated actively in the reform movement. It would have been hard not to compare Margaret Fuller's unconventional personal life and the "conversations" she held in Boston with Aspasia's intellectual salon and influence. "Aspasia, of Miletus, was the first woman who endeavored *systematically* to elevate the condition of her sex," Dall boldly proclaimed. She did not corrupt Athenian women but tried to educate them. Reminding her readers of the seclusion and ignorance in which Athenian women lived, Dall argued, "Aspasia used all her influence to draw the Greek women into the society of their husbands, and to awake in them love for literature and art." Dall defended Aspasia by comparing her to the women of modern reform movements. In a somewhat disconcerting and direct comparison to modern times, Dall described Aspasia's move from Miletus to Athens as a migration from the provinces to a great center of learning. Dall claimed that Aspasia "came up to Athens to see the distinguished men, with which the city swarmed, as country girls of our time have sometimes gone up to Boston, enamored of Orphic Alcott, the Greek Emerson, or Parker of the steady will." Dall urged her reform-minded readers to rethink the low opinion that had been broadcast about Aspasia by thinking of her in reference to their own challenges. "Look at the scandal of that day," Dall challenged them. "Was it not the counterpart of this of ours? At first, she was 'odd.' Then, 'bold, setting the conventions of decent society at defiance.' 'Who but a courtesan would sit in the presence of men unveiled?' " Dall encouraged her readers to think of Fuller and Aspasia in the same terms, and she also, in effect, encouraged them to use Aspasia to measure themselves. Aspasia, like Hypatia, had tried to use her learning to improve society. She had not kept her learning private but had behaved as a public intellectual. This was the sort of intellectual citizenship that women had practiced in the past, and that women in the present should seek to emulate, despite the discrimination that they had faced in both past and present.[31]

Dall used history to inspire women who were struggling for new rights, and she also used it to reach out to women who might be on the fence, women who were torn between the sort of domestic citizenship championed by Hale and the universal citizenship championed by advocates of woman's rights. To this end, she not only praised the direct activities of women such as Hypatia and Aspasia, but also attacked the idea of female

"influence" on men that was held out as an alternative. Advocates of domestic citizenship, of course, had championed women's influence as the appropriate way for them to approach political issues, facilitating the discussions of men, who would make the actual political decisions. But Dall argued just the opposite: women who worked indirectly through men were dangerous, exercising an immoral form of influence. Because no one had bothered to train them in the responsibilities of citizenship and political leadership, some women in history who had assumed tremendous power through family connections or through their lovers had created chaos. Dall's argument was not only a critique of writers such as Hale who championed female influence, but also a critique of histories that had dismissed women who became involved in politics as dangerous meddlers. The problem was not their female nature, but rather their lack of training.

Dall recognized that the arguments in support of female influence resonated particularly with women who felt comfortable in their domestic roles. They might sympathize with some of the issues that were raised by activists, Dall suggested, but they generally felt well represented by their husbands. Alluding to the most controversial aspects of the woman's movement, Dall acknowledged that these women had no interest in "going to conventions, making speeches, or wearing Grecian costume." Most of these women were concerned with propriety, but, as scholars such as Lori Ginzberg have pointed out, many elite women were quite successful in their attempts to influence their husbands and other elite men when they sought support for their charities or other civic undertakings. These were women who needed to recognize that their complacent acceptance of female influence had a dangerous underbelly. Not all women had used their influence for good. The study of women's history, Dall suggested, offered an excellent opportunity for understanding that problem.[32]

Clearly aware of arguments that had been advanced by eighteenth-century writers about women's corruption of politics, Dall was careful to argue that just because some women had exercised an unhealthy influence on politics did not prove that all women were innately incapable of such activities. In fact, they proved just the opposite. But because the only lines of participation usually open to them were through men they manipulated, examples of immoral women who enjoyed engaging in devious behavior tended to surface repeatedly. Speaking ominously of the kinds of influence women exercised in contemporary politics, Dall wrote in the pages of *The*

Una that "no woman can go to Washington with her eyes open, without seeing that it is by no means in the purest hands. To give every woman the political influence now possessed by a few from base causes, is surely a legitimate object; for in that way we should pour the holiest female influences into the molten metal of society as well as the more corrupt." Instead, because women had been historically denied the right to participate in politics, a long line of women who corrupted government could be produced. As Dall made clear in her later writings, they included women such as Olympia Maldachini, who exercised control over access to her lover, Pope Innocent X. Commenting on her portrait, Dall concluded, "The fierce, brow-beating aspect of the picture adds weight to the report, that she kept the whole conclave of cardinals in order, and poisoned the soup of Cardinal Patilla." Madame Pompadour wreaked similar havoc in the court of Louis XVI. More recently, Lady Hamilton had led Admiral Nelson to make disastrous political choices in Naples.[33]

Dall's association of female influence with female manipulation and deceit was aimed precisely at those women who saw themselves as protecting the purity of the nation at the same time that they protected their own purity. What Dall held up instead was a historical argument about the ways in which that commitment to influence could actually be quite corrupting, despite what many respectable matrons wanted to believe. As Dall began to publicly agitate for suffrage rights in the late 1850s, she used her critique of influence to structure three of her lectures focused on women of the French court in the seventeenth century.

Dall's lectures were based on Victor Cousin's extensive studies of women who had exercised their influence during the controversial and much-reviled reign of Anne of Austria. Cousin's volumes on Madame de Chevreuse and Madame de Hautefort, published in Paris in 1856, were particularly well known. Cousin romanticized their biographies to present two very different female responses to the political intrigues of court life. Madame de Chevreuse embraced the political causes of her lovers and became a key player in many of the political conflicts of her period. Madame de Hautefort, by contrast, could not escape many of the political intrigues surrounding her, but she always responded to politics with a concern for the personal well-being of her friends rather than with any political ambitions of her own. Madame de Chevreuse thus became the embodiment of scheming French women condemned by Antoine-Léonard Thomas, William Russell, and subsequent writers who used history to argue against

women's participation in politics. Madame de Hautefort, by contrast, became the example of how a virtuous woman should respond to political activities that unfolded around her: a women should attend to the personal well-being of her loved ones and support their wishes, without adopting a political position.[34]

The political significance of Cousin's work to contemporary debates was immediately clear to reviewers. The conservative British *National Review* described in detail Cousin's biographies of the two women in an 1856 review, and it concluded with a lengthy discussion about the application of these biographies to contemporary demands for woman's rights. De Chevreuse's problems with political intrigue occurred because she "could not reject her nature, which was to be subordinate, if not gracefully by submission of will, then disgracefully by wayward devotion of passion," the reviewer argued. De Hautefort, by contrast, possessed "an attractive radiance of *womanhood* . . . that charming subordination, which affects us less as the necessity of a weaker being than as the complaisance of a nature which would rather persuade than command." De Hautefort's biography presented not only a defense of aristocracy, but also a picture of true womanhood, in the face of demands for equal rights. "Of all the monstrous births of modern philosophy," the reviewer concluded, "sure none is so monstrous, so marked with *moral* ignorance and deterioration, as the doctrine of the equality of man and woman, in the form in which it is at present widely preached."[35]

Dall acknowledged her debt to Cousin in her lectures, but her interpretations of de Chevreuse's and de Hautefort's lives were quite different from Cousin's. Both women were flawed, Dall contended, because neither had been trained in the principles of citizenship, a deficiency that became lethal once their personal relationships meant that they would be able to influence politics. De Chevreuse, in particular, had the abilities of both a great stateswoman and a great financier. But her upbringing had led her to pursue a path of influencing her lovers rather than more directly assessing the needs of her government: "That she did not propose to herself a consistent end, grew out of no weakness. She was a far better financier than Mazarin & proved it, first by her able administration of her weak husband's Duchy & afterward by her quick appreciation of the great Colbert. But women in her day, as now, used their political power secretly without a thought of the responsibilities it involved. Had she been trained to the duties of a citizen, she could not have failed to see the danger of that step." Returning to the

problem of education in a succeeding lecture, Dall concluded that had de Chevreuse been properly instructed in "the duties & responsibilities of a citizen & the true aims of statesmanship" she probably would have turned out differently and so would have world history.[36]

However, while de Chevreuse's lack of preparation had led to political havoc, de Hautefort's lack of interest in politics had created even greater problems. Recognizing that de Hautefort was the character her audience was expected to admire, Dall went out of her way to argue that, despite her individual moral purity, de Hautefort's concern for her friends over the state had resulted in disastrous political consequences. Because she failed to understand politics, she put her personal feelings in the way of political assessments. According to Dall, "had she been clothed with 'open responsibility' & thought of her honor not only as a woman, but as a citizen of France, how different would have been her career." De Hautefort would have realized that her devotion to Marie de Medici (the mother of Louis XIII) threatened the peace of France. And she might have intervened in some of Anne of Austria's treasonous dealings with Spain.[37]

Dall's critique of Mmes. de Hautefort and de Chevreuse were woven into her campaign for woman's rights, whether they be educational, social, or civil (the "rights of citizenship," as she called them). Appearing before the Massachusetts legislature at the same time as she commenced these lectures, Dall presented petitions for woman's suffrage and reminded legislators not only of Hortensia speaking to the Roman Senate, and of Elizabeth's extended rule, but also of the women behind the scenes who manipulated men in Washington. "If women will meddle with politics, as they have from the beginning of time," Dall argued, "confer on them open and reputable channels of action, that you may be enabled to judge of their understanding and fruits." History demonstrated that government would flourish best with women's direct participation rather than through their indirect and untutored influence.[38]

History and Economic Citizenship

Dall's historical writings went beyond the allegories of intellectual and political citizenship that she used to legitimate the public activities of reform-minded women. Economic citizenship, even more than political rights, drove some of her most innovative history writing. If political citizenship

would allow women the right to direct participation in governance, economic citizenship would result from the recognition of the work that women were capable of doing, of a living wage, and of the access to professions now closed to them. To make that argument, Dall began to move beyond allegory in her historical writings and into a narrative framework that juxtaposed contemporary census data and statistics on female poverty against the economic activities of women in the past. Focusing on both the physical effort and economic value of women's labor in the past, Dall challenged Hale's and Ellet's celebrations of the moral nature of women's work. Moreover, she challenged Hale's triumphal march of domestic progress. Dall stressed the ways in which women had been active participants in the economies of the past even though they had often faced discrimination as they tried to pursue their vocations. Equally serious, though, Dall suggested that the historical trajectory for women had been one of decline, not progress.

Setting the stage for this historical perspective, Dall laid out the current problems faced by women who worked. Drawing heavily on the studies of Alexandre Parent-Duchâtelet in Paris and William Sanger in New York, Dall suggested that many of the women who became prostitutes had no choice if they wished to feed themselves or their children. Using the census of 1850, she pointed out that women were upholsterers, paper hangers, milliners, shoemakers, silver workers, nurses, and physicians, to name just a few occupations. As studies in Europe and the United States revealed, however, women were consistently paid half the wages of men for the same work, resulting in an income that they simply could not live on. It was ludicrous, she argued, to think that all men supported all women. The data made it clear that thousands of women worked for wages outside the home. Women often had a relationship to the economy that was independent of husbands, fathers, or brothers, but it was usually a lesser relationship.[39]

As Amy Stanley has noted, Dall focused her critique of female poverty on sexism rather than on the broader forces of capitalism that were resulting in widespread economic misery for all working people, a limitation that many activists of her generation shared. That said, though, she used her perspective to create an economic history of women's work. Dall argued that women had done almost every kind of labor imaginable in the past, but they often had gained only contempt for their endeavors. They had "from the beginning, done the hardest and most unwholesome work of the world in all countries whether civilized or uncivilized." Dall pointed out

that some of this hard labor was domestic, but it was equally important to recognize women's participation in "man's work," which was almost always erased from public consciousness. She noted, for example, that Bertha, a noblewoman in the tenth century, had reshaped the landscape of the Jura Mountains in France into vineyards and roads that she used not only for commerce but also for the defense of her people. Women as well as men had participated (and continued to participate) in the construction work there. In England, thousands of women continued to work in the coal mines. Yet, regardless of the physical strength they had shown and the importance of their labor, these women never received the respect for their hard work that the men had achieved. In England, she argued, some women were considered such beasts of burden that the practice of wife-selling (divorce) took place in the cattle market. Women had faced economic disenfranchisement in every possible way.[40]

Dall's rather grim historical perspective further dimmed as she turned her attention to the United States. It was here that Dall most seriously challenged historical portrayals by both Ellet and Hale, ignoring the domestic patriotism of women during the Revolution and decrying the celebration of domesticity as a moral category rather than as a form of work. Instead, Dall painted a picture of outright decline in the nineteenth century. Raising, perhaps for the first time, what would later come to be called the "golden age" argument about the colonial period, Dall suggested that women during the Revolution actually had participated actively in the economy and had been valued for their efforts. Ignoring the stories of women who had defended their homes and neighbors, Dall described the revolutionary period as a time in which women were active in commerce, behavior that had political implications. It was a tradition, she argued, that they had inherited as part of their European ancestry. "Then, as in France, the men went to war. Women of shrewdness and ability managed their husbands' affairs,— the shops and trades of the nation,—and grew so independent thereby that even Mrs. John Adams had to rebuke her husband for the absurd inequalities of privilege which his new government sustained." Dall detailed the activities of female printers and successful female merchants in New England. She also argued that, at the end of the Revolution, women still ran many establishments because the United States still retained British habits. Drawing on the recollections of Eliza Barney of Nantucket, Massachusetts, Dall maintained that "all the dry-goods and groceries were kept by women, who went to Boston semi-annually to renew their stock."[41]

However, if the republic had been born during an era in which women participated as economic citizens, the same could not be said of the period that had succeeded it: a period in which status demanded an end to (or at least ignorance of) female labor. Attacking the discourse on domestic citizenship, Dall argued that the contemporary discourse on women's work devalued their economic activities. Women worked, Dall pointed out, but "ladies" did not. And if women were to be ladies, they could not engage in the kind of work men did. "I believe that work is good for ladies," Dall contended. With this conclusion, Dall suggested not only that women's work had become increasingly devalued, but also that the theories of respectability promoted in ladies' magazines were the source of historical decline.[42]

The idea that women's work had been crucial to the building of society at the same time that it was devalued also carried over into her analysis of women's intellectual endeavors. As was the case with other woman's rights activists, women's education was not only a value in itself to Dall, but also something that took on meaning as women used it to improve their economies, societies, and governments. This was a kind of citizenship that had a long history. Dall began to develop this argument in 1853, in some of her earliest writings for *The Una*. In creating her sketch of the women of Bologna from the Renaissance through the Enlightenment, Dall argued that the public intellectual and artistic activities of the women of Bologna were a critical component in the political and economic success of the city. Discussing the accomplishments of artists such as Prosperzia de Rossi and Elsabetta Sireni as well as scientists such as Laura Bassi Veratti and Anna Morandi Manzolini, Dall suggested that their impact went far beyond the intellectual and artistic inspiration they brought to their city. By pursuing their activities in public, in educating their fellow citizens, they had helped to create an environment that led to success in various arenas. "Our sketches of Bolognese women," she concluded, "may bring some of our readers to reflect, as to what natural connexion there is between the presence of a large number of literary women within its walls, and the prosperity and mutual independence of Bologna La Grasse." Looking at the long history of intellectual vitality to which women had contributed and been welcomed, Dall argued, "Political economists would do well, perhaps, to consider what was and is the most literary city of all Italy, retains, in spite of political reverses, a position of thrift and activity not equaled on the peninsula."[43]

As Dall made clear in her lectures and writing at the end of the decade, women were not being allowed to advance the interests of society in the nineteenth century in the same way. While authors such as Sarah Josepha Hale suggested a narrative of progress in women's education and celebrated their impact on child rearing, teaching, and missionary work, Dall argued that a strong case could be made for a decline. The victories of female education in the United States were overrated, Dall contended. Looking back to the seventeenth century, Dall argued that in Germany, after the Thirty Years' War, middle-class women had become educated and had promoted learning throughout their society. In France, elite women had used their salons to foster intellectual discourse. In the nineteenth century, by contrast, women had found that doors shut in their faces, particularly as they sought the professional training that would allow them to affect their societies.[44]

Dall's three lectures on women and work were published separately in 1860 as *Woman's Right to Labor*, before their inclusion several years later in *The College, the Market, and the Court*. Her work on women and labor was widely praised for bringing important issues concerning discrimination against women in the workplace into the light. Dall's statistics had provided compelling evidence of the need of women to work and of their low pay. But most important, her writings were seen as more palatable than the critiques that were delivered at the woman's rights conventions. *Harper's Weekly*, in particular, noted the difference. "The question is not treated by her in the manner of the Woman's Rights Conventions, that is, by declamations and appeals; but by a calm presentation of copious facts, based upon very careful study and observation." *Harper's* singled out the effectiveness of her use of history, arguing, "By showing us what women have done, and what they are now doing, she reminds us how many spheres might yet be opened to them." The *Christian Examiner* made a similar point, enumerating the many occupations that women had taken up in the past. And the *North American Review* claimed approvingly that there was "no ultraism" in her work. When a second edition of *Woman's Right to Labor* quickly followed the first, A. G., in the *Nantucket Inquirer*, also praised the effectiveness of Dall's historical research. Dall had masterfully gathered facts "from the whole range of history, ancient and medieval, as well as from all ranks and orders of society as it now exists." Theories that seemed radical in the abstract seemed much less so when illustrated with facts. "Patiently following the thorny pathway of statistical research to sources of information

deeply imbedded in the past, she has opened new veins of thought, and rescued from oblivion facts of deep significance, which, from their complete isolation, have hitherto stood for nothing."

Equally telling, though, the *Chicago Press and Tribune* applauded not only her dignity but also her class position in celebrating her work. "She is a woman of the best social position and the highest culture," a background that was clear in her ability to analyze her facts and construct a convincing argument.[45]

The Loss of Audience

Dall's history writing and leadership in the woman's rights movement at the end of the 1850s suggest the ways in which politically informed history writing about the broad issues of female citizenship could be brought together successfully with an openly activist agenda. Dall's experience in the succeeding two decades, however, reveals just as clearly how that intellectual drive could collapse. There are two stories to be told here: one focuses on Dall's growing commitment to the ASSA in the 1860s and 1870s while the other is centered on Dall's rejection by various factions of the woman's rights movement.

Dall followed closely the activities of the British National Association for the Promotion of Social Science, which had been founded in 1857. She made one of her first moves to replicate the movement institutionally when she contacted George Ticknor in 1859 and asked him to create a Social Science section at the Boston Public Library in order to collect studies from around the world on issues such as poverty, education, and reform. In 1865, she became one of the founders (and few female leaders) of the ASSA. As Thomas Haskell has argued, the ASSA "was intended to construct safe institutional havens for sound opinion." Its appeal to Dall is obvious, for, as Haskell makes clear, this new organization would combat precisely the evils that attended the stagnant public opinion of a democracy. Over the next few decades, the work begun there would move away from the explicit concerns of reform to professional organization of the social science disciplines (focused on professional training and the collection of data), spurring the organization of the modern civil service, on the one hand, and the modern, professionally based university on the other. Training and facts would provide the basis for competent analysis and authority in a rapidly

changing society. Members such as Dall would use their data to confront the challenges of the world around them, from poverty and crime to gender inequality and class conflict.[46]

Dall was a key player in the founding of the movement. She drafted the original constitution of the organization and incessantly lobbied Frank Sanborn, the president of the ASSA, to make sure that women, and women's issues, were represented. In the fall of 1865, as the ASSA began to take shape, Dall badgered the male leadership to appoint women to the boards they were setting up on key topics such as health, education, and law. As the organization began to establish regional chapters, Dall made sure that women were included. An exasperated Frank Sanborn reassured her in 1868, for example, that the invitation that had been sent to interested "persons" to form a Midwest association had included women as well as men.[47]

The ASSA became a way for Dall to champion women's issues, a way to express her citizenship, and to bring some of those women along with her in a new institution where her leadership was acknowledged. She could become the public intellectual she had championed in her histories. Rather than writing history, she would live it. There is no doubt that Caroline Dall was in the forefront of a seismic shift in the nineteenth-century reform ethos, from romantic individualism to more institutional solutions. And those institutional solutions would be controlled by those with both education and a large supply of data. As William Leach has pointed out, this was precisely the sort of reform that appealed to Dall because educated elites such as herself would control the direction of reform. And certainly this was the sort of attitude that had led the *Chicago Tribune* to join praise of her work with an appreciation of her social standing. As Leach further points out, social science, at least in terms of reform, became women's work, something that Frank Sanborn had also recognized. Whether focusing on education, health and hygiene, or relief for the poor, women flocked to organizations informed by social science principles. In doing so, they laid the groundwork for much of the progressive reform that would follow in later years.[48]

While Dall had combined historical sketches with contemporary data in her lectures and in *The College, the Market, and the Court* to make some important and original arguments, she was transitioning away from historical modes of persuasion toward those rooted more explicitly in contemporary social science data. Even as she republished her early essays from *The Una* in *Historical Pictures Retouched*, Dall apologized for failing to spend

much time improving them. Her time was "now more seriously engrossed by social science," she explained. The difference between the two was the difference between observers and seekers: "It is the business of the Seekers to collect, collage, test, and simplify material; to decide what is worth saving, and what must be permitted to drift down the dark gulf of the past. It is the business of the Observers to make use of this material, and permit philosophic thought, general knowledge, and rare culture, to do their work with the accumulations so brought together." Dall was leaving the world of the seekers behind at least as early as 1859.[49]

The pull of the ASSA, however, was accompanied by the push—indeed shoves—that Dall experienced in the woman's rights movement. While her lectures and writings for *The College, the Market, and the Court* were lauded in the mainstream press, such as *Harper's*, for avoiding the rancor of the woman's rights conventions, some leaders of the movement were not so charitable. Indeed, the praise that Dall received for avoiding "ultraism" in her lectures in 1860 may have been a way in which some editors supported the challenge Dall was making to activists such as Elizabeth Cady Stanton. As Faye Dudden has shown, Dall challenged Stanton for leadership of the movement, particularly around the issues of sexuality and marriage, when Dall organized a separate convention in Boston in 1858. Stanton won that showdown, but she was clearly still seething a couple of years later. In 1860, Stanton criticized Dall for taking it upon herself to suggest that "the ladies of Boston" thought it was premature to take up the issue of divorce. "How can the women of Boston discuss the civil position of woman, without touching the subject of marriage and divorce?" Stanton demanded to know.[50]

Dall's travails with the woman's movement became even more serious after conflicts developed among activists in the early years of Reconstruction over whether or not to separate demands for African American rights from rights for women. Stanton, in particular, demonstrated how racist the rhetoric of the woman's rights movement could be when detached from its informal ties to the antislavery movement, creating a cloud that hung over her newly formed National Woman Suffrage Association. Given her conflicts with Stanton, Dall would seem a likely candidate to have joined with women such as Caroline Severance and Julia Ward Howe, who formed the Woman's Club of Boston and the competing American Woman Suffrage Association in the late 1860s. Indeed, there is some evidence that Dall tried to head in that direction. The leaders of the Woman's Club, however, wanted nothing to do with her. She went to one of the first meetings at the

end of 1868, only to discover that membership was not open to all. "They agreed upon a list of names today and sent out printed invitations, with 'Not transferable' upon them," a mortified Dall recorded in her journal. *"No such card came to me."* Stung by her rejection from both this organization and the Radical Club, another organization of reformers, Dall was mystified by her treatment. Apparently oblivious to her interactional shortcomings, Dall made repeated inquiries through numerous intermediaries as to why she had been blackballed. Thomas Higginson, clearly frustrated with the whole situation, at one point exclaimed, "I can't help it, Mrs. Dall, . . . [that] you're such an *intensely* unpopular person."[51]

Dall was finally invited to attend a few sessions of the Radical Club, but it did not go well and she soon stopped attending. In 1873, she delivered her three historical lectures on Mmes. de Chevreuse and de Hautefort and on female influence for one last time to members of the Radical Club, which met in the rooms of the Woman's Club. At the third lecture, Julia Ward Howe and a few other members of the Woman's Club not only attended but also brought Dall some flowers. "Did this mean I am sorry for the lies I wrote about you?" Dall scribbled on the first page of her lecture notes. "Nous serrons." The following week, one of Dall's friends noted that he had never seen Julia Ward Howe "show so much self restraint" and that "although she spoke gently, it was quite apparent that she wanted to speak sharply." A couple of weeks later, Dall bemoaned the fact that the *Woman's Journal* (edited by Howe) had ignored her lectures and that the woman's rights activists in Boston had appropriated her ideas without giving her credit. "Why then should they be so unwilling to allow me to live? For that is what it amounts to," Dall complained. "I am bound where I might be free, silent when I might speak."[52]

Although Dall had never been entirely comfortable with Elizabeth Cady Stanton, Susan B. Anthony, and the National Woman Suffrage Association, they at least tolerated her. Throughout the 1870s and beyond, she kept up sporadic contact with them, as Stanton and Anthony deflected Dall's insecurities and accepted what support she was willing to provide. "If you hadn't so emphatically said over & over that there were insurmountable reasons why 'shouldn't appear in public on the stage' with us 'shriekers' for suffrage here," Susan B. Anthony wrote to Dall in the 1880s, "I should venture to ask you to give us a short testimony."[53]

Dall's vexed relations with all sides of the woman's rights movement not only undermined her ability to articulate a vision of female citizenship

in her history writing, but also cost her a place in the movement's history. In the 1880s, when Harriet Hanson Robinson began to write her history of the woman's rights movement in Massachusetts, she contacted Dall for information. "I am a new comer into the suffrage reform," Robinson apologized, "and (it will not seem complimentary to you for me to say it) I never hear your name spoken as having been an originator of the woman's rights movement." Even worse, Dall was deeply stung a couple of decades later when Carrie Chapman Catt asked her to join in listening to "pioneers" of the woman's movement such as Susan B. Anthony, Julia Ward Howe, and Antoinette Brown Blackwell at the International Woman's Suffrage Conference in 1902. Although Catt asked her to sit on the platform with the "pioneers," the fact that Catt did not identify Dall as one cut her deeply, prompting her to write a lengthy response detailing her leadership in the early movement. In the end, feeling forgotten by her contemporaries, Dall took her last stab at writing herself into history: she offered to donate her voluminous collection of journals, scrapbooks, and letters to the Massachusetts Historical Society. It would be left to others to insert Dall into history.[54]

Epilogue

Dall may have given up on writing women's history, but others did not. Matilda Gage took up the mantle of trying to write a broader history of women with an activist's conscience. In 1868, she began publishing essays about the importance of female inventors in the pages of Stanton and Anthony's *Revolution*. Picking up on some of the issues of economic and intellectual citizenship that Dall had raised, Gage argued that women had been responsible for key inventions throughout history and that their contributions to the development of civilization had all too often been attributed to men. She republished those essays as a book in 1870 and in more condensed form as an article in the *North American Review* in 1883.[1]

In *Woman, Church, and State*, published in 1893, Gage also took on the historical trajectory laid out by authors such as Sarah Josepha Hale. Organizing her work around the argument that Christianity had restricted woman's liberty rather than fostering it, Gage argued that women in ancient civilizations had greater freedom than did women in modern society. Then, laying out the effects of canon law and common law on women, Gage developed her arguments about the declining status of women under Christianity. From changes in inheritance and marriage to the widespread prosecution of women for witchcraft, women had become dependent and despised.[2] Gage's work continued the tradition of writing and debate that had begun with Thomas and Russell in the eighteenth century and had been continued by Child, Hale, and Dall, among others. Eschewing archival research, she drew from the works of others, setting out a fresh perspective in a sweeping history of women that had broad political implications for understanding female citizenship.

By the 1890s, however, women's history also began to establish a small toehold with the academy. Lucy Maynard Salmon's history, *Domestic Service*, in particular, was a pathbreaking work in social history, and it also continued the analysis of women as independent economic citizens that

Dall had begun. Salmon brought her university training and the prestige of her academic position at Vassar to the construction of a history of housework that drew on the kinds of archival sources Dall had never known. But even as she brought her broader training in U.S. history to frame her study of the evolution of housework and domestic servitude in relationship to changes wrought by industrialization and immigration, Salmon engaged issues that Dall (and the first woman's rights movement) had brought up decades before. Perhaps most important, she gave housework an economic history that tied it to larger issues of participation in the production and consumption of goods within the nation as a whole. And in line with Dall's sense of economic history, she urged women to think about their activities as work that had economic value. As Julie des Jardins has argued, Salmon's choice of subject matter and her advocacy opened her to widespread criticism from male colleagues. But Salmon pioneered techniques that would ultimately have far-reaching effects within the discipline of history.[3]

Des Jardins has also documented the ways in which women's history continued to engage issues of women's rights and broad questions related to female citizenship in the first half of the twentieth century. Some scholars worked within universities, though they faced continued discrimination and challenges to the professionalism of their work. The problem was serious enough that, in the 1940s, Mary Beard rejected academic culture in her attempts to create a women's history that was more socially engaged. Her introduction to *Woman as Force in History* pointedly engaged the politics of Communists, Fascists, and the National Woman's Party. And as she fumed over the reluctance of another scholar, Carolyn Dexter, to take on a more wide-ranging history of women because of a lack of sources, Beard suggested her ties to activists a century earlier when she complained, "I wanted to ask how Lydia Maria Child got sources for her book on women in history which she published before 1848."[4]

In the middle of the twentieth century, independent scholars informed by the struggles for economic and racial justice produced women's history as part of their larger political agenda for broader citizenship rights. One of the most important of these works was Eleanor Flexner's *Century of Struggle*. Flexner, who had been involved in union campaigns and struggles for racial justice, published her work in 1959. Several years later, Betty Friedan used Flexner's work to shape a sustained historical narrative of women's activities in the past that framed her critique of "the problem that has no name." Friedan denaturalized the discourse that celebrated motherhood

and domesticity as the sole goal for women in chapters that detailed the struggles for women's rights in the past, as well as the professional dreams and accomplishments of women just a few decades before. Highlighting the importance of women's history for women's rights, Friedan argued that Flexner's book "should be required reading for every girl admitted to a U.S. college."[5]

Friedan's suggestion is a reminder of the power of women's history. In the wake of the women's rights movement that unfolded in the last several decades of the twentieth century and the growth of the academic field of women's history that accompanied it, perhaps it is a power that we now take for granted. Yet it is worth remembering just how important women's history can be and how important it was as debates about women's citizenship began to unfold in the late eighteenth century.

Given the close ties of the field of women's history to various (though often competing) arenas of women's politics, it is difficult to imagine the genre arising as part of an attempt to limit the citizenship of women. Yet, clearly and powerfully, this is what a popular strain of women's history did for more than a century. Tied to a defense of differentiated citizenship, these histories not only expounded upon the dangers of women to both scholarship and politics but also naturalized the social interactions and moral instruction that women could facilitate as the mark of a modern civilization. History was used to demonstrate the importance of domestic citizenship for women in a society where the very nature of citizenship was being created. As women had contested those boundaries of citizenship, first in a myriad of reform activities that had political significance and later in specific demands for full citizenship, the historical narrative of the late eighteenth century was challenged on a variety of fronts. Whether with anecdotes in the heat of debate or in the works of women such as Lydia Maria Child, Sarah Grimké, Margaret Fuller, or Caroline Dall, a new kind of women's history began to take shape. In different ways it lacked the triumphal sense of progress that would characterize so much of U.S. history writing during this period. But these new women's histories attempted to demonstrate possibilities for women's citizenship that went beyond the domestic. They would never have the popularity that writers such as Hale and Ellet achieved as they reworked the ideals of domestic citizenship around a historical narrative that was also meant to empower women. Hale and Ellet were swimming within mainstream narratives that joined the progress of domestic women with the progress of the nation. Yet even here, their

histories were part of a larger political debate. Both women wrote with an eye on the struggle for woman's rights in the 1850s and with the goal of creating an alternative to full citizenship for American women.

Questions about what full citizenship for women would mean have not been settled, in part because the very category of woman has been destabilized in recent decades. Political movements organized around a recognition that race, class, and sexuality have created inequalities among women have inspired scholarship about the past that has drawn upon and nourished those struggles for new understandings of both the limits and possibilities of citizenship. It would be easy enough to see the roots of that scholarship in the contemporary moment or in the experiences of women in the twentieth century. In fact, though, women's history is a genre that is woven into the very creation of the United States in the late eighteenth and nineteenth centuries. It did not emerge simply as a type of popular entertainment or expression of civic piety (though it could have elements of both), but more importantly it legitimated the terms by which women were included in the polity.

Notes

Introduction

1. Thomas Wentworth Higginson to Caroline Wells Healey Dall, March 27, 1854, Caroline Wells Healey Dall Papers, microfilm edition, 45 reels (Boston: Massachusetts Historical Society, 1981; cited hereafter as CDP, MHS), reel 2.

2. Nancy Isenberg, *Sex and Citizenship in Antebellum America* (Chapel Hill: University of North Carolina Press, 1998). Other scholars have also argued for viewing citizenship in similarly broad terms. See, for example, Lisa Lowe's discussion of the relationship of citizenship to nation in *Immigrant Acts: On Asian American Cultural Politics* (Durham, N.C.: Duke University Press, 1996), ix–x, 1–36; Evelyn Nakano Glenn's discussion of different forms of citizenship and the relationship of citizenship to race and gender in *Unequal Freedom: How Race and Gender Shaped American Citizenship and Labor* (Cambridge, Mass.: Harvard University Press, 2002), 18–55; and Lauren Berlant's summary of many of these different approaches to citizenship in "Citizenship," in *Keywords for American Cultural Studies*, ed. Bruce Burgett and Glenn Hendler, (New York: New York University Press, 2007), 37–42. Rogers M. Smith has delineated and analyzed conflicting ideals of ascriptive inequality versus liberal equality in the laws of U.S. citizenship from the time of the Revolution to the early twentieth century in *Civic Ideals: Conflicting Visions of Citizenship in U.S. History* (New Haven, Conn.: Yale University Press, 1997). For an important study of the ways in which citizenship laws operated differently for women, as opposed to men, see Linda K. Kerber, *No Constitutional Right to Be Ladies: Women and the Obligations of Citizenship* (New York: Hill and Wang, 1998).

3. Antoine-Léonard Thomas, *Essay on the Character, Manners, and Genius of Women in Different Ages*, trans. William Russell, 2 vols. (Philadelphia: R. Aitken, 1774); William Alexander, *History of Women*, 2 vols. (London: W. Stahan, 1779); A Friend to the Sex [John Adams], *Sketches of the History, Genius, Disposition, Accomplishments, Employments, Customs and Importance of the Fair Sex in All Parts of the World* (Philadelphia: Samuel Sanson, 1796).

4. Mrs. D. L. [Lydia Maria] Child, *History of the Condition of Women, in Various Ages and Nations*, 2 vols. (Boston: John Allen and Company, 1835); Elizabeth Ellet, *Women of the American Revolution*, 3 vols. (New York: Baker and Scribner, 1848 and

1850); Sarah Josepha Hale, *Woman's Record* (Philadelphia: Harper & Brothers, 1853); Mrs. [Carolyn] Dall, *Historical Pictures Retouched* (Boston: Walker, Wise, and Company, 1860).

5. Linda Kerber introduced the term "republican motherhood" into historical discourse to highlight the civic role of women as differentiated from that of men in the new republic in *Women of the Republic: Intellect and Ideology in Revolutionary America* (New York: W. W. Norton, 1980). Jan Lewis has complicated that term with the notion of the "republican wife," demonstrating the way in which marriage was invested with political meaning in this period in her article "The Republican Wife: Virtue and Seduction in the Early Republic," *William and Mary Quarterly* 44 (October 1987): 689–721. As Rosemarie Zagarri has stressed, many of these ideas had their origins in the Common Sense philosophy that was particularly powerful in Scotland, so that terming them "republican" or assuming that they were an outgrowth of revolutionary fervor is a bit misleading. See Zagarri, "Morals, Manners, and the Republican Mother," *American Quarterly* 44 (June 1992): 192–215. With Zagarri's point in mind, and with a view to the ways in which these ideals of civic identity would evolve in the nineteenth century, I am using instead the term "domestic citizenship" to refer to the constellation of political associations with the motherhood, marriage, and domestic life of women.

6. David Waldstreicher, *In the Midst of Perpetual Fetes: The Making of American Nationalism, 1776–1820* (Chapel Hill: University of North Carolina Press, 1997), 6–7. John Brooke also describes nationalism in the early republic as "a matter of civil rather than ethnic identity," in "Cultures of Nationalism, Movements of Reform and the Composite-Federal Polity: From Revolutionary Settlement to Antebellum Crisis," *Journal of the Early Republic* 29 (Spring 2009): 3.

7. Regardless of other differences about the nature of nationalism, most theorists of nationalism list a shared history as one of the key components necessary for creating nationalism. See, for example, Eric Hobsbawm and Terence Ranger, eds., *The Invention of Tradition* (New York: Cambridge University Press, 1992), 1–14; Craig Calhoun, *Nationalism* (Minneapolis: University of Minnesota Press, 1997), 4–5; Anthony D. Smith, *Myths and Memories of the Nation* (New York: Oxford University Press, 1999); and Anne McClintock, "Family Feuds: Gender, Nationalism, and the Family," *Feminist Review* 44 (Summer 1993): 61–80.

8. Julie des Jardins, *Women and the Historical Enterprise in America, Gender, Race, and the Politics of Memory, 1880–1945* (Chapel Hill: University of North Carolina Press, 2003); Kathryn Kish Sklar, "American Female Historians in Context, 1770–1930," *Feminist Studies* 3 (Autumn 1975): 171–184.

9. Nina Baym, *American Women Writers and the Work of History, 1790–1860* (Rutgers University Press, 1995), 214–239.

10. Ibid., 224–228.

11. Ibid., 219.

12. Kerber, *Women of the Republic*, 106–111; Peter Messer, "Writing Women into History: Defining Gender and Citizenship in Post-Revolutionary America," *Studies in Eighteenth-Century Culture* 28 (1999): 341–360.

13. Bonnie G. Smith, *The Gender of History: Men, Women, and Historical Practice* (Cambridge, Mass.: Harvard University Press, 1998), 39, 51.

14. Mary Kelley, *Learning to Stand and Speak: Women, Education, and Public Life in America's Republic* (Chapel Hill: University of North Carolina Press, 2006), 1–9. See also the articles in "Women in Civil Society," a special issue devoted to Kelley's book in *Journal of the Early Republic* 28 (Spring 2007).

15. Kelley, *Learning to Stand and Speak*, 15.

16. Thomas Wentworth Higginson, *Woman and Her Wishes; An Essay: Inscribed to the Massachusetts Constitutional Convention* (Boston: Robert F. Wallcut, 1853), 3.

Chapter 1

1. *Pennsylvania Gazette*, April 27, 1774; *Pennsylvania Packet*, May 2, 1774; *New York Gazette, and Weekly Mercury*, August 8, 1774. For a discussion of previous publications of this work, see Mary Catherine Moran, "L'Essai sur les femmes/Essay on Women: An Eighteenth-Century Transatlantic Journey," *History Workshop Journal* 59 (2005): 18.

2. *Pennsylvania Gazette*, April 27, 1774; *Pennsylvania Packet*, May 2, 1774. See also Caroline Winterer, *The Mirror of Antiquity: American Women and the Classical Tradition, 1750–1900* (Ithaca, N.Y.: Cornell University Press, 2007), 26, 34–38, for a discussion of the popularity of *Telemachus*, particularly among women in the colonies.

3. Bell advertised *Six Sketches on the History of Man* in *The Pennsylvania Ledger; or the Virginia, Maryland, Pennsylvania, & New Jersey Weekly Advertiser*, August 10, 1776. This was an abridged version of the four-volume *Sketches of the History of Man*. A few years later, *Sketches of the History of Man* was advertised in the *Royal Gazette* of New York on December 22, 1779, and in the *Connecticut Journal* on September 10, 1783. Alexander's *History of Women* was advertised in the *Royal Gazette* of New York on June 10, 1780; in the *New York Gazette, and Weekly Mercury* on August 26, 1782; and in the *Connecticut Courant* on March 8, 1785.

4. Cathy N. Davidson, *Revolution and the Word: The Rise of the Novel in America* (New York: Oxford University Press, 1986), 55–59; Clare Lyons, *Sex among the Rabble: An Intimate History of Gender and Power in the Age of Revolution, Philadelphia, 1730–1830* (Chapel Hill: University of North Carolina Press, 2006), 145–151. For a perceptive discussion of "the female reader," see Heidi Brayman Hackel and Catherine E. Kelly, eds., *Reading Women: Literacy, Authorship, and Culture in the Atlantic World, 1500–1800* (Philadelphia: University of Pennsylvania Press, 2008).

5. Isaiah Thomas, *The History of Printing in America with a Biography of Printers and an Account of Newspapers*, ed. Marcus A. McCorison (New York: Weathervane, 1970), 394–396, 401–402.

6. For a wide-ranging analysis of the relationship between commerce, sentiment, and gender, see G. J. Barker-Benfield, *The Culture of Sensibility: Sex and Society in Eighteenth-Century Britain* (Chicago: University of Chicago Press, 1992). For an important analysis of the significance of Common Sense thought on ideals of gender in the early republic, see Rosemarie Zagarri, "Morals, Manners."

7. Linda Colley, in *Britons: Forging the Nation 1707–1837* (New Haven, Conn.: Yale University Press, 1992), 237–281, particularly addresses the issue of women and British nationalism. The broader scholarship addressing gender and nationalism includes George Lachman Mosse, *Nationalism and Sexuality: Respectability and Abnormal Sexuality in Modern Europe* (Madison: University of Wisconsin Press, 1985); Anne McClintock, *Imperial Leather: Race, Gender, and Sexuality in the Colonial Contest* (New York: Routledge, 1995), 353–389; and Sita Ranchood-Nilsson and Mary Ann Tétreault, eds., *Women, States, and Nationalism: At Home in the Nation?* (New York: Routledge, 2000).

8. T. H. Breen, *The Marketplace of Revolution: How Consumer Politics Shaped American Independence* (New York: Oxford University Press, 2004), especially 78, 251, 303; Lawrence Glickman, *Buying Power: A History of Consumer Activism in America* (Chicago: University of Chicago Press, 2009), 52, 57. Both authors note parallels of the way consumer culture created an imagined community of shared buyers with Benedict Anderson's notion of the way in which print culture created an imagined community that was the prerequisite for modern nationalism. Moreover, it is important to remember that this process was not limited to the colonies.

9. For an important analysis of the conflicting ways in which various women encountered the commercial world of the late eighteenth century, see Ellen Hartigan-O'Connor, *The Ties That Buy: Women and Commerce in Revolutionary America* (Philadelphia: University of Pennsylvania Press, 2009).

10. Karin Wulf, *Not All Wives: Women of Colonial Philadelphia* (Ithaca, N.Y.: Cornell University Press, 2000), 119–151, esp. 142; Elaine Crane, *Ebb Tide in New England, Women, Seaports, and Social Change, 1630–1800* (Boston: Northeastern University Press, 1998), 101–105; Hartigan-O'Connor, *Ties That Buy*, 1–12. Advertisements for some of these women can be found in the *Pennsylvania Packet or the General Advertiser*, May 15, 1781; December 28, 1782; *Boston News-Letter*, July 8, 1773; *The Boston Gazette and Country Journal*, February 28, 1774. Women in England were also active in the retail trade. See Margaret R. Hunt, *The Middling Sort: Commerce, Gender, and the Family in England: 1680–1780* (Berkeley: University of California Press, 1996), 126–134.

11. Wulf, *Not All Wives*, 93; Lyons, *Sex among the Rabble*, 31–32; Crane, *Ebb Tide*, 12–16. Carole Shammas, in assessing the number of unmarried women in Philadelphia, notes that if unmarried daughters are added to the count of boarders, servants, slaves, and widows, that half the adult women in Philadelphia at any given time in the late eighteenth century were unmarried. Shammas, "The Female Social Structure of Philadelphia in 1775," *Pennsylvania Magazine of History and Biography* 107 (1983): 72–73.

12. Nancy F. Cott, *Public Vows: A History of Marriage and Nation* (Cambridge, Mass.: Harvard University Press, 2000), 24–47; Lyons, *Sex among the Rabble*, 43–114, 175–181. Lyons also argues that during the course of the eighteenth century, women became increasing vocal in newspaper ads about their decisions to leave husbands who physically abused them, or failed to sexually satisfy them. On marriage in Britain see John R. Gillis, *For Better, for Worse: British Marriages, 1600 to the Present* (New York: Oxford University Press, 1985). For premarital pregnancy rates in the colonies, see Robert Gross, *Minutemen and Their World* (New York: Hill and Wang, 1976), 99–100; Daniel Scott Smith and Michael Hindus, "Premarital Pregnancy in America, 1640–1971: An Overview and an Interpretation," *Journal of Interdisciplinary History* 5 (Spring 1975): 537–570. On illegitimacy in England, see Peter Laslett, Karla Oosterveen, and Richard Michael Smith, eds., *Bastardy and Its Comparative History: Studies in the History of Illegitimacy and Marital Nonconformism in Britain, France, Germany, Sweden, North America, Jamaica, and Japan* (Cambridge, Mass.: Harvard University Press, 1982).

13. Shammas, "Female Social Structure," 83; Hartigan-O'Connor, *Ties That Buy*, 39–145; Hunt, *Middling Sort*, 125–145.

14. Carole Shammas, "The Domestic Environment in Early Modern England and America," *Journal of Social History* 14 (1980): 3–24; Stephanie Grauman Wolf, *As Various as Their Land* (New York: HarperCollins, 1993), 49–70. For a discussion of changing patterns of consumption in the eighteenth century, in addition to Wolf, see Carole Shammas, *The Pre-industrial Consumer in England and America* (New York: Oxford University Press, 1990), particularly 157–193; and Richard L. Bushman, *The Refinement of America, Persons, Houses, Cities* (New York: Knopf, 1992), particularly 69–78.

15. Bushman, in *Refinement of America*, has stressed the way in which lower orders could emulate elites through practices of consumption in the eighteenth century (403–409). Other scholars have pointed out that more common folk might use consumption to create their own subcultures. See, for example, Shane White and Graham White, *Stylin': African American Expressive Culture from Its Beginnings to the Zoot Suit* (Ithaca, N.Y.: Cornell University Press, 1998), 5–37; and Hartigan-O'Connor, *Ties That Buy*, 172.

16. Breen, *Marketplace of Revolution*, 79–147.

17. Ibid., 172–182; Kate Haulman, "Fashion and the Culture Wars of Revolutionary Philadelphia," *William and Mary Quarterly* 62 (October 2005): 627–629. Winterer, in *Mirror of Antiquity*, analyzes how luxury and effeminacy were twin threats to republicanism, 5–6.

18. David S. Shields, *Civil Tongues: Polite Letters in British America* (Chapel Hill: University of North Carolina Press, 1997), 120.

19. Winterer, *Mirror of Antiquity*, 14–17; Harriett Guest, *Small Change: Women, Learning, Patriotism, 1750–1850* (Chicago: University of Chicago Press, 2000), 73.

20. For a recent discussion of the relationship between women and civil society, see Mary Kelley, *Learning to Stand and Speak: Women, Education, and Public Life in*

America's Republic (Chapel Hill: University of North Carolina Press, 2006), and the special issue devoted to both Kelley's book and the topic of women and civil society in the *Journal of the Early Republic 28* (Spring 2008). For the public sphere, see Jurgen Habermas, *The Structural Transformation of the Public Sphere: An Inquiry into a Category of Bourgeois Society* (Cambridge, Mass.: MIT Press, 1991), as well as various critiques including Nancy Fraser, "Rethinking the Public Sphere: A Contribution to the Critique of Actually Existing Democracy," *Social Text* 25/26 (1990): 56–80. For a discussion of how the salon could function as a locus for political discussion in the early republic, see Susan Branson, *These Fiery Frenchified Dames: Women and Political Culture in Early National Philadelphia* (Philadelphia: University of Pennsylvania Press, 2001), 125–142.

21. Sylvia Harcstark Myers, *The Bluestocking Circle: Women, Friendship, and the Life of the Mind in Eighteenth-Century England* (Oxford: Oxford University Press, 1990), 282–289; Elizabeth Egar, " 'The noblest commerce of mankind': Conversation and Community in the Bluestocking Circle," in *Women, Gender, and Enlightenment,* ed. Sarah Knott and Barbara Taylor (New York: Palgrave Macmillan, 2005), 288–305.

22. Dena Goodman, *The Republic of Letters: A Cultural History of the French Enlightenment* (Ithaca, N.Y.: Cornell University Press, 1994), 53–56, 99–111, 130; Shields, *Civil Tongues,* 120; Carolyn C. Lougee, "Noblesse, Domesticity, and Social Reform: The Education of Girls by Fenelon and Saint-Cyr," *History of Education Quarterly* 14 (Spring 1974): 87–90.

23. Jane Rendell discusses the relationship of concerns about commercial society to concerns about women by Scottish Enlightenment thinkers in her introduction to William Alexander, *The History of Women from the Earliest Antiquity to the Present Time,* vol. 1 (Bristol: Thoemmes, 1995), x–xi. See also Zagarri, "Morals, Manners," 195–199.

24. For a discussion of the theories of complementarity in Continental Europe, see Londa Schiebinger, *The Mind Has No Sex? Women in the Origins of Modern Science* (Cambridge, Mass.: Harvard University Press, 1989), 214–244. For a discussion of the different implications of ideas about the female nervous system in eighteenth-century Britain, see Barker-Benfield, *Culture of Sensibility,* 1–36.

25. Mark Salber Phillips, *Society and Sentiment: Genres of Historical Writing in Britain, 1740–1820* (Princeton, N.J.: Princeton University Press, 2000), 111–113.

26. Kames's four-volume *Sketches on the History of Man* was published in a shorter, one-volume version as *Six Sketches on the History of Man* in Philadelphia in 1776. Millar's *Origin of the Distinction of Ranks* was first published as *Observations Concerning the Distinctions of Rank in Society* (it had changed titles by the 1779 edition).

27. For a discussion of how Common Sense thinkers viewed this narrative as one of "female emancipation," see Karen O'Brien, *Women and Enlightenment in Eighteenth-Century Britain* (New York: Cambridge University Press, 2009), 87–97.

28. John Millar, *The Origin of the Distinctions of Ranks, or, An Inquiry into the Circumstances Which Give Rise to Influence and Authority, in the Different Members of*

Society (London: J. Murray, 1779), 28–40; Henry Home, Lord Kames, *Six Sketches on the History of Man* (Philadelphia: R. Aitken, 1776), 208.

29. Millar, *Distinctions of Rank*, 83–108.

30. Ibid., 107–109, 119.

31. Kames, *Six Sketches*, 242.

32. Ibid., 235, 252–253.

33. Millar, *Distinctions of Rank*, 81–86.

34. John Millar, *Observations Concerning the Distinctions of Rank in Society*, 2nd ed. (London: J. Murray, 1783), 94.

35. Millar, *Distinctions of Rank*, 121.

36. Guest, *Small Change*, 320–324; O'Brien, *Women and Enlightenment*, 11.

37. Kames, *Six Sketches*, 251–252. See also Zagarri, "Morals, Manners," 200.

38. Kames, *Six Sketches*, 255.

39. Ibid., 195.

40. Ibid., 195–196.

41. For a comparable argument being made in the colonies and the early republic, see Jan Lewis, "The Republican Wife: Virtue and Seduction in the Early Republic," *William and Mary Quarterly* 44 (October 1987): 689–721.

42. On Poullain de la Barre's distinctions between mind and body, see Schiebinger, *The Mind Has No Sex?*, 176–177; Siep Stuurman, *François Poulain de la Barre and the Invention of Modern Equality* (Cambridge, Mass.: Harvard University Press, 2004), 87–102.

43. Winterer, *Mirror of Antiquity*, 15–17.

44. On the shift away from exemplary history, see Timothy Hampton, *Writing from History: the Rhetoric of Exemplarity in Renaissance Literature* (Ithaca, N.Y.: Cornell University Press, 1990).

45. See, for example, Rogers M. Smith, *Stories of Peoplehood: The Politics and Morals of Political Membership* (New York: Cambridge University Press, 2003), 63–66; E. J. Hobsbawm, *Nations and Nationalism since 1780: Programme, Myth, Reality*, 2nd ed. (New York: Cambridge University Press, 1999), 37.

46. Anne McClintock has emphasized the way in which gender distinctions have been crucial in forming national histories in *Imperial Leather*, 352–389.

47. On the association between domesticity and national progress in Europe during the eighteenth century, see Bonnie S. Anderson, *Joyous Greetings: The First International Women's Movement, 1830–1860* (New York: Oxford University Press, 2000), 37–39.

48. For an alternative comparison of the works of Thomas and Russell with Alexander, see Miriam Elizabeth Burstein, *Narrating Women's History in Britain, 1770–1902* (Burlington, Vt.: Ashgate, 2004), 29–49.

49. Antoine-Léonard Thomas, *Essay on the Character, Manners, and Genius of Women in Different Ages*, trans. William Russell, 2 vols. (Philadelphia: R. Aitken, 1774), II: 46–72 (hereafter cited in text as *Essay*).

50. Mary Catherine Moran, "L'Essai sur les femmes/Essay on Women: An Eighteenth-Century Transatlantic Journey," *History Workshop Journal* 59 (2005): 17–32. See also Burstein, *Narrating Women's History*.

51. Mary Trouille, "Sexual/Textual Politics in the Enlightenment: Diderot and D'Epinay Respond to Thomas's Essay on Women," *Journal for Eighteenth Century Studies* 19 (March 1996): 7–10.

52. William Alexander, *History of Women*, 2 vols. (London: W. Stahan, 1779), II: 48–61.

53. A Friend to Sex [John Adams], *Sketches of the History, Genius, Disposition, Accomplishments, Employments, Customs, Virtues, and Vices of the Fair Sex in All Parts of the World Interspersed with Many Singular and Entertaining Anecdotes* (London, 1790).

54. *The Critical Review: or Annals of Literature*, ed. Tobias Smollett (1773), 378; *The Monthly Review, or Literary Journal*, ed. Ralph Griffiths and George Edward Griffiths (1790): 227.

55. Adams's *Sketches of the Fair Sex* was printed by Samuel Sansom, Jr., in Philadelphia in 1796; Evans indicates that Thomas C. Cushing of Salem advertised the book in 1796. Joseph Bumstead published the *Sketches* in Boston in 1807 and Robert Harpes published it in Gettysburg, Pennsylvania, in 1812. Alexander was published by J. H. Dobelbower in Philadelphia in 1795 and 1796; and his work was also published in London in 1779 and 1782 and in Dublin in 1779. His work was also translated and published in Paris in 1794.

56. "Extracts from Alexander's History of Women," *Litchfield Monitor; and Agricultural Register*, July 9, 1795; "On the happy Influence arising from Female Society, from Dr. Alexander's History of Women," *The Massachusetts Magazine; or Monthly Museum*, July 1795; "Various Modes of Courtship among different Nations, from Dr. Alexander's History of Women," *Weekly Magazine of Original Essays, Fugitive Pieces, and Interesting Intelligence*, February 17, 1798; "Origin of Fighting for the Fair Sex, from Alexander's History of Women," *Weekly Magazine of Original Essays, Fugitive Pieces, and Interesting Intelligence*, March 24, 1798.

57. O'Brien, *Women and Enlightenment*, 70–71, 106–107.

58. Zagarri, "Morals, Manners," 208–210; Winterer, *Mirror of Antiquity*, 5–9; Ruth Bloch, "The Gendered Meanings of Virtue in Revolutionary America," *Signs* 13 (Autumn 1987): 37–58; Lyons, *Sex among the Rabble*, 288–298, 305–307; Crane, *Ebb Tide*, 132–138.

Chapter 2

1. Abigail Adams to John Adams, June 17, 1782 (electronic edition), *Adams Family Papers: An Electronic Archive*, Massachusetts Historical Society.

2. See, for example, Barbara Clark Smith, "Food Rioters and the American Revolution," *William and Mary Quarterly* 51 (January 1994): 3–38; Branson, *These Fiery, Frenchified Dames*; Kate Haulman, "Fashion and the Culture Wars of Revolutionary

Philadelphia," *William and Mary Quarterly* 62 (October 2005): 625–662; Rosemarie Zagarri, *Revolutionary Backlash: Women and Politics in the Early American Republic* (Philadelphia: University of Pennsylvania Press, 2007).

3. On the association of patriotism with political values in eighteenth-century England, see Hugh Cunningham, "The Language of Patriotism 1750–1914," *History Workshop* 12 (Autumn 1981): 8–33. On the gendered differences in ideas of patriotism arising in the late eighteenth and early nineteenth centuries, see Kathleen Wilson, *The Sense of the People: Politics, Culture, and Imperialism in England, 1715–1785* (New York: Cambridge University Press, 1998), 70–78; Guest, *Small Change*, 181–192.

4. Kames, *Six Sketches*, 196.

5. Thomas Paine, "An Occasional Letter on the Female Sex," *Pennsylvania Magazine* (August 1775). See Moran, "L'Essai," 17–18.

6. Abigail Adams to John Adams, June 17, 1782.

7. Kate Davies, *Catherine Macaulay and Mercy Otis Warren: The Revolutionary Atlantic and the Politics of Gender* (New York: Oxford University Press, 2005), 198–211. For a more general discussion of women's patriotism during the Revolution, see Kerber, *Women and the Republic*, 73–113; Zagarri, *Revolutionary Backlash*, 20–23. Elaine Crane has noted Abigail Adams's reading of Russell, but she suggests that Adams is appropriating Russell's ideas rather than revising them. See Elaine Forman Crane, "Political Dialogue and the Spring of Abigail's Discontent," *William and Mary Quarterly* 56 (October 1999): 766–768.

8. Abigail Adams to John Adams, June 17, 1782.

9. Ibid.

10. Elaine Crane argues that Abigail Adams did not cite the authors she read because she wanted to avoid criticisms for misrepresenting their intentions. See Crane, "Abigail's Discontent," 761.

11. Philip Hicks, "Portia and Marcia: Female Political Identity and the Historical Imagination, 1770–1800," *William and Mary Quarterly* 62 (April 2005): 266–269. Hicks also notes that Linda Kerber, in *Women of the Republic*, has stressed the importance of historical precedent in pleas to women during the eighteenth century.

12. *The Sentiments of an American Woman* (Philadelphia: John Dunlap, 1780).

13. Philander, "The Female Advocate," originally published in the *New Universal Magazine* in November 1753 and republished in the *Pennsylvania Gazette*, June 20, 1754.

14. Rosemarie Zagarri, for example, has argued that although there were contesting visions of female rule in many of the histories that circulated, either way, they opened up a sense of female accomplishment (*Revolutionary Backlash*, 16).

15. For further discussion of this issue throughout Europe, see Anderson, *Joyous Greetings*, 34–37.

16. Millar, *Distinction of Ranks*, 62–68. The matrilineal social organization of many Native American tribes had become well known in Europe by the eighteenth century, particularly with the publication of *Moeurs des sauvages amériquains*

comparées aux moeurs des premiers temps by Abbe Lafitau in 1724. For more on this, see Jane Rendall, *The Origins of Modern Feminism in Britain, France, and the United States, 1780–1860* (New York: Schocken, 1985), 24.

17. Alexander, *History of Women*, II: 56 (hereafter cited in text as *HW*).

18. Dominique Godineau, "Masculine and Feminine Political Practice during the French Revolution, 1793–Year III," especially 62–72; and Darline G. Levy and Harriet B. Applewhite, "Women, Radicalization, and the Fall of the French Monarchy," both in *Women and Politics in the Age of the Democratic Revolution*, ed. Harriet B. Applewhite and Darline G. Levy (Ann Arbor: University of Michigan Press, 1993).

19. Smith, "Food Rioters and the American Revolution," 3–38; Branson, *These Fiery, Frenchified Dames*; Haulman, "Fashion and the Culture Wars"; Zagarri, *Revolutionary Backlash*; Judith Apter Klinghoffer and Lois Elkins, "'The Petticoat Electors': Women's Suffrage in New Jersey, 1776–1807," *Journal of the Early Republic* 12 (Summer 1992): 159–193; Jan Ellen Lewis, "Rethinking Women's Suffrage in New Jersey, 1776–1807," *Rutgers Law Review* 63 (Spring 2011): 1017–1035.

20. David Waldstreicher, *In the Midst of Perpetual Fetes: The Making of American Nationalism, 1776–1820* (Chapel Hill: University of North Carolina Press, 1997).

21. Zagarri, *Revolutionary Backlash*, 68–81.

22. On the participation of women in the informal politics of the early republic, see Jeffrey Pasley, "The Cheese and the Words: Popular Political Culture and Participatory Democracy in the Early American Republic," in *Beyond the Founders: New Approaches to the Political History of the Early Republic*, ed. Jeffrey Pasley, Andrew Robertson, and David Waldstreicher (Chapel Hill: University of North Carolina Press, 2004), 31–56; Waldstreicher, *In the Midst of Perpetual Fetes*, 177–245.

23. Branson, *These Fiery, Frenchified Dames*, 21–53.

24. Mary Wollstonecraft, "Article XXXVI," *The Analytical Review* 8 (1790), reprinted in *The Works of Mary Wollstonecraft* VII, ed. Janet Todd and Marilyn Butler (New York: New York University Press, 1989), 291.

25. Mary Wollstonecraft, *A Vindication of the Rights of Woman* (New York: Viking Penguin, 1985 [1792]), 95. The review was published, unsigned, in *The Analytical Review* 8 (September 1790): 100. For further discussion of this comment see Jane Rendall, "'The grand causes which combine to carry mankind forward': Wollstonecraft, History and Revolution," *Women's Writing* 4 (1997): 158.

26. Wollstonecraft, *Vindication*, 106–107.

27. Ibid., 152.

28. Ibid., 282–283.

29. For further discussion of the ways in which Wollstonecraft engaged the historical theories of the Scottish Enlightenment, see Rendall, "'The Grand causes which combine to carry mankind forward,'" 155–177; O'Brian, *Women and Enlightenment*, 173–200.

30. Branson, *These Fiery, Frenchified Dames*, 38–46; *Salem Gazette* 6 (October 16, 1992): 3; see also *Massachusetts Spy* (Worcester) XXI (October 4, 1792): 4; and XXI (November 22, 1792): 4.

31. Judith Sargent Murray, "On the Equality of the Sexes," *Massachusetts Magazine* II (March 1790): 133.

32. Judith Sargent Murray, *The Gleaner* (Schenectady, N.Y.: Union College Press, 1992 [1796–1798]), 703 (hereafter cited in text as *G*).

33. For an illuminating discussion of the ways in which these historical essays demonstrate how Murray had come to recognize that gender would play an important role in the way the politics of the early republic operated, see Jeanne Boydston, "Making Gender in the Early Republic: Judith Sargent Murray and the Revolution of 1800," in *The Revolution of 1800: Democracy, Race, and the New Republic*, ed. James Horn, Jan Ellen Lewis, and Peter Onuf (Charlottesville: University of Virginia Press, 2002), 254–256.

34. On republican womanhood, see Kerber, *Women of the Republic*; Jan Lewis, "The Republican Wife: Virtue and Seduction in the Early Republic," *William and Mary Quarterly* 44 (October 1987): 689–721. On the backlash against women in politics during this period, see Zagarri, *Revolutionary Backlash*. On the importance of voluntary associations as an arena for the exercise of rights in early America, see William J. Novak, "The Transformation of Citizenship in Nineteenth-Century America," in *The Democratic Experiment: New Directions in American Political History*, ed. Meg Jacobs, William J. Novak, and Julian E. Zelizer (Princeton, N.J.: Princeton University Press, 2003), 85–119.

35. Zagarri, *Revolutionary Backlash*, 82–85.

36. Ibid., 93–114; Waldstreicher, *In the Midst of Perpetual Fetes*, 232–235; John L. Brooke, *Columbia Rising: Civil Life on the Upper Hudson from the Revolution to the Age of Jackson* (Chapel Hill: University of North Carolina Press, 2010), 342–381.

37. Alexander Hamilton, James Madison, and John Jay, *The Federalist Papers*, ed. Clinton Rossiter, Letter VI (New York: New American Library, 1961 [1788]), 54–55. Linda Kerber discusses this allusion to Aspasia in *Women of the Republic*, 105. See also Lucubrator No. V, *New-Bedford Mercury*, December 18, 1807; James Wilson, *The Works of James Wilson*, vol. 1, ed. Robert Green McCloskey (Cambridge, Mass.: Harvard University Press, 1967), 86.

38. See, for example, *Washington Federalist* (Georgetown), June 10, 1801; *Farmer's Cabinet* (Amherst, N.H.), May 29, 1810; *Enquirer*, Richmond (January 5, 1811). Winterer, in *The Mirror of Antiquity*, 131–135, discusses the way in which Cornelia was seen not only as a virtuous mother, but also as a model in rejecting the temptations of luxury.

39. *Newburyport Herald*, September 22, 1801; *Providence Journal*, September 23, 1801. See also Philip Hicks, "The Roman Matron in Britain: Female Political Influence and Republican Response," *Journal of Modern History* 77 (March 2005): 65–69.

40. "Female Heroism," *General Magazine and Impartial Review of Knowledge & Entertainment* 2 (July 1798): 57; *Weekly Visitor, or Ladies' Miscellany* 2 (January 7, 1804): 55.

41. *Massachusetts Magazine* 1 (February 1789): 115; Alexander Garden, *Anecdotes of the Revolutionary War in America, with Sketches of Character of Persons the Most*

Distinguished, in the Southern States, for Civil and Military Services (Charleston: A. E. Miller, 1822), 226–230.

42. *The American Quarterly Review* 1 (March 1827): 32–34; letter from Mrs. Deborah Logan to Major Alexander Garden, September 26, 1822, *Collections of the Historical Society of Pennsylvania* I (1853): 118–121.

43. Peter Messer, "Writing Women into History: Defining Gender and Citizenship in Post-Revolutionary America," *Studies in Eighteenth-Century Culture* 28 (1999): 341–360; Linda Kerber, " 'History Can Do It No Justice': Women and the Reinterpretation of the American Revolution," in *Women in the Age of the American Revolution*, ed. Ronald Hoffman and Peter Albert (Charlottesville: University of Virginia Press, 1989), 40.

44. Carolyn Eastman, *A Nation of Speechifiers: Making an American Public after the Revolution* (Chicago: University of Chicago Press, 2009), 72–82.

45. *The Rise and Progress of the Young-Ladies Academy of Philadelphia: Containing an Account of a Number of Public Examinations & Commencements; The Charter and Bye-Laws; Likewise, Number of Orations delivered By the Young Ladies, And several by the Trustees of said Institution* (Philadelphia: Stewart and Cochran, 1795), 92–93.

46. Ibid., 94.

47. Anne M. Boylan, *The Origins of Women's Activism: New York and Boston, 1797–1840* (Chapel Hill: University of North Carolina Press, 1992), 17–21; Bruce Dorsey, *Reforming Men and Women: Gender in the Antebellum City* (Ithaca, N.Y.: Cornell University Press, 2002), 1–49.

48. Rosemarie Zagarri, "The Rights of Man and Woman in Post-Revolutionary America," *William and Mary Quarterly* 60 (April 1998): 203–230; Novak, "Transformation of Citizenship," 85–119.

49. H[annah] Mather Crocker, *Observations on the Real Rights of Women, with their Appropriate Duties, Agreeable to Scripture, Reason and Common Sense* (Boston: Printed for the Author, 1818), 22.

50. Ibid., 62, 34–37.

51. Ibid., 45–47.

52. Ibid., 20.

53. Ibid., 72.

54. Dorsey, *Reforming Men and Women*, 11–12.

Chapter 3

1. For a discussion of the significance of African American female abolitionists, including Maria Stewart, see Shirley Yee, *Black Women Abolitionists: A Study in Activism, 1828–1860* (Knoxville: University of Tennessee Press, 1992), especially 114–121. For a discussion of Stewart's use of domestic imagery in the context of creating a black nationalist ideology, see Laura Romero, *Homefronts: Domesticity and Its Critics in the Antebellum United States* (Durham, N.C.: Duke University Press, 1997), 52–69. Elizabeth McHenry analyzes the way in which female literary societies provided a space for

African American women to develop their own ideas for challenging the inequities of race and gender in *Forgotten Readers: Recovering the Lost History of African American Literary Societies* (Durham, N.C.: Duke University Press, 2002), 67–83.

2. "Mrs. Stewart's Farewell Address to Her Friends in the City of Boston," *Liberator*, September 28, 1833; reprinted in *Maria Stewart, America's First Black Woman Political Writer: Essays and Speeches*, ed. Marilyn Richardson (Bloomington: Indiana University Press, 1987), 68–69.

3. Grimké published portions of her *Letters on the Equality of the Sexes* serially in the *Spectator* and the *Liberator* in 1837, and she published them as a book in 1838. Fuller wrote "The Great Lawsuit" for *The Dial* in 1843 and then published an expanded version as *Woman in the Nineteenth Century* in 1844.

4. *Anti-Slavery Standard*, July 15, 1841.

5. Carroll Smith-Rosenberg, *Religion and the Rise of the American City: The New York City Mission Movement, 1812–1870* (Ithaca, N.Y.: Cornell University Press, 1971), 97–124; Mary Ryan, *Cradle of the Middle Class: The Family in Oneida County, New York, 1790–1865* (New York: Cambridge University Press, 1981), 53–70; Barbara Meil Hobson, *Uneasy Virtue: The Politics of Prostitution and the American Reform Tradition* (New York: Basic Books, 1987), 53–70; Ruth Borden, *Women and Temperance: The Quest for Power and Liberty, 1873–1900* (Philadelphia: Temple University Press, 1981); Barbara Epstein, *The Politics of Domesticity: Women, Evangelism, and Temperance in Nineteenth-Century America* (Middletown, Conn.: Wesleyan University Press, 1981), 89–95.

6. Susan Zaeske, *Signatures of Citizenship: Petitioning, Antislavery, and Women's Political Identity* (Chapel Hill: University of North Carolina Press, 2003), 25–26; Mary Herschberger, "Mobilizing Women, Anticipating Abolition: The Struggle against Indian Removal in the 1830s," *Journal of American History* 86 (June 1999): 15–40; Julie Roy Jeffrey, *The Great Silent Army of Abolitionism: Ordinary Women in the Antislavery Movement* (Chapel Hill: University of North Carolina Press, 1998), 134–170; Yee, *Black Women Abolitionists*, 86–111; Angelina Grimké, *Appeal to the Women of the Nominally Free States Issued by an Anti-Slavery Convention of American Women*, 2nd ed. (Boston: Isaac Knapp, 1838), 5–6.

7. Lori Ginzberg, *Women and the Work of Benevolence: Morality, Politics, and Class in the 19th-Century United States* (New Haven, Conn.: Yale University Press, 1990), 36–97; Anne M. Boylan, *The Origins of Women's Activism: New York and Boston, 1797–1840* (Chapel Hill: University of North Carolina Press, 2002), 20–24, 53–93; Nancy Hewitt, *Women's Activism and Social Change: Rochester, New York, 1822–1872* (Ithaca, N.Y.: Cornell University Press, 1984), 97–138.

8. Thomas Dublin, *Women at Work: The Transformation of Work and Community in Lowell, Massachusetts, 1826–1860* (New York: Columbia University Press, 1980), 58–74, 86–131; Christine Stansell, *City of Women: Sex and Class in New York, 1789–1860* (Urbana: University of Illinois Press, 1987), 130–154; Mary Blewett, *Men, Women, and Work: Class, Gender, and Protest in the New England Shoe Industry, 1780–*

1910 (Urbana: University of Illinois Press, 1988), 97–141; Teresa Anne Murphy, *Ten Hours' Labor: Religion, Reform, and Gender in Early New England* (Ithaca, N.Y.: Cornell University Press, 1992), 9–56, 191–221.

9. Kathryn Sklar, *Catharine Beecher: A Study in Domesticity* (New York: W. W. Norton, 1973) discusses the broad significance of domesticity in the writings of Catharine Beecher. See also Jeanne Boydston, *Home and Work: Housework, Wages, and the Ideology of Labor in the Early Republic* (New York: Oxford University Press, 1994), 120–163.

10. Carolyn L. Karcher, *The First Woman in the Republic: A Cultural Biography of Lydia Maria Child* (Durham, N.C.: Duke University Press, 1994), 126–132.

11. Karcher discusses Child's *Ladies' Family Library* in *First Woman in the Republic,* 146.

12. Karcher, *First Woman in the Republic,* 220–221; Bruce Mills, *Cultural Reformations: Lydia Maria Child and the Literature of Reform* (Athens: University of Georgia Press, 1994), 30–54.

13. Karcher discusses Child's use of Alexander in *First Woman in the Republic,* 221.

14. See also ibid., 225, on this point. Karcher argues that, in attending to issues of women's labor, political power, and sexual mores, Child anticipates many of the most important issues of the woman's rights movement.

15. Mrs. D. L. [Lydia Maria] Child, *The History of the Condition of Women, In Various Ages and Nations,* 2 vols. (Boston: John Allen &Co., 1835), I: 4, 6 (hereafter cited in text as *HCW*).

16. Millar, in particular, had criticized Egyptian men and women for transgressing the natural gender hierarchy.

17. Eric Foner, *Free Soil, Free Labor, Free Men: The Ideology of the Republican Party before the Civil War* (New York: Oxford University Press, 1970), 8–39.

18. Alexander Keyssar, *The Right to Vote: The Contested History of Democracy in the United States* (New York: Basic Books, 2011), 34–36.

19. When Child criticized the Burmese, she took a swipe at coverture by noting that women in Burma were also degraded because their legal evidence was not deemed equal to that of a man's. Her discussion of Aspasia was particularly interesting because the kinds of choices Aspasia made in becoming the mistress of Pericles were not all that different from those made by the young slave Harriet Jacobs, whose autobiography Child would help to edit a few years later. For a discussion of the ways in which Harriet Jacobs discussed her sexual liaison with a white slaveholder, see Hazel V. Carby, *Reconstructing Womanhood: The Emergence of the Afro-American Woman Novelist* (New York: Oxford University Press, 1987), 53–61. Jean Fagan Yellin discusses Child's influence on Jacobs's autobiography in the introduction to Harriet A. Jacobs, *Incidents in the Life of a Slave Girl, Written by Herself,* ed. Jean Fagan Yellin (Cambridge, Mass.: Harvard University Press, 2000), xxiv–xxxiii.

20. See also Winterer, *Mirror of Antiquity*, who emphasizes that Child depicted women as slaves and captives in all periods of history.

21. Dana D. Nelson, *National Manhood: Capitalist Citizenship and the Imagined Fraternity of White Men* (Durham, N.C.: Duke University Press, 1998), 105.

22. For a discussion of the various motives of working women in different industries, see Dublin, *Women at Work*, 21–57; Stansell, *City of Women*, 11–18; and Blewett, *Men, Women, and Work*, 44–67.

23. Karcher, *First Woman in the Republic*, 119.

24. Ginzberg, *Women and the Work of Benevolence*, 81; Karcher, *First Woman in the Republic*, 246–248.

25. *The Knickerbocker* 6 (July 1835): 84.

26. Anonymous [Sarah Josepha Hale], *American Ladies Magazine* 8 (October 1835): 588.

27. *Boston Pearl* 5 (October 3, 1835): 21.

28. *North American Review* 42 (October 1836): 513. Cushing is identified as the author by Octavius Brooks Frothingham in "Absent Friends," *North American Review* 128 (May 1879): 505.

29. Child's disclaimer did not show up in the 1838 edition of her *History of the Condition of Women*, but it was there beginning with the 1845 edition. Karcher, in *First Woman in the Republic*, notes the importance of Child's work for Grimké, Fuller, and other woman's rights activists (226–227).

30. For a discussion of Grégoire's and Odell's biographies of Wheatley, see Margot Minardi, *Making Slavery History: Abolitionism and the Politics of Memory in Massachusetts* (New York: Oxford University Press, 2010), 102–104. Grégoire's biography was reprinted in A. [Abigail] Mott, *Biographical Sketches and Interesting Anecdotes of Persons of Colour* (New York: Mahlon Day, 1826), 10–12, and later in *The Liberator* 7 (February 18, 1832): 28.

31. Minardi, *Making Slavery History*, 125–130; Miss [Catharine] Sedgewick, "Slavery in New England," *Bentley's Miscellany* 34 (1853): 417–424; William C. Nell, *The Colored Patriots of the American Revolution* (Boston: Robert F. Wallcut, 1855), 52–58, 64–73.

32. Minardi, *Making Slavery History*, 105; [Margaretta Odell], *Memoir and Poems of Phyllis Wheatley* (Boston: George W. Light, 1834), 20–24.

33. Sarah Grimké, *Letters on the Equality of the Sexes*, ed. Elizabeth Ann Bartlett (New Haven, Conn.: Yale University Press, 1988), 41, 51, 46.

34. Ibid., 59.

35. Ibid., 62.

36. Ibid., 53. Caroline Winterer has pointed out in *Mirror of Antiquity*, 166–180, that northern women in the antebellum period were increasingly less interested in taking the Roman matron as an example for behavior, both because of the matron's elite status and slaveholding.

37. Margaret Fuller, *Woman in the Nineteenth Century* (New York: W. W. Norton, 1971 [1845]), 47, 75–76.

38. Ibid., 64–65.

39. Ibid., 93–94, 72–78.

40. Ibid., 109–111.

41. Ibid., 116.

42. L. M. C. [Lydia Maria Child], "Woman in the 19th Century," *Broadway Journal* 1 (February 15, 1845): 97. In the context of analyzing *Woman in the Nineteenth Century* as an experiment in feminist discourse, Annette Kolodny discusses many of the critical reviews of the book in "Inventing a Feminist Discourse: Rhetoric and Resistance in Margaret Fuller's *Woman in the Nineteenth Century*," *New Literary History* 25 (Spring 1994): 356–357.

43. Edgar Allan Poe identified Briggs as the author of the unnamed review, criticizing the review as silly and disavowing any connection with the piece, no doubt because he was also a publisher of the *Broadway Journal* at the time. See *Godey's Magazine and Ladies Book* 33 (August 1846): 72.

44. [Charles F. Briggs], Reviews: "Woman in the Nineteenth Century," *Broadway Journal* 1 (March 1, 1845): 129; *Broadway Journal* 1 (March 8, 1845): 145.

45. [Orestes Brownson], "Woman in the Nineteenth Century," *Brownson's Quarterly Review* 2 (April 1, 1845): 249.

46. A. G. M., "The Condition of Woman," *Southern Quarterly Review* 10 (July 1846): 148.

Chapter 4

1. Elizabeth Cady Stanton, "Address of Elizabeth Cady Stanton to the Legislature of the State of New York, Feb 1854," in *Address to the Legislature of New-York, Adopted by the State Woman's Rights Convention, Held at Albany, Tuesday and Wednesday, February 14 and 15, 1854* (Albany, N.Y.: Weed, Parsons & Co., 1854), 4.

2. Nancy Isenberg, *Sex and Citizenship in Antebellum America* (Chapel Hill: University of North Carolina Press, 1998); Ginzberg, *Women and the Work of Benevolence*, 67–97.

3. Kelley, *Learning to Stand and Speak*, 75–76, 164, 257; Charles Rollin, *The Ancient History of the Egyptians, Carthaginians, Assyrians, Babylonians, Medes and Persians, Macedonians and Grecians* (Edinburgh: Charles Elliot, 1775), I: xiii, 331; VI: 250–251; Charles Rollin, *The Roman History from the Foundation of Rome to the Battle of Actium* (London: John and Paul Knapton, 1739), I: 48, 339; Sarah Pierce, *Sketches of Universal History* (New Haven, Conn.: Joseph Barber, 1811), II: 174–175.

4. Emma Willard, *A System of Universal History in Perspective* (Hartford, Conn.: F. J. Huntington, 1835), 249, 117–119, 104; Emma Willard, *History of the United States* (New York: White, Gallaher, &White, 1829), 34, 37, 51, 239–240.

5. Lucy Larcom, "Character and Institutions of the German Nations," 1849, Lucy Larcom Papers, Massachusetts Historical Society (hereafter cited as MHS).

6. Mary Haskell Thayer French Dyer, March 13, 1851, Allen French Papers, MHS; Lucy Chace, "The Comparison between Women of This Country and Those of Other Countries," Composition Books and Diaries, No. 7, and Diary Fragments, March 29, 1842, Chase Family Papers, American Antiquarian Society (hereafter cited as AAS); Caroline Barrett White, Journal, November 12, 1851, March 18, 1853, Caroline Barrett White Papers, AAS.

7. Wilson G. Richardson, *Catalogue of the Library of the University of Alabama, with an Index of Subjects* (Tuscaloosa, Ala.: M. D. J. Slade, 1848); *The Catalogue of the American Whig Society Library of the College of New Jersey* (New York: Charles Scribner, 1853); *Catalogue of the Public School and Lyceum Library of Municipality No. Two* (New Orleans, 1848); *Catalogue of the Books and Papers in the Library and Reading Room of the Ohio School Library of Cincinnati* (Cincinnati: C. F. Bradley & Co., 1856); *Catalogue of the Library of the Central High School* (Philadelphia: T. B. Brown, 1841); *Catalogue of the Public School Library in Poughkeepsie* (Poughkeepsie, N.Y.: Platt & Schram, 1851); *Catalogue of the Library of the Troy Young Men's Association of the City of Troy* (Troy, N.Y.: N. Tuttle, 1845); *Catalogue of Books Belonging to the Girls' Department of the Apprentices Library Company of Philadelphia* (Philadelphia, 1850).

8. *Speech of John Quincy Adams, of Massachusetts, upon the Right of the People, Men and Women, to Petition; on the Freedom of Speech and Debate in the House of Representatives of the United States; on the Resolutions of Seven State Legislatures, and the Petitions of More Than One Hundred Thousand Petitioners, Relating to the Annexation of Texas to This Union* (Washington, D.C.: Gales and Seaton, 1838), 66–67, 69, 76.

9. Ibid., 70–73.

10. Ibid., 75–76.

11. *Voice of Industry*, December 19, 1845, and January 23, 1846.

12. Ella [Harriet Farley], "Woman," *The Lowell Offering* 1 (April 1841): 131–134. On Lowell millworkers writing for *The Lowell Offering*, see Lise Vogel, "'Humorous Incidents and Common Sense': More on the New England Mill Women," *Labor History* 19 (1978): 280–286; Benita Eisler, ed., *The Lowell Offering: Writings by New England Mill Women (1840–1845)* (New York: Harper and Row, 1977), 13–41; Harriet H. Robinson, *Loom and Spindle, or Life among the Early Mill Girls* (New York: Thomas Y. Crowell, 1898).

13. Martha, *Voice of Industry*, May 8, 1846.

14. Sarah Bagley, *Voice of Industry*, June 5, 1845.

15. *Address by Elizabeth Cady Stanton on Woman's Rights*, September 1848, in Ann D. Gordon, ed., *The Selected Papers of Elizabeth Cady Stanton and Susan B. Anthony* (New York: Oxford University Press, 1997), I: 98. See the footnotes on pages 117–121 for many examples in the speech drawn from Child's *History of the Condition of Women*.

16. Rebecca Sandford, in *Proceedings of the Woman's Rights Convention Held at the Unitarian Church, Rochester, N.Y., August 2, 1848*, revised by Mrs. Amy Post (New

York: Robert J. Johnston, Printer, 1870; reprinted by Arno and the New York Times, New York, 1969), 6.

17. H. B. [Henry] Blackwell, in *Proceedings of the National Woman's Rights Convention, Held at Cleveland, Ohio, on Wednesday, Thursday, and Friday, October 5th, 6th, and 7th, 1853* (Cleveland: Gray, Beardsley, Spear, & Co., 1854), 46–48.

18. Ibid.

19. Lucretia Mott, in *Proceedings of the National Woman's Rights Convention, 1853*, 13.

20. Rufus B. Fowler, "Blackstone Literary Association Record Book, 1858–1860," Northbridge, Massachusetts, January 26, 1860, AAS.

21. Norma Basch, *In the Eyes of the Law: Women, Marriage, and Property in Nineteenth-Century New York* (Ithaca, N.Y.: Cornell University Press, 1982), 113–161; Suzanne Lebsock, *The Free Women of Petersburg: Status and Culture in a Southern Town, 1784–1860* (New York: W. W. Norton, 1984), 54–86.

22. Laurel Clark, "The Rights of a Florida Wife: Slavery, U.S. Expansion, and Married Woman's Property Law," *Journal of Women's History* 22 (Winter 2010): 39–63; Leonard L. Richards, *The California Goldrush and the Coming of the Civil War* (New York: Knopf, 2007), 77–78; Mark M. Carroll, *Homesteads Ungovernable: Families, Sex, Race, and the Law in Frontier Texas* (Austin: University of Texas Press, 2001), 129–130. For an interesting account of the way Ursuline nuns in New Orleans manipulated property law as control of Louisiana shifted from France to the United States, see Emily Clark, *Masterless Mistresses: The New Orleans Ursulines and the Development of a New World Society, 1727–1834* (Chapel Hill: University of North Carolina Press, 2007), 234–246.

23. Winterer, *The Mirror of Antiquity*, 5–8.

24. Ibid., 131–141.

25. See, for example, William Alexander's discussion of the declining morals of Roman women in his *History of Women*, I: 208–209.

26. Peregrine Bingham, *The Law of Infancy and Coverture* (Exeter, N.H.: George Lamson, 1824), 182–183.

27. [Caleb Cushing], "The Legal Condition of Woman," *North American Review* 26 (April 1828): 332–333. Lori D. Ginzberg discusses Cushing's discussion of property rights in *Untidy Origins: A Story of Woman's Rights in Antebellum New York* (Chapel Hill: University of North Carolina Press, 2005), 150. Cushing critiqued the political abilities of women in "The Social Condition of Woman," *North American Review* 42 (October 1836): 489–513.

28. [Cushing], "Legal Condition of Woman," 318. Joseph T. Buckingham's *The New England Galaxy* took note of Cushing's essay and offered qualified support, even as the newspaper fretted about domestic relationships. Agreeing with Cushing that a woman's property should be protected for her benefit, the newspaper nonetheless cautioned against setting the husband up as a villain in the marriage relationship. On the other hand, the newspaper seconded Cushing's criticisms of a double standard in

marriage law and women's vulnerability, particularly when married to a wastrel who squandered her fortune or carried on with other women. See X, "Legal Condition of Woman," *New England Galaxy* 11 (April 11, 1828): 2. Joseph T. Buckingham was the owner of the periodical until he sold it in November 1828. See Frank Luther Mott, *A History of American Magazines: 1741–1850* (Cambridge, Mass.: Harvard University Press, 1958), I: 127.

29. Mr. [Kimball] Dimmick, in J. Ross Brown, *Report of the Debates in the Convention of California, on the Formation of the State Constitution, in September and October, 1849* (Washington, D.C.: John T. Towers, 1850), 263.

30. Mr. [James McHall] Jones, *Report of the Debates in California . . . 1849*, 264.

31. O'Brien, *Women and Enlightenment*, 115–116; Winterer, *Mirror of Antiquity*, 137.

32. Baron de Montesquieu, *The Spirit of the Laws* (Dublin: G. and A. Ewing, and G. Faulkner, 1751), I: 133; II: 200–202.

33. [Cushing], "Legal Condition of Woman," 319–326.

34. Conrad Swackhamer, in *Report of the Debates and Proceedings of the Convention for the Revision of the Constitution of the State of New-York, 1846*, reported by William G. Bishop and William H. Attree (Albany, N.Y.: Office of the Evening Atlas, 1846), 1039. For the same argument about Roman women, see WJF, "Wives and Slaves; A Bone for the Abolitionists to Pick," *United States Magazine and Democratic Review* 17 (October 1845): 264.

35. For a discussion about how votes proceeded on married women's right to own personal property, see Richard William Leopold, *Robert Dale Owen: A Biography* (Cambridge, Mass.: Harvard University Press, 1940), 272–293.

36. Mr. [Christian] Nave, in *Report of the Debates and Proceedings of the Convention for the Revision of the Constitution of the State of Indiana, 1850* (Indianapolis: A. H. Brown, 1850), 469.

37. Nave, in *Report of the Debates . . . Indiana*, 484.

38. Mr. [William] Haddon, in *Report of the Debates . . . of Indiana*, 473.

39. Ibid.

40. Ibid., 474.

41. Mr. [Robert Dale] Owen, in *Report of the Debates . . . of Indiana*, 529.

42. Ibid.

43. Ibid., 530.

44. Ginzberg, *Untidy Origins*, 149; Leopold, *Robert Dale Owen*, 282.

45. Lucy Stone, *Pamphlet: The Proceedings of the Seventh National Woman's Rights Convention Held in New York City, at the Broadway Tabernacle on Tuesday and Wednesday, November 25th and 26th*, phonographically reported by Wm. H. Burr (Austin, Tex.: Jenkins Publishing, 1856), 44, retrieved July 8, 2008, http://asp6new.alexanders treed . com . proxygw . wrlc . org / wasm / wasmrest ricted / wasmfu llvolume / S10018233 .htm#S10018233-D0001.

46. Martha, *Voice of Industry*, May 8, 1846.

47. Paulina Wright Davis, in *Proceedings of the Woman's Rights Convention, Held at the Broadway Tabernacle, in the City of New York, on Tuesday and Wednesday, Sept. 6th and 7th, 1853* (New York: Fowlers and Wells, 1853), 26.

48. Ibid., 27–29.

49. As Catherine Hall points out, most people in Britain were shocked by the census findings from 1850 that showed how much women worked for wages. See Catherine Hall, *White, Male, and Middle Class: Explorations in Feminism and History* (New York: Routledge, 1992), 176.

50. Caroline Dall, in *Report of the Woman's Rights Meeting, at Mercantile Hall, May 27, 1859* (Boston: Urbina, 1859), 19–20.

51. Theodore Parker, "A Sermon of the Public Function of Woman, Preached at the Music-Hall, Boston, March 27, 1853," *Woman's Rights Tracts No. 2, Woman's Rights Tracts* (Boston: Robert F. Wallcut, 1854), 38.

52. Abby Price, in *Woman's Rights Convention . . . New York, 1853*, 34.

53. Elizabeth Cady Stanton, Letter, May 16, 1851, in *The Proceedings of the Woman's Rights Convention, Held at Akron, Ohio, May 28 and 29, 1851* (Cincinnati: Ben Franklin Book and Job Office, 1851), 34.

54. Lucretia Mott, in *Proceedings of the National Woman's Rights Convention, 1853*, 63.

55. Thomas Wentworth Higginson, *Woman and Her Wishes; An Essay: Inscribed to the Massachusetts Constitutional Convention* (Boston: Robert F. Wallcut, 1853), 3.

56. Ibid., 5–6.

57. Ibid., 15.

58. Mrs. E. Robinson, "Report on Education," *Woman's Rights Convention . . . Akron, 1851*, 21.

59. Thomas Wentworth Higginson, "Ought Women to Learn the Alphabet?" *Atlantic Monthly* 16 (February 1859): 144.

Chapter 5

1. *The Literary World* 6 (February 16, 1850): 152. This particular review was of Anita George's *Annals of the Queens of Spain*, but it also referred to works by Agnes Strickland, Lucy Aiken, and Elizabeth Ellet.

2. Mrs. [Elizabeth] Ellet, *Domestic History of the American Revolution* (New York: Baker and Scribner, 1850), v; *Graham's American Monthly Magazine of Literature, Art, and Fashion* 33 (November 1848): 298.

3. For a discussion of the changing meanings of Anglo-Saxonism during this period, see Reginald Horseman, *Race and Manifest Destiny: The Origins of American Racial Anglo-Saxonism* (Cambridge, Mass.: Harvard University Press, 1981). For a discussion of the ways in which white womanhood and domesticity can be woven into issues of nationalism, see McClintock, *Imperial Leather*, especially 352–396.

4. Lucy Larcom, "Character and Institutions of the German Nations," 1849, Lucy Larcom Papers, MHS. For a discussion of Child's view of Germanic women, see Chapter 3.

5. For a discussion of the ways in which a new ideal of history emerged in nineteenth-century Scotland, in which Enlightenment ideals of history that focused on measuring differences between past and present were replaced by a new approach of recovering the past and abolishing the distance between past and present through "transport," see Ian Duncan, *Scott's Shadow: The Novel in Romantic Edinburgh* (Princeton, N.J.: Princeton University Press, 2007), 62.

6. Cultural citizenship as it is used in contemporary discourse champions the ability of citizens to maintain cultural differences while sharing the same rights of citizenship as others, a goal that remains elusive for many minority groups. See, for example, Renato Rosaldo, "Cultural Citizenship, Inequality, and Multiculturalism," in *Race, Identity, and Citizenship: A Reader*, ed. Rodolfo D. Torres, Louis F. Mirón, and Jonathan Xavier Inda (Malden, Mass.: Blackwell, 1999), 253–261. It is important to recognize that the type of cultural citizenship championed by someone such as Hale was quite different. For an important analysis of the way in which nationalist thinking infused the nineteenth-century ideology of domesticity, see Kish Sklar, *Catharine Beecher*, especially 151–167.

7. Susan Phinney Conrad, *Perish the Thought: Intellectual Women in Romantic America, 1830–1860* (New York: Oxford University Press, 1976), 120; Mrs. [Elizabeth F.] Ellet, *Women Artists in All Ages and Countries* (New York: Harper & Brothers, 1859), 234.

8. Elizabeth Varon, *We Mean to Be Counted: White Women and Politics in Antebellum Virginia* (Chapel Hill: University of North Carolina Press, 1998), 124–136; David Moltke-Hansen, "Why History Mattered: The Background of Ann Pamela Cunningham's Interest in the Preservation of Mount Vernon," *Furman Studies* (1980): 34–42.

9. See, for example, *Godey's Lady's Book* 32 (February 1846): 94–95; 47 (July 1853): 84–85; 49 (November 1854): 460; 54 (February 1857): 179. See also Patricia Okker, *Our Sister Editors: Sarah J. Hale and the Tradition of Nineteenth-Century Women Editors* (Athens: University of Georgia Press, 1995), 72.

10. Sarah Josepha Hale, *Woman's Record; or, Sketches of all Distinguished Women, from "The Beginning" till* A.D. 1850 (New York: Harper and Brothers, 1855; originally published, 1852), xxxvii (hereafter cited in text as *WR*).

11. Varon, *We Mean to Be Counted*, 124–125, 135–136; Amy Kaplan, "Manifest Domesticity," *American Literature* 70 (September 1998): 581–606. For a discussion of similar issues with respect to Britain, see Marlon Ross, "Romancing the Nation-State: The Poetics of Romantic Nationalism," in *Macropolitics of Nineteenth-Century Literature: Nationalism, Exoticism, Imperialism*, ed. Jonathan Arac and Harriet Ritvo (Philadelphia: University of Pennsylvania Press, 1995), 56–85.

12. David Levin, *History as Romantic Art: Bancroft, Prescott, Motley, and Parkman* (Stanford, Calif.: Stanford University Press, 1959), 24–73.

13. For an analysis of the way in which Bridgman challenged the man who educated her, see Ernest Freeberg, *The Education of Laura Bridgman: First Deaf and Blind Person to Learn Language* (Cambridge, Mass.: Harvard University Press, 2001).

14. A. P. Leach, Records of the Jamaica Debating Society, December 14, 1838, Manuscript Collection, American Antiquarian Society.

15. Constantia [Judith Sargent Murray], "On the Equality of the Sexes," *The Massachusetts Magazine; or Monthly Museum, Containing the Literature, History, Politics, Arts, Manners & Amusements of the Age* 2 (April 1790); Crocker, *Real Rights of Woman*, 7–16; Grimké, *Letters on the Equality of the Sexes*, 33.

16. *New England and Yale Review* 11 (February 1853): 150; *North American Review* 76 (January 1853): 261–262.

17. Ann Douglas, writing of Hale's attempt to redeem historical figures such as Agrippina, deems the approach a "whitewash" in *The Feminization of American Culture* (New York: Knopf, 1977), 73–74.

18. *New England and Yale Review* 11 (February 1853): 151–152.

19. See McClintock, *Imperial Leather*; Kaplan, "Manifest Domesticity."

20. For a discussion of Bremer's trip to the United States and its impact on her later writing, see Brita K. Stendahl, *The Education of a Self-Made Woman: Frederika Bremer, 1801–1865* (Lewiston, N.Y.: Edward Mellon Press, 1994), 85–119.

21. Scott E. Caspar emphasizes that Ellet situates the patriotism of women in their homes and families in *Constructing American Lives: Biography and Culture in Nineteenth-Century America* (Chapel Hill: University of North Carolina Press, 1999), 166. [William Gilmore Simms], *Southern Quarterly Review* (July 1850): 314–354.

22. Elizabeth Ellet, *The Women of the American Revolution* (New York: Haskell House, 1969 [1850]), I: 24–35, 18 (hereafter cited in text as *WAR*).

23. Ellet, *Domestic History of the Revolution*, 139, 307.

24. For previous references to this incident, see David Ramsay, *The History of the American Revolution* (Trenton, N.J.: James J. Wilson, [1789] 1811), II: 317; and Alexander Garden, *Anecdotes of the Revolutionary War in America, with Sketches of Character of Persons the Most Distinguished, in the Southern States, for Civil and Military Services* (Charleston, S.C.: A. E. Miller, 1822), 226–230.

25. Kerber, "'History Can Do It No Justice,'" 40.

26. On the political importance of plantation novels and southern domestic novels in promoting reconciliation, see Varon, *We Mean to Be Counted*, 103–136; Nina Baym, *Woman's Fiction: A Guide to Literature by and about Women in America, 1820–1870* (Urbana: University of Illinois Press, 1993), 175–207; Elizabeth Moss, *Domestic Novelists of the Old South: Defenders of Southern Culture* (Baton Rouge: Louisiana State University Press, 1992).

27. Ellet's use of dialogue speaks to the issue of sentiment that Scott Caspar has identified and analyzed in Ellet's work: a strategy that left women affected by the events of history, but unable to affect them. See Caspar, *Constructing American Lives*, 177.

28. On antislavery fairs, see Deborah Van Broekhoven, "'Better than a Clay Club': The Organization of Anti-Slavery Fairs, 1835–1860," *Slavery and Abolition* 19 (April 1998): 24–45.

29. *Christian Inquirer* 3 (November 18, 1848): 24; *Home Journal* 40 (September 30, 1848): 2; *The Independent . . . Devoted to the Consideration of Politics, Social and Economic Tendencies, History, Literature, and the Arts* 1 (December 28, 1848): 16.

30. *The United States Magazine and Democratic Review* 23 (December 1848): 565.

31. [William Gilmore Simms], "Ellett's Women of the Revolution," *Southern Quarterly Review* 1 (July 1850): 328.

32. Ibid., 314, 319–20.

33. Ibid., 318.

34. Moltke-Hanson, "Why History Mattered," 34–35.

35. *Godey's Lady's Book* 21 (November 1840): 237.

36. Varon, *We Mean to Be Counted*, 126–129; *Godey's Lady's Book* 51 (August 1855): 177–178; *Southern Literary Messenger* 21 (October 1855): 629.

37. *Southern Literary Messenger* 21 (September 1855): 562.

38. Ibid., 564.

39. Ibid., 563.

40. Varon, *We Mean to Be Counted*, 125.

Chapter 6

1. Caroline Wells Healey Dall Journal, December 28, 1852, CDP, MHS, reel 34.

2. Dall, "Bologna and Its Women," *The Una* II (March 1854): 238. For a discussion of the concerns about public opinion in the woman's rights movement, see Isenberg, *Sex and Citizenship*, 77–78. For a similar concern expressed by Rebecca Hicks, the editor of the Southern women's newspaper the *Kaleidoscope*, see Varon, *We Mean to Be Counted*, 123.

3. *The Liberator* 21 (November 7, 1851): 179.

4. *The Liberator* 22 (October 15, 1852): 167.

5. *The Liberator* 22 (October 29, 1852): 175.

6. Paulina Wright Davis to Caroline Wells Healey Dall, December 18, 1852, CDP, MHS, reel 2.

7. Paulina Wright Davis to Caroline Wells Healey Dall, January 2, 1853, CDP, MHS, reel 2.

8. Paulina Wright Davis to Caroline Wells Healey Dall, May 19, 1853. CDP, MHS, reel 2.

9. Isenberg, *Sex and Citizenship*, 73.

10. Mari Jo Buhle and Paul Buhle, eds., *The Concise History of Woman Suffrage* (Urbana: University of Illinois Press, 1978), 89; Sylvia D. Hoffert, *When Hens Crow: The Woman's Rights Movement in Antebellum America* (Bloomington: Indiana University Press, 1995), 19–22.

11. *The Una* I (February 1853): 4.

12. Paulina Wright Davis to Caroline Wells Healey Dall, January 2, 1853, CDP, MHS, reel 2.

13. *The Una* I (February 1853): 1.

14. *The Una* III (September 15, 1855): 142.

15. Caroline Wells Healey Dall Journal, August 25, 1853, CDP, MHS, reel 34.

16. Circulation figures of *Godey's Lady's Book* can be found in Patricia Okker, *Our Sister Editors: Sarah J. Hale and the Tradition of Nineteenth-Century American Women Editors* (Athens: University of Georgia Press, 1995), 56. For circulation figures for *The Una*, see Caroline Wells Healey Dall Journal, September 29, 1855, CDP, MHS, reel 34.

17. Dall criticized Hale in several of her essays in *The Una*. See, for example, "Bologna and Its Women," 238; and "The Countess Matilda," *The Una* II (June 1854): 285. Her comments on Kingsley can be found in her review in *The Una* II (February 1854): 220–221; and her criticism of Lady Morgan is in "Bologna and Its Women," 238.

18. Thomas Wentworth Higginson to Caroline Wells Healey Dall, March 27, 1854, CDP, MHS, reel 2; Paulina Wright Davis to Caroline Wells Healey Dall, June 1, 1853, CDP, MHS, reel 2; Caroline Wells Healey Dall to William Lloyd Garrison, June 11, 1858, Caroline Dall Papers, Schlesinger Library, Harvard University (hereafter cited as CDP, SL); "The Rights of Woman," *Liberator* 28 (February 19, 1858): 30.

19. Report from the *Worcester Spy* reprinted in *Liberator* 29 (March 18, 1859): 43; Caroline H. Dall, *The College, the Market, and the Court, or Woman's Relation to Education, Labor, and Law* (Boston: Lee and Shepard, 1867), 49. For the importance of classics in college curricula during this time, particularly in relation to women, see Winterer, *Mirror of Antiquity*, 202–203.

20. Dall, *The College, the Market, and the Court*, 49.

21. Ibid., 54.

22. Ibid., 60.

23. Ibid., 72.

24. Ibid., 61.

25. Dall, *Historical Pictures Retouched*, 252, 256, 257, 261.

26. Ibid., 253, 262, 263.

27. Dall, *The Una* III (February 1855): 25–26; Dall, *Historical Pictures Retouched*, vi.

28. Iron [Dall], "Hypatia," *The Una* I (May 1853): 51.

29. Ibid.

30. See also Isenberg, *Sex and Citizenship*, 41–74.

31. Dall, "Aspasia," *The Una* I (April 1853): 44–45. As Helen Deese notes, Dall attended one season of Fuller's conversations in 1841 but was always considered an outsider. See Deese, "Transcendentalism from the Margins: The Experience of Caroline Healey Dall," in *Transient and Permanent: The Transcendentalist Movement and Its Contexts*, ed. Charles Capper and Conrad Edick Wright (Boston: Massachusetts Historical Society, 1999), 128–129. Madeline Henry has noted that Caroline Dall referred "contemptuously to Ischomachus as running off to 'the saloon of Aspasia,'" but it seems likely her contempt was for Ischomachus's treatment of his wife, not for

Aspasia's salon. See Madeline M. Henry, *Prisoner of History: Aspasia of Miletus and Her Biographical Tradition* (New York: Oxford University Press, 1995), 106.

32. *The Una* II (August 1854): 307; Ginzberg, *Women and the Work of Benevolence*, 44–46, 75–77.

33. *The Una* II (August 1854): 308, 333–334.

34. Victor Cousin, *Madame de Hautefort et Madame Chevreuse: Nouvelles études sur les femmes illustres et la société du XVII siécle*, 2 vols. (Paris: Didie et Cie, 1856).

35. *National Review* VI (October 1856): 328, 339–340.

36. Caroline Wells Healey Dall, "Mme. Chevreuse," lecture first delivered February 1, 1858, 11, 49–50, CDP SL; "Woman's Claim," lecture first delivered February 15, 1858, 10, CDP, SL.

37. Dall, "Mme. Hautefort."

38. Dall, "Woman's Claim," CDP, SL; Caroline Dall, "Address before the Massachusetts Legislative Committee, in Support of a Memorial Petitioning for the Right of Universal Suffrage," *The Liberator* 28 (March 5, 1858): 40.

39. Dall, *The College, the Market, and the Court*, 140–155, 175, 203–207. Dall drew on William W. Sanger, *History of Prostitution: Its Extent, Causes, and Effects throughout the World* (1858) and Alexandre Parent-Duchâtelet, *De la prostitution dans la ville de Paris* (1836).

40. Dall, *The College, the Market, and the Court*, 47, 156, 160–161; Amy Stanley, *From Bondage to Contract: Wage Labor, Marriage, and the Market in the Age of Slave Emancipation* (New York: Cambridge University Press, 1998), 231.

41. Dall, *The College, the Market, and the Court*, 73–89.

42. Ibid., 157.

43. Dall, *The Una* II (March 1854): 238, 229.

44. Dall, *The College, the Market, and the Court*, 19.

45. Comments from *Harper's Weekly*, *Christian Examiner*, and *North American Review*, all reprinted in *Liberator* 30 (February 17, 1860): 28; comments from the *Chicago Press and Tribune* reprinted in *Liberator* 30 (May 11, 1860): 75; comments from the *Nantucket Inquirer* reprinted in *Liberator* 30 (November 2, 1860): 176.

46. Thomas L. Haskell, *The Emergence of Professional Social Science: The American Social Science Association and the Nineteenth-Century Crisis of Authority* (Urbana: University of Illinois Press, 1977), 98, 47–62, 75; Caroline Wells Healey Dall to George Ticknor, March 25, 1859, CDP, MHS, reel 41; William Leach, *True Love and Perfect Union: The Feminist Reform of Sex and Society*, 2nd ed. (Middletown, Conn.: Wesleyan University Press, 1989), 298–299.

47. Frank Sanborn to Caroline Wells Healey Dall, September 16, 1868, CDP, MHS, reel 5. See also Caroline Wells Healey Dall to Frank Sanborn, September 24, 1865, CDP, MHS, reel 41; and Caroline Wells Healey Dall Journal, December 14, 1865, CDP, MHS, reel 36. For an additional discussion of Dall's support of women in the ASSA, see Leach, *True Love*, 280; and Nancy Bowman, "Caroline Healey Dall, Her

Creation and Reform Career," in *Women of the Commonwealth: Work, Family, and Social Change in Nineteenth-Century Massachusetts*, ed. Susan L. Porter (Amherst: University of Massachusetts Press, 1996), 138.

48. Leach, *True Love*, 288–289, 298–299, 316–319, 344–346. See also Caroline Wells Healey Dall Journal, September 6, 1865, CDP, MHS reel 36; and Caroline Dall to Franklin Sanborn, September 24, 1865, CDP, MHS, reel 41.

49. Dall, *Historical Pictures Retouched*, vi, viii.

50. Faye Dudden, *Fighting Chance: The Struggle over Woman Suffrage and Black Suffrage in Reconstruction America* (New York: Oxford University Press, 2011); ECS [Elizabeth Cady Stanton], "Mrs. Dall's Fraternity Lecture," *Liberator* 30 (November 16, 1860): 182.

51. Caroline Wells Healey Dall Journal, May 29, 1868, CDP, MHS, reel 29; Higginson, cited in Helen Deese, "'My Life . . . Reads to Me Like a Romance': The Journals of Caroline Healey Dall," *Massachusetts Historical Review* 3 (2001): 122. For further discussion of Dall's rejection by the Boston women, see Dudden, *Fighting Chance*, 63. See also Ellen Carol DuBois, *Feminism and Suffrage: The Emergence of an Independent Women's Movement in America, 1848–1869* (Ithaca, N.Y.: Cornell University Press, 1978), 79–104.

52. Dall, "Woman's Claim," March 10, 1873 (mismarked 1872), CDP, SL; Caroline Dall Journal, March 17, 1873; and Caroline Dall to A. W. Stevens, April 1, 1873, CDP, MHS, reel 29.

53. Susan B. Anthony to Caroline Dall, n.d. (January 1884 folder), CDP, MHS, reel 13.

54. Harriet Hanson Robinson to Caroline Dall, March 15, 1881, CDP, MHS, reel 11; Carrie Chapman Catt to Caroline Dall, February 3, 1902, CDP, MHS, reel 24; Caroline Dall to [unknown], October 26, 1873, CDP, MHS, reel 29.

Epilogue

1. Mrs. M[atilda] E. Joslyn Gage, *Woman as Inventor* (Fayetteville, N.Y.: F. A. Darling, 1870); Matilda Gage, "Woman as an Inventor," *North American Review* 136 (May 1883): 478–489.

2. Matilda Joslyn Gage, *Woman, Church, and State: A Historical Account of the Status of Woman through the Christian Ages, with Reminiscences of Matriarchate* (Chicago: C. H. Kerr, 1893).

3. Lucy Maynard Salmon, *Domestic Service* (New York: Macmillan, 1897); Des Jardins, *Women and the Historical Enterprise*, 269.

4. Mary R. Beard, *Woman as Force in History: A Study in Traditions and Realities* (New York: Macmillan, 1946), 1–19; Des Jardins, *Women and the Historical Enterprise*, 80–88, 218–219. Beard's comment on Child is quoted in the latter work on page 256.

5. Des Jardins, *Women and the Historical Enterprise*, 260–261; Betty Friedan, *The Feminine Mystique* (New York: W. W. Norton, 1963), 380.

Index

Acknowledgments

As someone who has written women's history, I have been fascinated by the ways in which the authors who produced early women's histories, particularly in the nineteenth century, engaged key questions of political development and wrote for a wide range of readers with very few resources to support them. This realization has helped me to be acutely aware of the privileges I have experienced in being able to write with the support of my university, colleagues, funding agencies, and the very knowledgeable staffs of a wide range of universities and libraries. I could not have completed my work without them. I finished this book in Yogyakarta, where I was a Fulbright Scholar at UIN Sunan Kalijaga. I thank both the Fulbright Commission and my colleagues in Indonesia for their support. I am also deeply grateful to the Massachusetts Historical Society for awarding me the Ruth R. Miller Fellowship, which allowed me the time that I needed to examine the many facets of the society's excellent collections. This process was further aided by the hospitality of Stanford University, which offered access to its library collections for three summers, and the Department of American Civilization at Brown University, where I was a visiting scholar during another summer. I also thank the George Washington University Facilitating Fund, which offered me summer support early in this project.

I have benefited from the assistance of the staff at many libraries and historical societies, including Stanford Library, the Library of Congress, the Yale archives at Sterling Library, the John Hay and Rockefeller libraries at Brown, the Rhode Island Historical Society, the Historical Society of Pennsylvania, and the American Antiquarian Society. I wish to extend special thanks to the interlibrary loan staff of Gelman Library at George Washington University (GW) for its speedy and professional service. Likewise, Conrad E. Wright and his staff at the Massachusetts Historical Society were

extremely helpful in directing me to sources. Finally, the staff of the Schlesinger Library at the Radcliffe Institute for Advanced Study provided invaluable aid in my final stages of research.

During the many drafts of these pages, I have relied extensively on good friends and colleagues. I am particularly grateful to Susan Smulyan for her general good sense and her help in making it possible for me to conduct research at Brown. I also thank Ann Fabian for her close reading of this manuscript at an early stage and for her excellent advice my writing drew to a conclusion. Many thanks to other scholars for their comments and casual conversations: David Moltke Hansen, Lori Ginzberg, Rosemarie Zagarri, Barbara Smith, John Vlach, and the late Roy Rosenzweig. Mari Jo Buhle and Jane Gerhard, my collaborators in writing a textbook on women's history at the same time that I worked on this project, helped me to create a historical narrative that is a crucial element of this work as well. My colleagues at GW—Phyllis Palmer, Jim Miller, Melani McAlister, and Chad Heap—have made sure to send research assistants my way when they could. I also thank my research assistants for their contributions to this project: Amy Bowles, Betsy Wiley, John O'Keefe, Dave Kieran, Craig Allen, and Grace Kuipers. I am deeply grateful to the two anonymous readers for this manuscript who provided such valuable and detailed suggestions for improvement. Finally, I thank Erica Ginsburg and the staff at the University of Pennsylvania Press. Peter Agree, my editor for this project, has known both what to say and what not to say—always at the right time.

Of course, my family has lived with this book more than anyone else besides me. My children, Max, Nicholas, and Grace Kuipers, have been extremely patient with me in this endeavor. My husband, Joel Kuipers, has encouraged this project from its inception and cheered me on. I thank them all for their support and their pride in my work.